Good Practice in Safeguarding Children

Good Practice in Health, Social Care and Criminal Justice Series

Edited by Jacki Pritchard

This series explores topics of current concern to professionals working in social care, health care and the probation service. Contributors are drawn from a wide variety of settings, both in the voluntary and statutory sectors.

also in the series

Good Practice in Safeguarding Adults
Working Effectively in Adult Protection
Edited by Jacki Pritchard
ISBN 978 1 84310 699 9

Good Practice in the Law and Safeguarding Adults
Criminal Justice and Adult Protection
Edited by Jacki Pritchard
ISBN 978 1 84310 937 2

Good Practice in Brain Injury Case Management
Edited by Jackie Parker
Foreword by David J. Price
ISBN 978 1 84310 315 8

Good Practice in Adult Mental Health
Edited by Tony Ryan and Jacki Pritchard
ISBN 978 1 84310 217 5

Good Practice in Risk Assessment and Management 1
Edited by Jacki Pritchard and Hazel Kemshall
ISBN 978 1 85302 338 5

Good Practice in Risk Assessment and Risk Management 2
Key Themes for Protection, Rights and Responsibilities
Edited by Hazel Kemshall and Jacki Pritchard
ISBN 978 1 85302 441 2

Good Practice in Risk Assessment and Risk Management 2 volume set
Edited by Hazel Kemshall and Jacki Pritchard
ISBN 978 1 85302 552 5

Good Practice in Counselling People Who Have Been Abused
Edited by Zetta Bear
ISBN 978 1 85302 424 5

Good Practice in Health, Social
Care and Criminal Justice

GOOD PRACTICE in
Safeguarding Children
Working Effectively in Child Protection

Edited by **Liz Hughes** and **Hilary Owen**

Jessica Kingsley Publishers
London and Philadelphia

The editors and publishers are grateful to the proprietors listed below for
permission to quote the following material:
The 'Safeguarding Offer' by the Yewlands Family of Schools. Reprinted by permission of the Yewlands
Family of Schools' Project, Sheffield. The 'Child Protection Information' by Whiteways Junior School.
Reprinted by permission of Whiteways Junior School, Sheffield. Adapted extracts from Sheffield City
Council, Safeguarding Children Service. Used by permission of Safeguarding Children Service, Children
and Young People's Directory, Sheffield City Council. Sample frontsheet from 'Developing a Whole School
Policy on Child Protection' by Child Protection in Education (CAPE). Reprinted by permission of CAPE.
'Assertive Behaviour' table from p.5 of *The Assertive Social Worker* by Patricia McBride.
Copyright © Patricia McBride, 1998, Ashgate.

Crown copyright material is reproduced with the permission of the Controller of HMSO
and the Queen's Printer for Scotland.

First published in 2009
by Jessica Kingsley Publishers
116 Pentonville Road
London N1 9JB, UK
and
400 Market Street, Suite 400
Philadelphia, PA 19106, USA

www.jkp.com

Copyright © Jessica Kingsley Publishers 2009

Library of Congress Cataloging in Publication Data
Good practice in safeguarding children : working effectively in child protection / edited by Liz Hughes and
Hilary Owen.
   p. cm. -- (Good practice in health, social care, and criminal justice)
Includes bibliographical references and index.
   ISBN 978-1-84310-945-7 (pbk. : alk. paper) 1. Social work with children--Great Britain. 2. Abused
children--Services for--Great Britain. 3. Child abuse. 4. Child abuse--Prevention. I. Hughes, Liz. II.
Owen, Hilary.
   HV751.A6G794 2009
   362.7--dc22
                              2008033476

British Library Cataloguing in Publication Data
A CIP catalogue record for this book is available from the British Library

ISBN 978 1 84310 945 7

Printed and bound in Great Britain by
Athenaeum Press, Gateshead, Tyne and Wear

CONTENTS

INTRODUCTION

HILARY OWEN AND LIZ HUGHES

Incredibly, it is 16 years since the original *Good Practice in Child Protection* manual for professionals (Owen and Pritchard 1993) launched the JKP 'Good Practice' series. We had a Conservative government then, and their Children Act 1989 was a stunningly well drafted piece of legislation that has stood the test of time. The subsequent Labour governments acknowledged this and only added to it. However, there has been a steep increase in the complexity of the work for practitioners, compounded for many by their unfamiliar working environments created by structural and organisational changes. The Labour party in government decided to pin their agenda for children's services onto the findings of the enquiry into the death of Victoria Climbié (Laming 2003). The emphasis in their Children Act 2004 is on integrating services around meeting the needs of children and their families, wherever possible. This means that many practitioners are working directly alongside colleagues from other professions and agencies in a team, often being line managed and/or supervised by the same manager. There are consequences for how information is shared and for how practitioners work together. There are risk management issues to be addressed, particularly in relation to ensuring managers have the skills necessary to manage these inter-agency teams. Senior officers in all agencies delivering services to children and/or parents need to be innovative, flexible and skilful to get it right. Some are not used to inter-agency working.

Integration is the key to children's services at every level, including in strategic planning and budget setting. Inter-agency strategic partnerships (or Children's Trusts) have become responsible for developing and delivering local Children and Young People's Plans. These are based on the five outcomes identified by the government's 'Every Child Matters' agenda as necessary for children's wellbeing: stay safe; be healthy; enjoy and achieve; make a positive contribution; achieve economic wellbeing. One of these outcomes, 'staying safe', inspires most children's services' safeguarding activity. There is so much more to deliver these days than protection from abuse by parents/carers. In the latest version of the 'Working Together' statutory guidance, there is a definition which is fundamental to all our current work:

> Safeguarding and promoting the welfare of children is defined for the purposes of this guidance as:
>
> - protecting children from maltreatment
>
> - preventing impairment of children's health or development
>
> - ensuring that children are growing up in circumstances consistent with the provision of safe and effective care
>
> ...and undertaking that role so as to enable those children to have optimum life chances and to enter adulthood successfully... Effective safeguarding is essential as part of wider work to safeguard and promote the welfare of children. However, all agencies and individuals should aim proactively to safeguard and promote the welfare of children so that the need for action to protect children from harm is reduced. (HM Government 2006, pp.34–35)

Section 11 of the Children Act 2004 makes it clear that both agencies providing services to children and agencies providing services to adults have a statutory responsibility to ensure they safeguard children and promote their welfare, in the way that they deliver their services. It also makes it clear that Safeguarding Children Boards have a statutory responsibility to monitor and evaluate these services.

This new volume in the 'Good Practice' series brings you up to date with the practice implications of these new developments. Reflecting the move from protection to safeguarding, we start with a chapter which updates you on legislation and statutory guidance. It does not matter which agency you work in, or which sector, statutory or voluntary/community; if you work with children or parents or both, this chapter will ensure you know the business.

Reflecting the emphasis that the Department for Children, Schools and Families has put on the overall contribution that schools should be making towards achieving the five outcomes for children, our second chapter by Flora Bandele describes a model of how a school can fulfil its safeguarding responsibilities proactively, creating a safe environment, and also how it can help recognise individual vulnerable children and protect them.

Many children's services have experienced changes resulting in a reduction of contact with children in their homes. As services struggle to meet their targets, contact increasingly takes place in clinics, children's centres and schools. When a practitioner does visit a child in his/her home, it needs to be treated as a rich and valuable opportunity to assess any vulnerability in detail. Practitioners need to use all the skills at their disposal to get the most out of the visit. We include a chapter that demonstrates how to do this.

There is now a great deal of evidence that children's physiological development is affected by the way in which their parents relate to them emotionally. Dipti Aistrop's chapter on safeguarding infant mental health shows how practitioners can actively support attachment between children and their parents/carers.

Attempting to engage parents in safeguarding their child is not always easy because their own difficulties and past experience often get in the way of a positive relationship with practitioners. This can be scary, because all the evidence shows that the more engaged parents are with their child's protection plan, the better the outcome for the child. In Chapter 5 Ruth Pearson gives some practical suggestions about how to improve difficult relationships with service users.

Many of the research findings in the field have emphasised that it is often the impact of carers' behaviour that renders children vulnerable or compounds their difficulties.

Assessing the impact of carers' problematic behaviour and finding ways of ameliorating it and supporting the children are the subjects of several chapters in this new volume. Rosie Jakob contributes a chapter on working with parents who have a learning disability, and shows how many can be supported to become safe parents.

In Chapter 7 Mandy Craig describes good inter-agency practice in relation to working with parents who misuse substances. Sue Peckover describes how to risk assess situations where children are living with domestic abuse, and shows how to develop safety plans for them. There has always been tension between those providing mental health services to adults and those responsible for safeguarding the welfare of children of those adults. This is largely due to the sensitive nature of both areas of work and the sometimes conflicting needs of parents and children. The new world requires the development of active working relationships between adult and children's services which depends on a greater understanding and respect of each other's roles and responsibilities especially with regard to information sharing. Karen Johnson's chapter includes a case study which illustrates the way in which difficulties between practitioners and clients arise and analyses the underlying factors in both clients and workers which contribute to misunderstandings and conflict.

Some areas of practice are very specialised and require particular collaboration with services outside your usual brief. Recent government action has addressed the issue of attempting to safeguard children who are trafficked. This is of particular concern to services operating near air or sea ports. Emma Kelly describes good practice in this difficult field in Chapter 10.

The agencies with a statutory responsibility to investigate child abuse have not changed, even though the methods they use have. Jeff Boxer's chapter allows you to think through the ways in which the police can safeguard children, and provides support to police officers making difficult decisions in the community. Rosie Jakob describes ways in which social workers can ensure the assessments they undertake are evidence based and the judgements they make are safe.

We include a chapter which brings managers up to date on good practice in supervision, so important for ensuring practitioners feel safe enough to practice in environments which challenge them on a number of different fronts. Finally, we make suggestions for improving the management of serious case reviews, which at the moment seem to be adding nothing to our ability to prevent tragedies and are exacerbating unnecessarily the anxiety that the practitioners involved naturally experience.

We cannot cover all the relevant issues in a single volume: the children's agenda is huge and new issues are emerging all the time. Indeed, since this book was written, further events in Haringey have called into question the extent to which the 'Every Child Matters' agenda is being embedded in local services, following the convictions for the death of Baby P. However, it is essential that practitioners feel confident and supported in working with complex and uncomfortable situations, or we shall lose them. Practitioners need to know their practice is based on collective experience and evidence from research. This book adds to the resource available and provides kind encouragement to those practitioners. Safeguarding children is one of the most important activities anyone can undertake: we congratulate the children's workforce on their increasingly skilled and committed contribution to our society's future.

REFERENCES

HM Government (2006) *Working Together to Safeguard Children*. London: Stationery Office.

Laming, H. (2003) *The Victoria Climbié Inquiry: A Report of an Inquiry by Lord Laming*. London: Stationery Office.

Owen, H. and Pritchard, J. (1993) *Good Practice in Child Protection*. London: Jessica Kingsley Publishers.

STATUTES

The Children Act 1989 (2004). London: The Stationery Office.

The Children Act (2004). London: Stationery Office.

CHAPTER 1

FROM PROTECTION TO SAFEGUARDING: BRINGING YOU UP TO DATE ON STATUTORY RESPONSIBILITIES

HILARY OWEN

INTRODUCTION

This chapter brings together recent legislation and statutory guidance which every practitioner working with children or parents, whatever their professional background, needs to know about in order to practise competently and confidently. It describes the development of key government initiatives which provide practitioners with powerful tools to do their jobs well. It reveals some of the complexities of the work and how thoughtful, intelligent and imaginative practitioners sometimes need to be to achieve good outcomes for families. Other chapters in this book describe these complexities in more detail and demonstrate how to work with them safely and successfully.

Initiatives in one part of a complex human system always produce unforeseen consequences in another part, particularly when resources are tight. Many parts of our safeguarding system are improving: a few are deteriorating. I shall draw attention to some issues of concern which practitioners in all sectors, statutory, private, voluntary and community, might take responsibility for raising with their managers and indeed government ministers whenever the opportunity arises.

First, a point of interest. All specialisms have their fashionable jargon, and safeguarding children is no exception. The language of government guidance in safeguarding children has become more sophisticated and expresses very precisely the nuances of changing ideologies and politicians' intentions. The clearest example of this is the extension of the work from 'child protection' (protecting children from maltreatment) to 'safeguarding children' (ensuring that children are growing up in circumstances consistent with the provision of safe and effective care). Safeguarding is a wider range of activities, often preventative and proactive. It ranges from taking children into care because of maltreatment by parents to putting strategies in place to prevent knife and gun crime amongst young people, from prosecuting paedophiles to ensuring agencies use safe recruitment and employment practices. A more hidden example is the change from 'child protection register' to 'list of children who need a child protection plan' (HM Government 2006a). Lists work in just the same way that registers did but, for a parent, the sting of hearing that your child has been 'registered' has been removed. The emphasis now is all on the child protection plan, the future, the support to be offered; rather than on the past, the injury, the cry for help. Considering carefully the terminology of government guidance will reveal the ideas, debates and current (if sometimes short-lived) consensus behind it.

> Listen for the language: the guidance means very precisely what it says.

The recommendations of Lord Herbert Laming (2003) and Sir Michael Bichard (2004) have provided the framework for the Labour government's approach to safeguarding children. The government's helpful emphasis on *outcomes* for children, rather than service *outputs*, is expressed as its Every Child Matters agenda (Department for Education and Skills 2004), which has five aspirational high-level outcomes for children, underneath which all performance indicators now sit:

1. stay safe
2. be healthy
3. enjoy and achieve
4. make a positive contribution
5. achieve economic wellbeing.

The Every Child Matters agenda, whilst framed by the Children Act 2004 and the Education Act 2002, is without boundaries. It is not a single strategy or initiative; it is a 'systems approach' which is meant to ensure that safeguarding children is considered at every level of every organisation offering services to children and/or parents. This includes strategic documents, policies and procedures, individual job descriptions and person specifications, supervision arrangements and practice. It has arguably been characterised by four principles: accountability, information sharing, integration and the move from protection to safeguarding. Each of these principles has been applied at all levels of organisations, affecting government departments, chief executive officers, local structures, management, professions and practitioners alike. As can be imagined, an initiative as thoroughgoing as this produces a huge number of changes, and the pace of change is very rapid. It is difficult to distinguish those new practices which will last from those which will fall by the wayside after a year or two. One of the first changes to be made, in 2003, was the removal of overall responsibility for safeguarding children from the Department of Health to the Department for Education and Skills, which was renamed (on 28 June 2007) the Department for Children, Schools and Families (DCSF) (note the order of the words and the significance of schools in the government's agenda for children). The statutory functions of the posts of Director of Education and Director of Social Services were combined to form a single post of Director of Children's Services, ensuring that accountability is very clear and integrating management of all local authority services for children. Joint commissioning arrangements have been put into place to deliver integrated Children and Young People's Plans.

The effects of organisational change can take a long time to filter down and alter the quality of practice. Some of the things that are changing are good. The DCSF has energy and resources to put into children's issues because their only concern is children: children were only a small part of the responsibilities of the Department of Health. However, the DCSF's initiatives are all about schools and school-aged children, and pre-school children seem to have been left behind, with health visiting services being cut by many Primary Care Trusts (PCTs). This is an issue because these children are the ones most likely to die from maltreatment. The UNICEF report *Child Maltreatment Deaths in Rich Nations* published in 2003 indicated that 'the risk of death from maltreatment [is] approximately three times greater for the under-ones than for those aged one to four, who in turn face double the risk of those aged 5–14' (reported in the *Guardian*, 18 September 2003). Joined-up government is as essential as joined-up services.

The Laming Report (Laming 2003) made a recommendation to the police which was intended to improve their response to crimes against children. Lord Laming's view was that a crime against a child should be treated just as seriously as a crime against an adult, and therefore the police should very much take the lead in investigating and prosecuting child abuse offences (Laming 2003, Recommendation 97). However, in many areas this has led to a loss of impetus in the social work role in investigation developed since the Cleveland Inquiry (Butler-Sloss 1988), and to a deterioration in close joint working between police and social workers. This counters the integration of professional teams working with children recommended elsewhere in the Laming report (see, for example, Recommendation 14). It is early days as yet in the life of the Every Child Matters agenda, given the number and depth of the changes required, and it is important that practitioners, managers and service commissioners keep a close eye on how it is developing.

Despite the unforeseen consequences above, many of the changes brought about by the government's response to the Laming and Bichard reports are evidence-based and are contributing to clear improvements in practice. Which legislation and statutory guidance does today's practitioner working with children and/or their carers need to know in order to achieve best practice? There is an impressive amount of practice guidance, case study material and examples of good practice available on the government's 'Every Child Matters' website. However, the number of national documents conscientious practitioners might feel they need to look at is now slightly overwhelming, particularly since they need to follow their own local procedures as well. I have made an attempt below to simplify things, and present the key issues for practitioners.

LEGISLATION AND STATUTORY GUIDANCE TO KEEP AT YOUR FINGERTIPS

1. The Children Act 1989

This is still the most important piece of legislation in the practitioner's toolbox. It remains the basis of our safeguarding system, defining the threshold for state intervention in family life to protect children from abuse. The definitions it contains of 'significant harm' (section 31) and of a 'child in need' (section 17) are still current.

It is still the case that a local authority (children's social care) has a duty to investigate whenever it receives information which gives reasonable cause to suspect significant harm (section 47). Agencies (like health services and schools) still have a duty to co-operate with a local authority making investigations under this section (47 {11}).

2. The Adoption and Children Act 2002

A) DOMESTIC ABUSE

Whilst lawyers were very happy with the definition of harm contained in the Children Act 1989 (section 31{9}), feeling that it was very inclusive and covered all aspects of children's health and development, the Labour government was mindful of consistent research findings demonstrating that domestic abuse could cause emotional harm to children witnessing it (see, for example, Mullender *et al.* 2002). It wanted to emphasise that agencies had a duty to assess harm whenever domestic abuse was present, and so included in the Adoption and Children Act 2002 an amendment to the definition: 'impairment suffered from seeing or hearing the ill-treatment of another'.

This is notable because it takes account of evidence from children and young people that they are often in the position of overhearing abuse to a parent in another part of the house, whilst the parent believes they do not know about it because they are not seeing it. Since this Act, the indications are that some areas of the UK (see, for example, Sheffield Safeguarding Children Board 2007) have seen a rise in the numbers of children referred to Child Protection Registers/Lists of Children with Child Protection Plans in the category of emotional abuse because of domestic abuse. However, whilst it is obviously an improvement that harm to children as a result of domestic abuse is being assessed properly, there has as yet been no increase in resources for services to assist them and those who commission children's services are having to consider what can be done to improve their response within current budgets. Likewise, adult services commissioners are having to think again about how to offer effective programmes to perpetrators and protective services to victims. In some areas, there are so many referrals to children's social care because of domestic abuse that they cannot be looked at and risk assessed. An improvement in one part of the system again is producing unforeseen consequences in another.

B) PARENTAL RESPONSIBILITY

This legislation also contributed a further amendment to the Children Act 1989 in respect of fathers' parental responsibility. A basic piece of information which all practitioners, particularly early years, school and social care staff, working with a child should know is who has parental responsibility. The Children Act 1989, whilst an excellent piece of legislation in most respects, contained the odd piece of Conservative Party ideology that did not sit well with its overall aim of putting children first. One of these was the refusal to allow unmarried fathers parental responsibility except in limited circumstances. As our child protection system developed, however, children's social workers became used to looking at which adults in a family had real relationships with children, rather than just those whom the Conservative Party would like to have relationships with them. The Adoption and Children Act 2002 reflected this reality, and provided an additional key, easy method for unmarried fathers to acquire parental responsibility: having their name registered on the birth certificate. The current situation is that the following now have parental responsibility:

- the child's mother
- the child's father if married to the mother
- the child's unmarried father if registered as such on the child's birth certificate
- the child's unmarried father if there is a parental responsibility agreement with the mother

- a step-parent if there is a parental responsibility agreement with all those who already have parental responsibility
- someone with a parental responsibility order from the court
- someone with a residence order from the court
- someone who becomes the child's guardian on the mother's death
- someone who adopts a child.

3. The Sexual Offences Act 2003

This piece of legislation helpfully clarified some of the more ambiguous aspects of illegal sexual behaviour and applied it consistently to both genders. It criminalises an adult who buys sex from someone under the age of 18 years, even when they can demonstrate that they believed the young person to be 18 years old. This puts the onus of responsibility upon the adult to find out the age of the young person before they act. It sets the age of consent for sex at 16 years for both young men and women. It deems a child under the age of 13 years unable to consent to sexual activity. This clarification led to a sensible piece of statutory guidance for practitioners working with sexually active young people being published as part of *Working Together to Safeguard Children* (HM Government 2006a). A tension has always existed between the need to protect young people from paedophiles and pimps and the need to offer them confidential healthcare services which they feel confident about accessing. The statutory guidance treads a tightrope, but nevertheless promotes excellent practice. It indicates that an offence under the Sexual Offences Act 2003 involving a child under 13 'should be taken to indicate a risk of significant harm to the child' (HM Government 2006a, p.105) and therefore should *always* be discussed with the child protection lead in the practitioner's organisation, with a presumption that the case will be reported to children's social care. Children's social care will always consult with the police.

Where a young person aged 13–15 is involved, the Working Together guidance (HM Government 2006a, p.106) describes a number of factors which should be taken into account in assessing risk of harm. Where there are concerns, the practitioner should discuss the case with his/her agency's child protection lead, and then with other agencies if concerns remain. Confidentiality can be maintained if the practitioner believes this is necessary, although access to other agencies' information will then be problematic: it is impossible to make an accurate risk assessment without the full picture. Specifically, where the sexual partner is identified, a check can be made with the police, who should share any relevant information, in line with recommendations 8–13 of the Bichard Enquiry Report (Bichard 2004). Whilst sexual activity with someone under 16 years is an offence, it does not always entail harm.

Many services may be offered to the young person to promote their safety, welfare and health. A referral should be made to children's social care only if there is reasonable cause to suspect significant harm, or s/he appears to be a child in need under section 17 of the Children Act 1989.

4. The Children Act 2004

Having indicated that the Children Act 1989 remains the key piece of legislation, it is important to explain the contribution of the main piece of the Labour government's children's legislation. The Children Act 2004 is primarily about new statutory leadership roles, joint planning and commissioning of children's services, and how organisations ensure their functions are discharged in a way which safeguards children and promotes their welfare. Section 11 (and section 175 of the Education Act 2002, where schools are concerned) particularly details what organisations should have in place to do this (including those which provide services to adults, like NHS mental health trusts, and have contact with children through the parents/carers they work with). It is also about the establishment of local safeguarding children boards, the statutory replacements for area child protection committees. The hope is that these new arrangements will significantly improve services to children, and outcomes for children, over time. However, the Children Act 2004 also has a direct effect on the practitioner's working day, improving practice, as the following new initiatives demonstrate.

A) THE CHILDREN'S INFORMATION SHARING INDEX/CONTACTPOINT

It was Recommendation 17 of the Laming Report (2003) that the government should investigate the feasibility of operating a national database of all resident children in order to facilitate the sharing of information between agencies, particularly where a child is made vulnerable by being moved around from place to place. The Children Act 2004 laid the legal foundations for this, and local databases have been trialled in some areas. Preparations are underway for the national (England) child index to be implemented by the end of 2008, although as with all complex enterprises, it is quite possible this timescale will change. The information the national database contains is very basic: name, date of birth, address, GP, school, possibly health visitor, but also, crucially, the names and contact details of practitioners involved with the child. Children's details will be kept on ContactPoint unless the child or parent is aware of their right to request its removal, and actively requests that they be removed. Where sensitive services, like sexual health, are concerned, contact details are held only with the young person's active consent, and access to them is controlled. No case records are held. No information is held about the adults in the household. All practitioners who need to use the database for their work will have had an enhanced Criminal Records Bureau check. A high level of security applies to the data, and some children's details are 'shielded' if there are concerns that a member of the family could be endangered if their location is revealed (for example, if there has been domestic abuse). Practitioners' use is monitored to ensure they do not abuse the system (for example, to look up a child's details for reasons other than work) and issues are raised with the individual concerned and dealt with by their line manager. If a practitioner has carried out a common assessment (see below) the fact of this (not the detail of it) can be logged on the system, so that work is not duplicated. As well as providing a basic co-ordinating tool for integrated working, supporting early intervention to safeguard children, this system can be used to trace and protect children who may be at risk.

Whilst the fact that no case records are kept on ContactPoint is cited as a positive safeguard to children's privacy, a further development, the Electronic Common Assesement Framework (e-CAF), will mean that case material about vulnerable children (a much smaller group of children) is kept and shared electronically. Practitioners should be aware that exactly the same consents need to be obtained for sharing confidential information held electronically, as for information held on paper. The *Guardian* newspaper has been very active in criticising the government's interest in computerising personal records (see, for example, 'Who lost our data expertise?' by Michael Cross, 2007). There is no doubt that there are many threats to the maintenance of confidentiality in relation to electronic data, not the least of which is human error. It remains to be seen whether the benefits of ContactPoint and the e-CAF outweigh the risks.

B) PRIVATE FOSTERING ARRANGEMENTS

A private fostering arrangement is where a child under the age of 16 years (or under 18 if disabled) is living with someone other than a parent or close relative with the intention that s/he will be there for 28 days or more. Recommendation 11 of the Laming Report indicated that the government should review the law (the Children Act 1989) on private fostering, as it left local authorities without a statutory duty to assess the arrangements made for the child. Obviously, these children are potentially vulnerable. The Children Act 2004 and subsequent regulations, The Children (Private Arrangements for Fostering) Regulations 2005, addressed this, and also added a local authority responsibility to publicise parents' and private foster carers' legal responsibility to notify them of the arrangements they intended to make for the child. The Children Act 1989 originally placed a duty on teachers, health and other professionals to notify the local authority if they came across a private fostering arrangement. The Children Act 2004 (and the statutory guidance which followed, contained in *Working Together to Safeguard Children*, HM Government 2006a) brings this duty into focus: all practitioners need to be aware of it in the course of their work with families. The British Association for Adoption and Fostering (BAAF) estimates that between 15,000 and 20,000 children in the UK are privately fostered (BAAF 2008).

5. Working Together to Safeguard Children (HM Government 2006a) – statutory guidance

The Labour government chose to continue updating the 'Working Together' statutory child protection guidance originally published in 1988, because the model of inter-agency working it provided remains the basis of our system for safeguarding children. In 1991, following implementation of the Children Act 1989, the guidance was much expanded, then updated on the basis of research findings (see the excellent summary *Child Protection: Messages from Research*, Department of Health 1995) in 1999, and finally revised in line with the Every Child Matters agenda in 2006.

Working Together to Safeguard Children (HM Government 2006a), despite being statutory guidance, is sometimes curiously ambiguous about key issues, reflecting, I think, unresolved struggles between powerful interests. The government clearly expects that practitioners should be using the Common Assessment Framework (CAF) for early identification of need and co-ordination of services. However, *Working Together to Safeguard Children* falls short of saying it should be used. It states only that: 'The Common Assessment Framework offers a basis for early referral and information-sharing between organisations' (p.104).

This may reflect the unwillingness of some powerful professions, like the medical profession, to use the CAF. Some organisations like the National Probation Service and police forces have made a decision that their staff will not be involved in instigating a CAF, but will contribute to an assessment carried out by another agency. However, use of the CAF is so very important to the way practitioners in children's services should be working, whatever their professional background, that it needs to be detailed here (see below), despite the fact that it is not statutory.

Working Together to Safeguard Children describes how agencies should co-operate, and most significantly how local safeguarding children boards should operate. It describes significant aspects of joint working that have to be included in local policies and procedures, and sets out an inter-agency child protection training strategy. It includes the essential child protection process (largely unchanged from 1999), which is also summarised in the booklet *What to Do If You're Worried a Child is Being Abused* (Department for Education and Skills 2003). It summarises more detailed statutory guidance supplemental to the essential child protection process which has been published since 1999, on children abused through prostitution, fabricated or induced illness, investigating complex (organised or multiple) abuse, female genital mutilation and forced marriage. There is a completely new area of work relating to situations where children die unexpectedly, which I detail below. It also contains very helpful non-statutory practice guidance in Part 2 which is informed by research findings.

A) THE COMMON ASSESSMENT FRAMEWORK AND INTEGRATED PRACTICE

The Common Assessment Framework is a model of assessment developed from the evidence-based *Framework for the Assessment of Children in Need and their Families* (Department of Health 2000) and simplified to enable its use generically by any agency for any vulnerable child. Completing a common assessment should ensure that the practitioner works according to 11 principles identified by research as resulting in good outcomes for children. *Working Together to Safeguard Children* (HM Government 2006a) describes these principles in detail, indicating that work to safeguard and promote the welfare of children should always be:

- child-centred
- rooted in child development
- focused on outcomes for children
- holistic
- ensuring equality of opportunity
- involving of children and families
- building on strengths as well as identifying difficulties
- multi- and inter-agency in approach
- a continuing process, not an event
- providing and reviewing services
- informed by evidence.

Practitioners should consider undertaking a common assessment whenever it seems that a child's needs cannot be met from within their own agency. The CAF entails collection of information and assessment in three different 'domains': the child's developmental needs, parenting capacity, and family and environmental factors. Where a number of agencies need to be involved to assist a child to achieve the five outcomes of the Every Child Matters agenda, then a 'lead professional' (the person who works most closely with the child) should co-ordinate the activity by means of a clear plan agreed by all the agencies, parents/carers and the child, if they are of sufficient age and understanding. The plan is developed and reviewed at agreed intervals via meetings with the family. This way of working means that consent to sharing family information with specific agencies has to be sought before the work can take place. Workers have to be open with family members about concerns, be clear with them how different agencies can help them, what they themselves need to do to ensure their child's situation improves to a reasonable standard, and be specific about timescales.

B) CHILD DEATH PROCESSES

It is estimated nationally that 22 per cent of children's deaths are preventable. New arrangements detailed in Chapter 7 of *Working Together* (HM Government 2006a) aim to identify how future similar deaths can be prevented. Local safeguarding children boards have to have in place a 'rapid response' to all unexpected deaths of children and young people (up to the 18th birthday) led by a designated doctor. A rapid response team made up of those professionals who have been involved with the family, plus those who need to become involved with them (including bereavement support), is brought together in all cases. These teams have their normal agency responsibilities when a child dies unexpectedly, but they must also:

- make immediate enquiries into the death and evaluate the reason it happened

- collect information about the death in accordance with a nationally agreed (and very extensive) dataset

- maintain contact with the family to ensure they are kept up to date with information about the death.

In most cases, the team will just evaluate information available, rather than reviewing services provided. Obviously, any practitioner working with a child or a parent could be part of a rapid response team at some point in their career. The designated doctor ensures that all the information about the death is sent to a multi-agency child death overview panel, which is a subgroup of the local safeguarding children board. All deaths, both expected and unexpected, are reviewed by the panel and any patterns or trends are identified. Action is taken to try and prevent similar deaths in future. Preventative action might be in relation to sudden unexpected death in infancy ('cot death'), or road traffic, for example.

6. Information Sharing: Practitioners' Guide (HM Government 2006b)

This non-statutory guidance is based on the relevant parts of the Data Protection Act 1998, the Human Rights Act 1998, the Children Act 2004 and the Education Act 2002. It forms the basis on which inter-agency work to safeguard individual children can be carried out. The Data Protection Act and the Human Rights Act allows the sharing of confidential information in particular circumstances. Section 11 of the Children Act 2004 (and sections 175 and 157 of the Education Act 2002) indicates that agencies have to ensure that their staff know how to share information to achieve positive outcomes for children and to protect them from significant harm. In practice it seems that there has always been a tendency for practitioners to become confused very quickly about what should be shared and with whom. Whilst this guidance is 23 pages long, explaining the details behind its final position, it does contain a single page with six key points on it which encapsulate good practice (HM Government 2006b, p.5). My summary of the legal position is:

> If the information is confidential, you need consent to share it. However, if by not sharing it a child is likely to suffer significant harm then the information should be shared. It is good practice to seek consent to share in the first instance, if this puts no one at risk, but if consent cannot be obtained in a timely manner, then it should be shared anyway. The information shared should be relevant and proportionate: it is not appropriate to share the whole contents of someone's record if only a small part of it relates to the risk of significant harm.

7. Local Authority Social Services Letter (LASSL 2005) Identification of Individuals Who Present a Risk to Children

The Home Office began a review in 2004 of so-called 'Schedule 1' offences (Schedule 1 of the Children and Young Persons Act 1933). It identified that the term 'schedule 1 offender', used for many years to identify people who pose a risk to children, lacked clarity, defining people by their offending history rather than by any risk they pose to children. A schedule 1 offender can be someone who was convicted as a 14-year-old of an assault offence against a classmate in the playground, whilst Ian Huntley, who murdered schoolchildren Jessica Chapman and Holly Wells had never been convicted of a schedule 1 offence, although he had come to the attention of the police for allegations of no less than eight separate sexual offences before the murders took place. Therefore, this Local Authority Social Services Letter indicated that in future reference should only be made to individuals who present a risk to children. Children's social care is the agency which makes the assessment of risk to specific children, using all available information from all agencies, sometimes with information presented at a meeting convened under multi-agency public protection arrangements (MAPPA). They work with the family concerned in an open way to produce recommendations about the person's contact with the children. It is good practice for practitioners from other agencies to raise any concerns they have with social care about an individual's contact with children, share any information they have appropriately, and contribute to any child protection plan developed.

8. Safeguarding Children and Safer Recruitment in Education (Department for Education and Skills 2006)

This final piece of new statutory guidance updates the responsibilities of all local authority education services, schools and further education colleges. In particular, it introduces new high standards of employment practice in the light of the Bichard Report (2004) and a new role of 'Local Authority Designated Officer' (LADO), who is responsible for the oversight and monitoring of any allegations of child abuse made against any member of the children's workforce. It is important to note that whenever an allegation is made against any member of the workforce (from police officer to doctor to volunteer working in a children's charity organisation) then the situation has to be referred to the LADO. An allegation is defined comprehensively. It is when someone has:

- behaved in a way that has harmed a child, or may have harmed a child

- possibly committed a criminal offence against or related to a child

- behaved towards a child or children in a way that indicates s/he is unsuitable to work with children (pp.57–58).

The LADO advises on the process and is required to monitor the investigation and outcomes of all allegations, particularly timescales. There may be a total of four investigative processes going on: an employer's disciplinary, criminal, section 47 social work enquiries under the Children Act 1989, and finally that by a professional body like the General Medical Council, for example. The purpose of this work is to ensure that all allegations are dealt with fairly, transparently and expeditiously, and it is work that has been informed by many years of good practice by schools. Related to this area of work are new arrangements for recording and sharing information about individuals who should not work with children, for which the Safeguarding Vulnerable Groups Act 2006 provides the foundation. All practitioners should have clear information about their employer's expectations about their behaviour, and need to be aware of their responsibility to share any concerns they have about colleagues in relation to their contact with children.

WATCH THIS SPACE

This has been a tour of current legislation and statutory guidance which has relevance for all practitioners working with children and/or their carers. Today's practitioner needs to know much more than was the case 15 years ago, and much decision-making is more exposing because it is, rightly, done on an inter-agency basis with families' involvement. However, many of the latest initiatives, although grounded in research findings, need to be monitored closely to ensure the outcomes for children are the ones we expect. Attrition and lack of communication between different professions, between central and local government, and between different central government departments can create unanticipated difficulties. Practitioners have a key role in this monitoring process.

REFERENCES

BAAF (British Association for Adoption and Fostering) (2008) 'Private fostering: 'Promoting awareness of the notification requirements.' Available at http://74.125.77.132/search?q=cache:CNrGRMx01KsJ:www.dcsf.gov.uk/consultations/downloadableDocs/Promoting%2520Awareness%2520of%2520the%2520Private%2520Fostering%2520Notification%2520Requirements.doc+private+fostering:+promoting&hl=en&ct=clnk&cd=1&gl=uk, accessed 17 December 2008.

Bichard, M. (2004) *The Bichard Inquiry Report*. London: Stationery Office.

Butler-Sloss, E. (1988) *Report of the Inquiry into Child Abuse in Cleveland 1987*. London: HMSO.

Cross, M. (2007) 'Who lost our data expertise.' *Guardian*, 29 November.

Department for Education and Skills (2003) *What to Do If You're Worried a Child is Being Abused*. London: Stationery Office.

Department for Education and Skills (2004) *Every Child Matters: Change for Children*. London: Stationery Office.

Department for Education and Skills (2006) *Safeguarding Children and Safer Recruitment in Education*. London: DfES Publications.

Department of Health (1995) *Child Protection: Messages From Research*. London: HMSO.

Department of Health (2000) *Framework for the Assessment of Children in Need and Their Families*. London: Stationery Office.

Guardian (2003) '*UK child abuse deaths could be double official figures, says UN*.' 18 September.

HM Government (2006a) *Working Together to Safeguard Children*. London: Stationery Office.

HM Government (2006b) *Information Sharing: Practitioners' Guide*. London: Stationery Office.

Laming, H. (2003) *The Victoria Climbié Inquiry: A Report of an Inquiry by Lord Laming*. London: HMSO.

LASSL (2005) *Identification of Individuals Who Present a Risk to Children*, Home Office, Circular 16/2005. London: Home Office.

Mullender, A., Kelly, L., Hague, G., Malos, E. and Iman, U. (2001) *Children's Perspectives on Domestic Violence*. London: Routledge.

Sheffield Safeguarding Children Board (2007) 'Responding to the needs of children and young people in Sheffield who are affected by domestic abuse: Findings from a gap analysis for the Sheffield 0–19+ Partnership.' Available at www.safeguardingsheffieldchildren.org.uk/welcome/safeguarding-children-board/research-and-evaluation, accessed 7 July 2008.

STATUTES

The Adoption and Children Act (2002) London: Stationery Office.

The Children Act 1989 (2004) London: Stationery Office.

The Children Act (2004) London: Stationery Office.

The Children (Private Arrangements for Fostering) Regulations (2005) London: Stationery Office.

Children and Young Persons Act (1933) London: HMSO.

The Data Protection Act (1998) London: Stationery Office.

The Education Act (2002) London: Stationery Office.

The Human Rights Act (1998) London: Stationery Office.

Safeguarding Vulnerable Groups Act (2006) London: Stationery Office.

The Sexual Offences Act (2003) London: Stationery Office.

CHAPTER 2

THE CONTRIBUTION OF SCHOOLS TO SAFEGUARDING CHILDREN

FLORA BANDELE

INTRODUCTION

This chapter intends to draw together information from various government guidelines, as well as give examples of how a number of schools in Sheffield have incorporated this guidance into practice. Readers will be given a practical overview of how schools can fully contribute to the safeguarding of children.

The *Every Child Matters* green paper identified the five outcomes that are most important to children and young people:

1. being healthy
2. staying safe
3. enjoying and achieving
4. making a positive contribution
5. achieving economic wellbeing.

The five outcomes are universal ambitions for every child and young person, whatever their background or circumstances. Improving outcomes for all children and young people underpins all of the development and work within children's trusts.

The outcomes are mutually reinforcing. For example, children and young people learn and thrive when they are healthy, safe and engaged, and the evidence shows clearly that educational achievement is the most effective route out of poverty.

PART 1: SAFER SCHOOLS = SAFER CHILDREN

It is a Department for Children, Schools and Families requirement that every educational establishment in the country should have a senior member of their leadership team designated as having key responsibility for safeguarding and protecting children. Each local authority should keep a list of these designated staff. Safeguarding and promoting the welfare of children is now a statutory duty for all education staff (Education Act 2002 s175 and s157). *Working Together to Safeguard Children* (HM Government 2006, pp.34–35) defines safeguarding and promoting the welfare of children and young people as:

- protecting children from maltreatment

- preventing impairment of children's health or development

- ensuring that children are growing up in circumstances consistent with the provision of safe and effective care

- undertaking that role so as to enable those children to have optimum life chances and to enter adulthood successfully.

Education takes up a major proportion of a child's life and therefore, staff in nurseries, schools and colleges are particularly well placed to contribute to the delivery of the five outcomes for children. They are also the people most likely to be able to identify when these outcomes are not being met for a particular child, or when a child is at risk of harm or significant harm.

Safeguarding children and young people and promoting their wellbeing is more than just child protection. In order to safeguard children and young people and ensure their personal development, we need to have safeguarding at the heart of schools' purpose and therefore need to offer the following:

GOOD PRACTICE POINTS

- A positive and preventative curriculum: a curriculum that teaches children and young people how to make good choices about healthy, safe lifestyles and how and who to ask for help if their safety is threatened.

- Partnership with parents and carers: a commitment to an open and honest relationship and involvement of parents and carers at all stages of a child or young person's education and care.

- A safe learning environment: where it is okay to talk and children and young people will be listened to; where learners feel safe in a secure environment; where they do not endure bullying, racism or sexual harassment; where medical needs are met.

- Inclusive practices: so that all learners will be helped to fulfil their potential in an ethos/culture where every child and young person feels included, particularly those not achieving the five Every Child Matters outcomes.

- Safeguarding policies, procedures and guidance: easily accessed documents that are understood and used by all staff, are in accordance with local authority guidance and are reviewed annually.

- Integrated practice: a commitment to the early identification of children and young people with additional needs and speedy intervention involving multi-agency co-operation and common methods of sharing information and assessing need, i.e. use of the Common Assessment Framework, the Child Index (ContactPoint) and the Lead Professional role.

- Well trained staff and management: who have had appropriate levels of training and are clear and confident about what is expected of them in their day-to-day work in order to safeguard children and young people.

- Safe recruitment, selection and management practices: that help to deter, reject or identify people who might abuse children or young people or are otherwise unsuited to work with them.

(www.safeguardingsheffieldchildren.org.uk
The Safeguarding Children 'Offer')

PART 2: WHAT MAKES AN EFFECTIVE DESIGNATED OFFICER FOR CHILD PROTECTION/SAFEGUARDING?

The key contributory factors to being an effective child protection/safeguarding officer are commitment, dedication and time. It cannot be stressed enough how important these are, especially time. In most circumstances, it is simply not possible for a child protection/safeguarding officer to perform the role effectively whilst having a full-time teaching commitment. In some areas, the role will be a full-time job in itself.

As required by the Department of Children, Schools and Families (DCSF), a child protection/safeguarding officer in school needs to be able to:

- refer cases to appropriate agencies

- offer support and advice to all staff

- liaise within and have knowledge of the safeguarding children system

- identify children who are vulnerable, in need of additional services or at risk of significant harm

- ensure that *all* staff in school are aware of safeguarding issues and what to do if they are concerned about a child

- manage clear, accurate, secure records

- access resources for children and their families

- ensure that all staff, including themselves, are trained and regularly updated to an appropriate level in safeguarding matters

- ensure that parents are properly involved from the outset. For example, it is advisable to outline the school's safeguarding responsibilities in the school prospectus, and refer to this during admissions interviews/assemblies

- ensure that all relevant school policies are reviewed and updated in line with new legislation/guidance on an annual basis

- with the head teacher, provide such information to the local authority as required. The Sheffield safeguarding children website has an example of an annual safeguarding report. It asks questions under five headings:

  ○ Policies and procedures

  ○ Recruitment

  ○ Training

  ○ Information sharing

  ○ Other good safeguarding practice. (Adapted from Department of Children, Schools and Families (2006, p.83)

It can be an onerous and very lonely job, particularly in areas where abuse and need are identified efficiently, thus exposing the staff member to ongoing distressing circumstances. It can also be very difficult for those officers, perhaps less skilled, or successfully hoodwinked by plausible adults, who miss signs and indicators, and inevitably feel that they have somehow failed the children in their care. It is therefore concerning that it would appear that one of the main gaps in provision for many child protection/safeguarding officers is proper support and supervision in safeguarding for themselves (as distinct from line management).

GOOD PRACTICE POINT

- The Yewlands family of schools in Sheffield is looking to develop a post that will perform this role for their child protection/safeguarding officers. If it proves to be feasible, the model will be suggested to other families of schools across Sheffield. (The family of schools is made up of a secondary school, its main feeder primaries, plus any local early years settings, faith primaries, sixth-form colleges, or special schools as appropriate.)

PART 3: STAFF TRAINING: CONFIDENCE AND COMPETENCE

Government guidance (see DCSF 2006) expects that all members of staff working with children should have training in safeguarding and protecting children at stipulated regular intervals. This includes office/administrative staff, kitchen staff, and other ancillary workers such as cleaners (if they are on site whilst children are present); as well as teaching and support staff. Temporary staff and volunteers who work with children should be made aware of the school's child protection/safeguarding procedures, as well as their own responsibilities therein. Some schools extend this to providing a safeguarding statement for all visitors to the school to sign that they have read and understood. The following is an example from Whiteways Junior School in Sheffield:

XXX School

Child Protection Information

Our school believes it is essential that every child has a right to protection from abuse of any kind. We therefore take any allegations of child abuse very seriously and as a visitor/worker at XXX you will need to know the following information in relation to child protection.

- The Child Protection Lead Teacher (CPLT) is XXX.
- The Deputy Child Protection Lead Teacher is XXX.
- Both the CPLT and Deputy can be contacted via the school office.
- Any suspicions or incidents relating to any child protection matter should be immediately referred to one of the above staff members.
- Details of such incidents should be written down and passed on as soon as is practicable.
- **All adults** in school have a responsibility to report any suspicions or incidents.
- **Please remember all such reports are strictly confidential**.
- Please do not put yourself in vulnerable situations, e.g. do not work alone with a child in an enclosed space or touch a child inappropriately.

> In the instance of a child being at immediate risk or danger, staff are authorised to take any reasonable steps necessary to protect the child.
>
> For more information please refer to the school's Child Protection Policy which is available in the school office.

However, members of staff will need different levels of training depending on their levels of involvement with children. In Sheffield, a training audit tool has been devised that can be adapted by schools and other local authorities in order to facilitate this task. It provides a table in which staff members can be grouped by role, and then indicates by insertion of date, when/if a member of staff has received the available safeguarding training suitable for their role. For more information see www.safeguardingsheffieldchildren.org.uk, Training Audit Tool.

PART 4: SCHOOL PROCEDURES: EVERYONE NEEDS TO KNOW HOW TO...

Safeguarding policies and procedures

An effective whole school child protection/safeguarding policy is one that provides clear direction to staff and others about expected codes of behaviour in dealing with child protection/safeguarding issues. An effective policy also makes explicit the school's commitment to the development of good practice and sound internal school/service procedures. This ensures that child protection/safeguarding concerns and referrals may be handled sensitively, professionally and in ways that support the needs of the child. It needs to contain information in the following areas:

- introduction and purpose
- legal framework and supporting national and local guidance and procedures
- safeguarding and child protection roles of the child protection/safeguarding officer, the head teacher and the governing body
- training and support offered to staff
- professional confidentiality and its limits
- records – collation, storage, access, transfer
- attendance at case conferences and other multi-agency safeguarding meetings
- monitoring and support of pupils with additional needs, or who have been abused

- use of the Common Assessment Framework

- in-school procedure flowcharts on what to do if a child has additional needs, a child is/is suspected of being abused either by adults or other children, and where an allegation of abuse of a child, or other wrongdoing, has been made against a member of staff.

Information on much of the above can be found on the Sheffield Safeguarding Children website: www.safeguardingsheffieldchildren.org.uk. See below for a sample front sheet taken from a guidance document on writing a child protection policy compiled by a regional group called Child Protection in Education (CAPE):

Practice example of front sheet

Child Protection/Safeguarding Policy

School . . . .

A. Named staff/personnel with designated responsibility for Child Protection

Academic year	Designated person	Deputy Designated person	Nominated Governor

B. Review dates for this policy

Review date	Changes made	By whom

(www.cape.org.uk – Writing a Child Protection Policy: a Framework for Schools)

Allegations against staff

Statutory guidance around allegations against staff and volunteers was issued in October 2006 in *Working Together to Safeguard Children* (HM Government 2006). It sets out in detail what is expected of employers and the statutory authorities. Its key points are outlined as follows:

SCOPE OF PROCEDURES

The procedures will apply where a person who works with children has:

- behaved in a way that has harmed or may have harmed a child

- possibly committed an offence against or related to a child

- behaved towards a child or children in a way that indicates that s/he is unsuitable to work with children.

They will also apply where:

- concerns arise about the person's behaviour with regard to her/his own children

- concerns arise about the behaviour in private or community life of a partner, member of the family or other household member.

INVESTIGATIONS

There may be three strands to an investigation:

- police investigation of a possible criminal offence

- a child protection investigation by children's social care (could include the children of the member of staff in certain circumstances)

- disciplinary action by the employer.

It is possible for all three strands to run together but, as a general rule, the police investigation and any prosecution will take precedence. What is new and helpful, however, is the fact that statements taken by the police and children's social care can be made available to the employer, subject to consent which will be obtained at the outset.

KEY FEATURES

- It covers all employees and volunteers.

- Each employer must designate a senior manager to deal with such matters (and a deputy to cover for absence).

- Allegations against head teachers will be dealt with by the chair of governors (deputy in their absence).

- There is a requirement to notify the Local Authority Designated Officer (LADO) within one working day of receipt of an allegation. Different authorities have different arrangements regarding the identification of the LADO. It is important that you find out what your own authority's arrangements are, particularly if you are a head teacher, deputy head teacher or chair of governors.

- The nature of any investigation and actions will be determined by the LADO in consultation with the employer and, where appropriate, the police.

- Cases will be dealt with 'expeditiously and fairly' (for both the alleged victim and the alleged perpetrator).

- There will be a definite outcome from all investigations, even if alleged perpetrators resign.

- Detailed records will be kept on personnel files for ten years or until normal retirement age, whichever is the longer, and mentioned in employment references.

- Regulatory bodies will be notified where appropriate.

GOOD PRACTICE POINTS

The following checklist will be useful for staff:

- Is action required to secure the immediate safety or wellbeing of a child/children? The child/children may need medical attention or to be removed from the scene of an incident. It may be necessary to assign a member of staff to look after them until parents arrive.

- Record dates/times of alleged incidents, the names of those involved and those of any potential witnesses.

- Secure any evidence such as written reports, emails or photographs given to you. Remember that taking statements is a specialist role of the police and you could undermine their work if you are not careful. It is reasonable to listen to a child in a sympathetic way and encourage them to speak but not lead them. Questions such as 'tell me what happened' or 'what happened next?' are OK, but questions such as 'did Mr X hit you on the head yesterday?' are not. You need to ask just enough questions to make a decision.

The member of staff would then pass the matter directly to the head teacher (or chair of governors) who would then:

- Verify that the alleged event(s) could have happened. Was the member of staff on duty and present when the alleged incident took place? Are there credible witnesses who are able to confirm what happened?

- Contact the Local Authority Designated Officer.

- Inform parents where appropriate, but what is said may need to be guided by the LADO/police.

- Contact the relevant Human Resources Provision if suspension or other action is being considered pending investigation.

- Decide what, if anything, is told to other staff members.

(Adapted from www.safeguardingsheffieldchildren.org.uk
'Allegations against staff and volunteers in schools
and early years settings' DCSF 2006)

Restraint policies and procedures

Physical contact with children and young people may be appropriate and necessary in some circumstances and where necessary reasonable force can be used to control or restrain pupils. The law forbids any degree of physical contact which is deliberately intended to punish a pupil or which is primarily intended to cause pain, injury or humiliation in any educational setting or circumstances. All schools must have a policy about the use of force to control or restrain pupils which is available to and understood by the governing body, staff, volunteers, parents and pupils. It should include general information such as the following, as well as information pertinent to the particular school/establishment.

If a school is aware that a pupil may behave in way that is likely to require physical control or restraint, they should plan for this situation and include:

- a risk assessment of the situation

- strategies to manage the pupil

- the involvement of parents/carers

- briefing the staff

- ensuring additional support is available

- medical advice if the child has specific health needs.

The plan should be recorded as part of the child's Individual Behaviour Plan and shared and agreed with parents/carers.

Qualified teachers as well as staff authorised by the head and trained to physically control pupils can use such force as is reasonable to prevent a pupil from:

- committing a criminal offence

- injuring themselves or others

- causing serious damage to property including their own

- engaging in any behaviour prejudicial to maintaining good order and discipline at the school.

If a pupil is at immediate risk of serious injury or on the point of inflicting serious injury on someone else any member of staff is entitled to intervene. Everyone has the right to defend themselves against an attack provided they do not use a disproportionate degree of force to do so. Before intervening physically, the member of staff should try to communicate calmly and clearly with the pupil about their behaviour and consequences. If the member of staff requires help or if there is a risk of injury they should remove other pupils, summon assistance and/or call the police. Incidents should be clearly recorded and placed in a numbered Incident Book and the head teacher as well as parents/carers informed as soon as possible. Any complaint about such an incident should be dealt with under disciplinary or LADO allegations against staff procedures. (Adapted from Department of Children, Schools and Families (2007))

Children and young people who abuse

Children can abuse each other emotionally, physically or sexually. Any such abuse should be taken seriously and action taken straight away. It must be borne in mind that children who abuse are likely to have considerable needs themselves and/or may need some form of protection.

GOOD PRACTICE POINTS

Taking action – emotional/physical abuse (bullying)

- Use in-school anti-bullying policies and procedures, unless a child has suffered or is likely to suffer significant harm, in which case refer to police/children's social services.

- Inform parents/carers.

- Support victim(s), and perpetrators where necessary.

- Deal appropriately with perpetrator(s).

- Consider the need for extra services for any of the children involved.

- Record incidents and action taken.

- Tackle anti-bullying in your curriculum.

Taking action – sexual abuse (including non-consensual 'horseplay')

- Refer to police/children's social services.

- Inform parents/carers as advised by police/children's social services.

- Contribute to any subsequent investigation.

- Support the children concerned.

- Consider the need for extra services for any of the children involved.

- Consider the risk the perpetrator poses to other children in the school.

- Convene a risk management meeting where appropriate.

- Record incidents and actions taken.

- Tackle sexual abuse in your curriculum.

(www.safeguardingsheffieldchildren.org.uk
Children and Young People who Abuse)

RISK MANAGEMENT OF YOUNG PERSONS POSING A RISK TO CHILDREN

One of the more difficult tasks for schools to deal with is the management of children who have abused other children, especially if the abuse is sexual. Sheffield Children and Young People's Directorate are in the process of developing guidance for schools. Below are some of the areas we believe important to consider and record when assessing and managing the risk from and to such pupils:

Practice example

- Introduction – to include name, address and date of birth of perpetrator; Reason for Risk Management Evaluation (RME); agencies to be invited to the RME meeting

- Perpetrator's behaviours of concern

- Perpetrator's level of personal responsibility taken for behaviour of concern

- Perpetrator's attitude towards victims

- Openness and engagement of perpetrator

- Therapeutic input history

- Perpetrator's family and environmental factors, both positive and negative

- Relevant information on the victim(s) and family(ies), e.g. any relation to or out of school interaction with perpetrator and/or family

- Analysis of the risk based on above information

- What support and monitoring mechanisms are available both in and out of school – including the limitations of said support/monitoring

- The agreed plan of action

- Recording, storage and distribution of information.

(Adapted from Person Posing a Risk (PPR) Guidance-Assessment Framework, Sheffield Safeguarding Children Board Protocol)

Procedures for boarding schools

There are a number of essential safeguards important for all schools, but particularly important in situations where children are living away from home in boarding schools. Schools with boarding facilities may find the following additional checklist useful:

GOOD PRACTICE POINTS

- Children living away from home particularly need to feel valued and respected, and their self-esteem promoted.

- The school and its boarding facility should be open to external scrutiny (including from families and the wider community).

- As in any other school, staff should be trained in all aspects of safeguarding children.

- Children should be listened to and their views/concerns responded to. Staff should recognise the importance of understanding how individual children communicate; and if there may be any cultural constraints.

- Children should have ready access to a trusted adult outside the institution and must not feel intimidated about using such access.

- Complaints procedures should be clear, effective, user friendly and readily accessible to children and young people, including those with disabilities and those for whom English is not a first language. These procedures should address informal or 'minor' complaints as seriously as formal or major ones.

- Bullying must be swiftly and effectively dealt with, especially as the children are in a situation where there is no 'let up' or safety valve of being able to go home and leave it behind for a few hours.

- Recruitment and selection procedures should be rigorous and create a high threshold of entry to deter abusers, in particular for staff recruited to work in the boarding facility.

- Clear procedures and support systems should be in place to respond to staff concerns whether about conditions or about other staff. The procedures should guarantee that the 'whistle-blower's' position and prospects are not prejudiced.

- There should be effective supervision and support for all staff.

- Staff should be alert to the risks to children in the external environment from people prepared to exploit the additional vulnerability of children living away from home.

- Contractor staff must be effectively checked and supervised when on site or in contact with the children.

(Adapted from HM Government 2006, pp.193–4)

PART 5: NO SCHOOL IS AN ISLAND: EFFECTIVE LINKS WITH OTHER SCHOOLS AND AGENCIES

Transitions and other transfers of information

It is vital that safeguarding information (as well as general information) about pupils is promptly and accurately shared between schools in a number of circumstances. At each stage of transition (from early years provision/pre-school services to primary school, from primary to secondary, and from secondary to tertiary), or when a pupil moves schools, provision should be made for a comprehensive handover of information and records that highlight vulnerability or risk. At the very least, there should be a face-to-face meeting between relevant child protection/safeguarding officers for all children within a local authority area for whom a child protection record exists. Where a child moves out of the local authority area, these records should be sent recorded delivery to the named child protection/safeguarding officer of the receiving establishment, preferably with a follow-up telephone call to ensure receipt and clarify any questions raised. Different schools will have different methods of transferring information for those children about whom there are concerns that fall short of significant harm. However, consideration still needs to be given to the particularly personal and sensitive nature of such information. Some schools in Sheffield are using an adapted version of the Government's Pre-CAF checklist with all their transitioning children to identify vulnerability on intake as well as to pass information to receiving schools.

Practice Example: Birley Spa Primary School, Sheffield

Birley Spa Primary have chosen to use a checklist identifying positive and inhibiting factors across all the five outcomes for children as an in-class tool for all children in the school. They then apply a 'traffic light system' with red being high concern. Two reds would trigger a full Common Assessment. Any confidential information or child protection concerns are recorded and stored with the Child Protection Liaison Officer (CPLO). Once every term, class teachers use non-contact time to update and check over all their checklists, which then form the basis for transition to the next teacher, and eventually to the relevant secondary school.

This system has been very successful in alleviating parental anxiety about assessment of needs. The children also enjoy taking an active part in adding to their 'purple file' as it is referred to. Issues included are things like joining the Brownies, always forgetting PE kit, frequent loss of 'golden time', or bereavement in the family.

Positives:

- Staff are now finding that it is easy to relate dips in attainment to issues happening in a child's life.

- Children and parents are fully involved at a very early stage.

- Concerns and worries are identified very early.

- Concerns are not overlooked in children who shine in one area, but may be lacking in others.

- It is easy to update all kids when someone new comes in, or supply cover is used.

- It replaces disparate forms, thereby reducing duplication.

In Sheffield, when schools do not know where children who have left have gone to, they are referred to Sheffield's Children Missing in Education Team. The CME team has two core functions:

- to identify Children Missing from Education (Clause 4 of the Education and Inspections Act 2006)

- to support the exclusions and re-integration of vulnerable children.

The work primarily consists of:

- locating children who have become 'missing or lost' from schools

- identifying children who do not have a school place or other provision

- supporting parents/carers to secure a school place or appropriate education provision

- fast admission of Looked After Children into Sheffield schools

- admission and management of the In Year Fair Access Policy (formerly 'Hard to Place Pupil Protocol').

Once children have been located, then files can be transferred in the usual way.

Building a 'family of schools'

A pilot project within the Parson Cross/Ecclesfield Service District of Sheffield is looking at building closer links between a selected secondary school, its feeders, and the special schools, faith schools and tertiary college in the immediate surrounding area with a view to improving communication and consistency of systems, and sharing good practice between all the schools involved. In phase one of the Yewlands' project, the schools worked closely with the Sheffield Safeguarding Children Service to pull together a consistent safeguarding 'offer' that all in the family of schools agreed to (see *Good Practice Points* in Part 1 above). A web-based summary version of policies, procedures and information documents designed to help and support child protection/safeguarding officers in performing their role effectively was produced. Phase two of the project is looking at the creation and joint funding of a post that will provide safeguarding supervision and support for all the child protection/safeguarding officers across the family of schools.

Even without having the above systems in place, it is vital that effective communication within and between schools takes place routinely in cases where safeguarding is an issue. Too often, safeguarding staff in schools never think to check with siblings' schools or previous schools of children they are concerned about, even when they think to consult with partner agencies.

PART 6: RECORDING AND RECORD KEEPING

Dos and don'ts

Clear and accurate factual recording of all safeguarding concerns/incidents is vital to the effective safeguarding of children and, in some cases, the apprehension and prosecution of perpetrators. It is important to realise that safeguarding records are kept until the child has reached their twenty-fifth birthday. Therefore, records must be as meaningful in 20 years time as they are at the time of writing.

All records should be:
- factual and evidenced
- concise and complete
- accurate and objective
- dated and signed
- securely stored.

Basic principles

A safeguarding file should be opened by the relevant member of staff (e.g. early intervention – Special Educational Needs Co-ordinator (SENCO), Learning Mentor, Education Welfare Officer etc; child protection – Child Protection Liaison Teacher (CPLT)/Child Protection Officer (CPO)) when any cause for concern has been identified.

Where possible all records must include the:
- child's full name, address, date of birth
- details of anyone with parental responsibility
- details of any other significant adults

- details of any siblings, and their addresses if different

- names and contact details of any involved professionals.

They should also include:
- date and time of writing the record

- date and time you obtained the information

- date and time of any alleged incident and/or when your concern was triggered

- nature of your concerns, what gave rise to them, and any conversations you have had about this

- any action you have taken

- extent and nature of any involvement by others, and their full name, position and relationship to the child.

Don't forget:
- If a disclosure is made, you must thoroughly record the content of the disclosure and any responses you made.

- Stick to the facts as you know them, and give reasons for your professional opinions.

File contents – Organised in date order

- front-sheet summary with basic details of the child:

  ○ a chronology of the contents of the file, updated after each new entry

  ○ copies of reports and ongoing log of discussions, meetings, etc.

  ○ a copy of any completed pre-assessment checklist, and/or Common Assessment Form

  ○ reports to and minutes of all formal meetings (e.g. multi-agency meetings, case conferences, core groups meetings, etc.)

  ○ a copy of the child's safeguarding action plan(s) (e.g. multi-agency action plan, child protection plan, etc.)

  ○ confirmation that the child is subject to a child protection plan, if appropriate.

Storage

- All individual safeguarding records/files/ information should be collated and stored in a locked cabinet separate from any other recorded pupil information.

- Access to child protection records/files is managed by head teacher/manager, the child protection/safeguarding officer and the deputy child protection/safeguarding officer.

Sharing information within your establishment

- Information will need to be shared with other colleagues where this is in the best interest of the child or young person.

- It is the responsibility of the child protection/safeguarding officer, their deputy and the head teacher/manager to decide who has access to safeguarding information.

- They may provide a wider group of staff with limited information so that they are able to respond appropriately to the child in school.

Transferring files/records

- All safeguarding files must be transferred immediately to the new establishment and a receipt for the file should be returned to the transferring establishment.

- Where possible, transfers should take place in a face-to-face meeting.

- Where the child is moving out of the city, files should be transferred by recorded delivery to the named, relevant practitioner with designated responsibility for child protection.

- Each establishment must keep a copy of the front-sheet summary to ensure they have sufficient knowledge of the case and their involvement, should this be required at a later date, until the child becomes 25 years old.

- Where more than one child of the family attends the establishment, consideration will need to be given to splitting or copying files. Permission to copy documents that have not originated in school (e.g. case conference minutes) must be sought from the relevant agency.

- Where secondary pupils do not continue into further education, the secondary school/college must ensure that the safeguarding records are archived securely until the young person is 25 years old.

- All child protection/safeguarding officers receiving current or closed files must keep all the contents and not remove any material. (*Record Keeping and the Transfer of Files.* Available at www.safeguardingsheffieldchildren.org.uk)

PART 7: SAFER RECRUITMENT
Recruitment and vetting checks

Those who employ people to work in schools must carry out the following recruitment and vetting checks on intended new appointees:

- identity checks

- List 99 checks

- CRB disclosures

- qualifications checks

- checks to confirm the right to work in the United Kingdom

- where the appointee has lived outside the United Kingdom, further checks may be necessary to establish suitability to work with children

- seek references

- check previous employment history.

(Adapted from Department for Children, Schools and Families (2006) p.37)

Volunteers/parent helpers

Education establishments should adopt similar recruitment procedures for volunteers to those they use for paid staff where they are undertaking an ongoing voluntary role with children on a regular basis (regular is seen as three or more times in a 30-day period, once a month or more, or overnight).

- If checks have not been completed satisfactorily, the volunteer must not be left alone with children.

- For one-off roles, such as school outings, it is recommended that the CRB risk assessment guidance available on the LEAF (Local Education Authority Federation) website at www.leafonline.co.uk is used.

- If volunteers are recruited by another organisation to work in your setting, obtain assurance that the person has been properly recruited and vetted, and obtain an agreement in respect of supervision and support for the volunteer.

- Ensure that the volunteer role is defined and understood by all and that it does not involve the provision of personal care to children and young people.

- Make sure that volunteers have sufficient information about the establishment and its ethos in order to properly safeguard children and themselves.

Governors should be seen as volunteers in this context and:
- governors who have regular contact with children should be asked for a CRB disclosure

- any governor giving cause for concern should be asked for an enhanced CRB disclosure

- all other governors should be asked for a signed declaration confirming their suitability to fulfil the role. (*Volunteers*, adapted from and accessed at www.safeguardingsheffieldchildren.org.uk)

PART 8: CONCLUSION

In conclusion, it is worth remembering that children and young people spend a substantial amount of their lives in school. For some it will be their only chance to access the appropriate role modelling required to grow up 'healthy, happy, wealthy and wise'. For others, it is our vigilance and appropriate intervention that will enable them to grow up at all. We are an important part of the whole of their lives, their achievement of *all* the five outcomes for children, not just their teaching and learning.

We *can* make a difference. Let's do that.

REFERENCES

Child Protection in Education (CAPE) (2004) 'Writing a Child Protection Policy: A Framework for Schools.' Available at: www.cape.org.uk/downloads.php, accessed 9 December 2008.

Department for Children, Schools and Families (2006) *Safeguarding Children and Safer Recruitment in Education*. London: Stationery Office.

Department for Children, Schools and Families (2007) *The Use of Force to Control or Restrain Pupils*. London: Stationery Office.

HM Government (2006) *Working Together to Safeguard Children: A Guide to Inter-agency Working to Safeguard and Promote the Welfare of Children*. London: Stationery Office.

Sheffield Safeguarding Children Service (2008) 'Allegations against Staff, Governors and Volunteers in Schools.' Available at http://www.safeguardingsheffieldchildren.org.uk/sys_upl/templates/AssetBrowser/AssetBrowser_disp.asp?ItemID=1842&basketPage=&basketItem=&pgid=114650&tid=186&page=1 , accessed 25 November 2008.

Sheffield Safeguarding Children Service (2008) 'Children and Young People Who Abuse.' Available at http://www.safeguardingsheffieldchildren.org.uk/sys_upl/templates/AssetBrowser/AssetBrowser_disp.asp?ItemID=1845&basketPage=&basketItem=&pgid=114650&tid=186&page=1, accessed 25 November 2008.

Sheffield Safeguarding Children Service (2008) 'The Person Posing a Risk to Children Assessment Framework – (PPRTC Assessment Framework).' Available at http://www.safeguardingsheffieldchildren.org.uk/sys_upl/templates/AssetBrowser/AssetBrowser_disp.asp?I temID=3445&basketPage=&basketItem=&pgid=122390&tid=186&page=2 , accessed 25 November 2008.

Sheffield Safeguarding Children Service (2008) 'Record Keeping and the Transfer of Files.' Available at http://www.safeguardingsheffieldchildren.org.uk/sys_upl/templates/Asset Browser/AssetBrowser_disp.asp?ItemID=1864&basketPage=&basketItem=&pgid= 114650&tid=186&page=3, accessed 25 November 2008.

Sheffield Safeguarding Children Service (2008) 'The Safeguarding Children "Offer".' Available at http://www.safeguardingsheffieldchildren.org.uk/sys_upl/templates/AssetBrowser/Asset Browser_disp.asp?ItemID=1870&basketPage=&basketItem=&pgid=114650&tid= 186&page=4, accessed 25 November 2008.

Sheffield Safeguarding Children Service (2008) 'Safeguarding Children Training Audit for Schools.' Available at http://www.safeguardingsheffieldchildren.org.uk/sys_upl/templates/ AssetBrowser/AssetBrowser_disp.asp?ItemID=1871&basketPage=&basketItem=&pgid= 114650&tid=186&page=4, accessed 25 November 2008.

Sheffield Safeguarding Children Service (2008) 'Volunteers.' Available at http://www.safe guardingsheffieldchildren.org.uk/sys_upl/templates/AssetBrowser/AssetBrowser_disp.asp?I temID=1877&basketPage=&basketItem=&pgid=114650&tid=186&page=5, accessed 25 November 2008.

USEFUL ORGANISATIONS

Child Protection in Education, www.cape.org.uk

Department for Children, Schools and Families, www.dcsf.gov.uk

Every Child Matters, www.everychildmatters.gov.uk/resources-and-practice/

Local Education Authority Foundation, www.leafonline.co.uk

Sheffield Safeguarding Children Service
Floor 4, Palatine Chambers, 18–28 Pinstone Street
Sheffield S1 2HN
or Floor 2, Redvers House, Union Street
Sheffield S1 2JQ
www.safeguardingsheffieldchildren.org.uk

Teachernet, www.teachernet.gov.uk

CHAPTER 3

MAKING THE MOST OF A HOME VISIT

LIZ HUGHES

This chapter refers mostly to health visitors, but is equally relevant for practitioners from other disciplines and agencies whose job it is to visit families in their homes. There are references to the academic literature, but most of the ideas were generated by health visitors and school nurses in Sheffield who took part in a Delphi style exercise (Gordon 2004) designed to achieve consensus about the issues to be considered when visiting vulnerable children at home.

WHY VISIT AT HOME?

Visiting at home allows the professional the opportunity to observe the environment in which children and families live in order to assess the likely impact of that environment on the children's health, development and wellbeing and the parents'/carers' capacity to meet their needs (Department of Health 2000). A recent Serious Case Review which received a high level of media interest criticised community nursing staff for not having seen the children's bedrooms. Reports in the media described the living room where the parents spent most of their time as well equipped and 'state of the art', whereas conditions in the bedrooms were found to be appalling (Cantrill 2005).

It is probably fair to assume that if the condition of the living accommodation gives cause for concern, the bedrooms are likely to be as bad if not worse. However it is clearly not safe to assume that good conditions in the living room prevail throughout the house.

There is a tension between what may be perceived as inappropriately imposing middle class standards and accepting lower standards because that is the norm for the area (Reder, Duncan and Gray 1993). The participants in this study were keen not to take on the role of social policemen and strongly agreed that it may not be appropriate to routinely ask to see rooms in the house other than the one into which they have been invited, for example the children's bedrooms. This is obviously a sensitive issue, which should not be ignored, especially if there are concerns about the general state of the house.

The Children Act (1989 s47) requires professionals to compare the child in front of them with other children of similar age and development and to consider what constitutes reasonable parenting. A useful question to consider is whether this child's circumstances would be acceptable for our own children. If the answer is 'no', then intervention is needed.

Judgement should be made regarding the urgency for immediate action balanced with the possible benefit of taking some time to develop a working relationship with the parents before challenging their home conditions. Discuss options with your supervisor or manager.

WHO TO VISIT AT HOME?

In these times of changing lifestyles, increasing workloads and decreasing resources, professionals have to be able to prioritise. It is no longer possible or, in the opinion of some critics, useful to visit all families with young children at home (Department of Health 2007; Hall and Elliman 2003). Studies have shown that home visiting programmes in the past have benefited some families but not others and have improved some outcomes but not others. Olds et al. (1999) suggest that programmes which focus on families where there are factors which indicate increased risk of poor outcomes are more likely to demonstrate success.

MAKE THE MOST OF A RARE OPPORTUNITY; YOU MIGHT ONLY HAVE ONE CHANCE

Organisational, caseload and workload pressures nowadays mean that for many practitioners visiting clients in their own homes is limited to one initial contact. Unless obvious concerns are recognised at this visit, parents and carers are thereafter expected to attend clinic or the practitioner's work base to access services, seek advice and gain support. Historically, regular home visits to families with pre-school children by the health visitor was routine and gave the practitioner the opportunity to get to know the family, to get a sense of their relationships, attitudes, beliefs and support systems and an understanding of what life might be like for the children. It also offered the family the opportunity to develop a relationship with the practitioner based on familiarity and trust (Browne et al. 2000).

Changes in circumstances, improvements or deterioration in home conditions, the quality of attachment and bonding (Bacon and Richardson 2001; Howe et al. 1999) and parental mental health (Falkov 1996; Hetherington et *al.* 2002). The comings and goings of male partners (Scourfield 2006) and so on would be observed and noted. Appropriate interventions would be planned, implemented, monitored and reviewed (Appleton and Cowley 2003; Douglas and Ginty 2001; Macdonald 2001).

There have always been families who prefer not to have professionals visit them at home; it may be that they do not wish to have their environment observed and their privacy invaded, or risk being exposed to judgement and criticism which would not be the case in the clinic setting (Reder and Duncan 1995). The professional has to decide whether this is appropriate or whether it raises the level of concern. The problem with the 'one-off' visit, especially in the early post-natal period, before the rosy glow of new parenthood has been clouded by sleepless nights and before visitors who flocked to see the infant have gone away, is that the assessment made could be limited and possibly inaccurate.

The situation observed at two weeks post partum may be significantly different at six weeks when the impact of incremental sleep deprivation and other losses which are experienced after the birth of a baby are more evident and the reality of caring for the infant is not what the parents were expecting (Cox, Holden and Sagovsky 1987; Rosenblatt 1993).

Possible problems

- Loss
- Sleep
- Freedom
- Body image
- Relationship with partner
- Income
- Expectations
- Image of 'baby'

Many parents do not expect to have ambivalent or negative feelings about their children. Having a baby is supposed to be a joyful experience, especially if the pregnancy has been carefully planned and longed for. Most parents are able to put on a 'brave face' in public, so their presentation at clinic may be very different from what it would be in the home. The current medical model of baby clinic based on immunisation, growth monitoring and health assessment does not readily facilitate the development of a relationship with a professional that would encourage the sharing of intimate and sensitive information and feelings. Most parents feel pressure to appear to be coping, especially in front of those who may be perceived to be in a position to remove their children (Goffman 1959). They value the opportunity to tell their story in an unhurried way, to discuss hopes, fears and disappointments and to express their feelings in an environment where they feel comfortable and safe. For most people, the best place to do this is at home.

VISIT BY APPOINTMENT OR 'DROP IN'?

This is a sensitive and possibly contentious area; some argue that it is more respectful to the family to visit only by appointment. Clients may be embarrassed if the house is untidy or they are still not dressed in the middle of the morning, as is very common in the first few weeks of an infant's life. Parents sleeping late may become an issue of concern if children are missing nursery or school.

Managers would probably say that in terms of cost efficiency it is better to visit by appointment, there being, theoretically, less risk of the client not being at home. It is of course possible that the appointment system gives clients who are reluctant to engage the opportunity to be out when the practitioner knocks on the door.

The 'drop in' visit is likely to afford the practitioner a more realistic impression of the family, which may facilitate more effective assessment and intervention. It is good practice to ask the family if they mind being 'dropped in' on, though a negative response may mean that a useful opportunity is no longer an option. It is ultimately a matter of professional judgement: what are the risk factors and how much higher would anxiety levels be in this event? It is important to remember that it is a privilege to be invited into clients' homes; no one has statutory right of entry without an order from the court (Human Rights Act 1998).

Remember that the law requires that the threshold of significant harm is reached before there can be compulsory intervention in family life (The Children Act 1989). Remember too that the health visiting service is optional for families; they do not have to engage. However, most families with young children do engage and it is important to think about the reasons why they may not want to. It would be a good idea to discuss concerns with your safeguarding children supervisor or manager before making a decision about action. Your employing organisation is likely to have a policy for addressing the issue of clients who do not wish to access universal health services. The local safeguarding children board child protection procedures may include a protocol for managing unco-operative families. If in doubt discuss it with your manager or safeguarding children supervisor.

INFORMATION GATHERING

Familiarise yourself with professional and government guidance and your agency/trust's policy on information management (Department for Education and Skills 2005; Health Visitors Association 1994; Royal College of Nursing and Midwifery Council (NMC) 2007).

Health practitioners are likely to have some kind of written record for the family, maybe only a copy of an ante-natal letter or a hospital discharge letter, but possibly a significant record of involvement, intervention and outcomes. Check your local multi-agency Information Sharing System to find out whether the child is known to other agencies.

Read the records

There is all manner of information to be gleaned from the records. Try not to make a home visit without first reading the family record thoroughly. There are some families where it may be inappropriate to visit at home, for example where there is known to be a history of violence or a dangerous dog. The decision not to visit at home must be taken only after careful consideration of the concerns and assessment of risk. If it is not safe for a professional to visit the home, what might it be like for a child to live there?

Be aware of risk factors that may render children vulnerable to abuse and neglect

Remember that these are risk factors, not indicators of abuse. A combination of two or more of these factors is likely to increase the level of risk.

Is there a chronology of significant events that includes concern about safeguarding issues? Has a Common Assessment Form been completed? Have any additional needs been identified? If so what action has been taken? What interventions have been tried and what resources have been offered to and taken up by the family? Are there any obvious child protection/child in need records; case conference minutes; a current child protection/child in need plan?

Child protection minutes are often printed on coloured paper to make them easy to identify. In some areas records of children who are the subjects of child protection plans or referred for discussion in supervision are filed in distinctive folders for the same reason. Be aware of practice in your local safeguarding children board area.

Risk factors

- Substance/alcohol misuse
- Adult mental health problems
- Learning disabilities
- Domestic abuse
- Disabled child
- Homelessness/frequent house moves
- Asylum seekers
- Young unsupported parents
- Step/reconstituted family

Check that the address given is correct

It may be obvious to a practitioner who knows the area that no such address exists. In these circumstances it would be worth a phone call to your local child health department or to the GP practice to clarify.

Note changes of address

Changes of address may mean that the family has financial difficulties or that they are attempting to avoid contact by agencies (Reder and Duncan 1995). For older children it may mean that their education is being affected by disrupted school attendance and they may not have the opportunity to make friends.

Other issues to consider

- What other information would be helpful?
- Where might you find it?
- Who else might have information that would contribute to your knowledge of the family?
- Is there a contact number for the family or a grandparent?

There should be a record of names and contact details of practitioners previously involved with the family who may be able to share useful information.

Is it possible from the records to determine members of the household?

There should be names and dates of birth of family members, which will tell you how many children there are in the household, their ages and spacing. You may discover that there are siblings living elsewhere or perhaps a child has died or has been removed from the parents' care because of abuse or neglect.

Is there evidence of changes of partner? (*Disappearing Men*, Scourfield 2006). It may be apparent that the children have different surnames, common in Asian families, but it may indicate that the mother has had a succession of partners. In this case it is worth considering whether the older children's situation in the family is different to that of the children of the current relationship.

Is there anyone who definitely should not be in the household?

Has anyone been identified as a person posing risk to the children, the term now used in place of 'schedule 1 offender' to describe an adult who may or may not have a conviction for an offence against a child (Home Office 2004)? An enquiry to your local Information Sharing Index might be helpful.

Family history

There may be a family health needs assessment that would tell you about particular issues that have been identified and how they have been addressed. That would be a useful starting point for your visit and may indicate to the family that you have taken the trouble to find out something about their needs. Individual children's records may contain a history of contact with practitioners from several agencies. There should be a history of growth and development, immunisation, identified health needs, disabilities, planned interventions and outcomes based on the Framework for the Assessment of Children in Need or the Common Assessment Framework (CAF).

There may be information regarding attendances at accident and emergency departments and other hospital facilities, defaulted appointments and liaison letters from other professionals.

Is there reference to anything that might suggest domestic abuse, for example records of attendance of the mother (usually) at Accident and Emergency departments with facial (or other) bruising? Is there any evidence that the question has been asked? Is there reference to extended family support and social networks?

BEFORE YOU SET OUT ON THE VISIT

Dress sensitively and appropriately. Wear something in which you would not mind being touched by sticky fingers. Parents may be offended if you appear unwilling to have their child climb on your knee and the child may be reluctant to engage with you. But do not deliberately 'dress down', that may be equally offensive.

What do you want to achieve?

- Be clear about your reason for visiting.
- Write a list of objectives.
- How do you expect to achieve them?
- What will you do if you don't/can't?

Based on the information you have gathered, decide whether it is safe to visit alone, if in doubt arrange for a colleague to go with you, even if just to sit in the car.

Visit procedures

- Let your colleagues know where you are going and what time to expect you back.

- Have a plan for action if you do not return as planned, for example, let your colleagues know if you have safely finished the visit but are not returning to base, it may save unnecessary anxiety and emergency action.

- Carry a mobile phone with a fully charged battery and programmed with speed dial numbers.

- Ensure that you park your car in a situation from which it is easy to drive away, try to reverse into parking spaces where possible, it's usually quicker to drive out forwards.

Observing the house or flat in the context of other homes in the same area

- Do all the houses on the road look the same or does this one stand out as different?

- Does it appear well maintained?

- Are the curtains open or closed?

- Is there evidence of damage to windows or doors?

- Is the garden tidy or full of rubbish?

- Is there a large dog on a chain which might be long enough to reach anyone setting foot on the premises?

- What might it be like to live next door to this family?

- Are there people coming and going from the property?

- Do you feel comfortable visiting this household?

Curtains which remain closed during the daytime may or may not be a significant sign. Reder and Duncan (1995) refer to a phenomenon that they call 'closure', a feature in some of the historical cases of child deaths from abuse. The term refers to behaviour which families employ as a defence against the outside world in general and child welfare practitioners in particular. Habitually closed curtains in families who are difficult to engage is of concern. Do not assume that they are still in bed and go away. Visiting unco-operative families is very stressful for professionals. Your local safeguarding children boards' child protection procedures may include guidance for managing families who are difficult to engage and your employer may have a policy of zero tolerance of abuse of their employees that may be helpful.

First impressions

- What are your first impressions?
- Are you hoping that they will not be at home when you call?
- Is your concern about a particular individual?
- Is there any evidence that your concern is justified?

It is worth sitting in the car for a few minutes to observe comings and goings. It may be that the family has many attentive friends, but it could also be a sign that attempts are being made to collect debts or that the property is being used to deal drugs or for the purposes of prostitution.

Be especially concerned about young people coming and going when they should be at school.

GETTING IN

In order to achieve your objectives you have to get over the threshold and that means knocking on the door and engaging with whoever answers. It sounds easy, but it may cause some anxiety especially if there is a history of the family being unco-operative or difficult to engage. Rehearse what you plan to say and perhaps take something to offer, for example health promotion material appropriate to the age of the child. As you approach the house, note signs of people being at home, for example open windows, a car in the drive and the sound of children playing/crying.

Front door or back door?

There is an argument for using the back door on the grounds that you are more likely to be led through the kitchen into the living area, thus being able to see where food is prepared and to observe the standard of hygiene, however, this could be construed as being inappropriately nosey. Again it depends on the level of concern.

There is a knack to knocking on doors

Some families dread a knock on the door; it could be someone they do not want to see, perhaps someone demanding money. So do not knock too loudly, aggressively or persistently.

It is useful to carry something that identifies you to anyone watching, for example the baby weighing scales. Always carry and show agency identification.

Getting in

- Listen very carefully before you knock, can you hear the TV or voices?
- Listen again after knocking, can you hear footsteps or has it gone quiet?
- It may be worth announcing yourself through the letterbox.

NOT GETTING IN: THE 'NO ACCESS' VISIT

Some organisations have specific guidance about what constitutes a no access visit. Familiarise yourself with local guidance and act accordingly. No access visits have featured in many Serious Case Reviews and public inquiries into child deaths from abuse and neglect (Reder *et al.* 1993). No access visits therefore cause anxiety for front line workers, especially when children are believed to be vulnerable. For the purpose of this discussion the following examples are included, but there are no doubt other situations that could be defined as no access.

No access

- There is no one at home for an opportunistic drop in visit.
- There is no one at home for a visit which was made by appointment with the family.
- There is someone at home but they don't open the door.
- The door is opened but you are not invited in.

Options for action

It depends on the level of concern. Is this the first time you have failed to gain access or have you tried several different days and times? Are there signs that the property is lived in? Are the parents likely to be taking/collecting children from school? How anxious are you? What are you anxious about?

Options for action

- Leave a card stating when you plan to call again.
- Try to contact them by phone.
- Leave a card with contact details and wait for the client to get in touch.
- Ask neighbours when the client is likely to be in.
- Revisit at another time of day.
- Liaise with school/nursery re child's attendance/concerns.

- Liaise with other workers.
- Discuss with your manager/safeguarding children supervisor.

The 'doorstep' visit

- The door is answered but you are not invited in.
- You are told that the person/child you want to see is not at home.
- The family is just going out.
- The door is answered by a child.
- The door is answered by an adult male who is at home alone.

Options for action

Again it depends on the level of concern; you will have to make a professional judgement. Does it raise your level of anxiety? In the first three examples, it may be possible to negotiate another, more convenient, time. In the case of the door being answered by a child, how old is the child? Is s/he home alone, this could be evidence of neglect. Is the parent still in bed? This may indicate poor supervision. Or is the parent simply engaged on the telephone or feeding a baby? Exceptionally, it may not be appropriate to enter. A female worker should be very cautious about going into a house where she will be alone with an adult male especially if he is not known to the worker. Fathers are of course entitled to be offered the health visiting service but it is unlikely that he will be the primary target of the visit and it would be more effective and possibly safer to make another arrangement to visit with a colleague when the child is at home or to invite them to clinic.

Male workers should be equally cautious when visiting women who are alone at home; this may not be culturally acceptable to some families, and it is possible that the worker may be vulnerable to allegations of professional malpractice. Remember that parents do not have to engage with the health visiting service. Reasons for refusal or reluctance to do so should be explored with the parents if possible and other ways of accessing the service offered. Some families prefer to see their GP, perhaps because they mistakenly believe that they are guaranteed absolute confidentiality. Liaison with the GP may be useful in a situation where there are concerns about vulnerable children and non-engagement with services; it may help to decide what action to take.

DURING THE VISIT

Be punctual; if it's not possible to keep to the agreed appointment time try to let the family know. Be polite and respectful, you are a guest in their home and you would like to be invited in again. Remember that you are in a position of power in relation to the family that may affect communication.

Tell the family why you're there

One of the first things that is taught in nurse training is the importance of telling the patient what you're going to do. This usually refers to treatment in hospital, but it is very important in any setting. Fear of the unknown makes people feel powerless and vulnerable and affects the way they behave. Introduce yourself and your service; show your professional identification card. Tell them why you are visiting and what you would like to achieve during the visit, ask them what they expect from your service and what they would like to talk about. Be prepared to be flexible and responsive to circumstances, but beware of being inappropriately distracted from your agenda.

Setting boundaries

It is important to remember that your aim is to establish and develop a professional working relationship with the family, not a friendship. It may be difficult to challenge parents who think you are their friend. Be a friendly professional, not a professional friend. How are you going to address each other? First-name terms seem to be the norm these days, but this can blur the boundary of the relationship. It is respectful to ask the client how they would prefer to be addressed. Agree the length of time available for the visit; they (and you) may have other pressing commitments.

Engaging with the parents

It is important to find common ground. Most clients are interested in your personal professional credibility, especially when you are commenting on their parenting style and homemaking capacity. You don't have to be a parent yourself, but it helps! At least you will be seen to have experienced the most fundamental aspects of parenthood. Remember though, that your own personal experience may not be relevant to others. Those who are not parents will find other ways of making connections with the family. Simply showing an interest in the children and the family's needs and a commitment to working with them to achieve their goals may be enough.

It may be useful to ask them about their previous experience of your agency or other services, it may help to understand reluctance to engage and facilitate more effective ways of working.

What other information do you need? Decide whether it is appropriate to ask today and what would be best left until your next contact.

See the child/children

It sounds obvious, but it is possible to do several visits to the home and not see the children. Perhaps they are at nursery or taking a nap; babies and toddlers usually sleep in the daytime. But it is possible that the parents are deliberately not allowing you access. Ask the parents when is the best time to see the children. It is good practice to use the Common Assessment Framework format incorporating the Framework for the Assessment of Children in Need in discussion with the parents to assess the children and to identify needs (Department for Education and Skills 2005).

During the first visit

- Assess development, measure growth.
- Assess attachment, quality of care, etc.
- Assess parenting style/capacity.
- Identify family health needs, raise their awareness of those needs.
- Assess need for more than core service; is this possible after this visit?
- Identify issues of concern.
- Agree a plan of intervention.
- Give contact numbers, etc.

Keep the focus on the children

It is easy to become so involved with the parents' agenda that the children's situation is not addressed. This could be because the parents have immediate needs, but it could also be that the parents are deliberately diverting the professional's attention away from the children. It is important to recognise that this may be happening and find ways of bringing the focus back to the children.

Assess parenting capacity

Are the children's basic needs catered for? How do the parents speak to the children? How do the parents speak about the children? The effects of 'low warmth, high criticism' parenting on children are well documented in the literature (Department of Health 1995).

Home environment

- Is it warm enough and clean enough?
- Do they have the basic essentials?
- Are there age-appropriate toys?
- Are there animals in the house? Do they appear well cared for?
- Is there evidence of cigarette smoking in the house?
- Is there anything that suggests illicit drug or alcohol use?
- Are there half-empty feeding bottles and dirty nappies lying around? These could pose a risk of gastro-enteritis.

Signs of safety

It is important to balance risk of harm with mitigating factors (Turnell and Edwards 1999). It may be that although there are factors in the parents' lifestyle that may result in harm to the children, there are others in the family and social network who have an interest in the children and will look out for them. Do not assume, however that the existence of extended family and friends necessarily means that they are supportive. Possibly the most important sign of safety is the parents' recognition of risk, acknowledgement of their responsibility to prioritise the children's needs and engagement with support services.

Addressing concerns

It is best practice to be open and honest with parents about concerns from the outset: if they don't understand what the problems are, how can they be expected to change? This should be done gently but firmly in a non-judgemental way, there is no need to be brutal or confrontational. Parents need to understand exactly what is expected of them, by when and what action may be necessary in the event of their failure to engage and continuing concern. Be aware that some parents know what professionals want to hear, so expressed commitment to change should be evidenced by actual change within the given time frame.

Getting out, having a plan

Openly keep your eye on the time; it is easy for clients to become engrossed in telling you their story. Don't try to sneakily look at your watch, they will notice and they may think you are not interested in them. Remind them of the time you agreed to finish the visit and what time you have to leave. It sometimes happens that a client will tell you something really significant just as you are about to leave; resist the temptation to be drawn into further discussion now unless you think that the risk of not doing so is too great. Offer another appointment or signpost the client to an alternative appropriate service.

Getting in again

Very often there is good reason to go back, especially if you have not achieved your original agenda, perhaps you were not able to see the children. Explain this to the parents and negotiate a date and time which is convenient for them and when the children will be at home or awake.

AFTER THE VISIT

Reflection: 'Two heads are better than one'

This is probably most effectively done with a colleague or child protection/safeguarding supervisor who may challenge perceptions and assessments. Having another person's objective and/or expert perspective may add to the quality of the analysis. Try to make time for this process as soon as possible after the visit, before impressions have faded. Make notes of important points.

Reflection after the visit

- Were you able to achieve your objectives? If not, why not?
- How did it make you feel?
- Who/what made you feel this way?
- What action do you need to take?
- Do you need to seek/share information? What, with whom?

Record keeping

Records must be kept in line with professional codes of conduct and local policies.

Records are a tool for practice and should reflect assessment, planning and evaluation. It is very useful to keep a chronology of significant events, it can be a reminder of how long the family has been known to services, what issues have been identified and resources provided or offered and rejected. It is a time-consuming exercise but well worth the effort.

WHEN THINGS GO WRONG

Best practice doesn't necessarily result in happy endings. Working with vulnerable families is known to have a high emotional impact on staff, especially when they are reluctant to engage and difficult to work with (Morrison 1994). Use your colleagues as a supportive resource; look after each other. It is vital that staff engage in regular proactive supervision with a manager or safeguarding children supervisor and that workload issues are addressed appropriately.

REFERENCES

Appleton, J. V. and Cowley, S. (2003) 'Valuing professional judgment in health visiting practice.' *Community Practitioner* 76, 6.

Bacon, H. and Richardson, S. (2001) 'Attachment theory and child abuse: an overview of the literature for practitioners.' *Child Abuse Review* 10, 377–397.

Browne, K., Hamilton, C.E., Hegarty, J. and Blisset, J. (2000) 'Identifying need and protecting children through community nurse home visits.' *Representing Children* 13, 2, 111–123.

Cantrill, P. (2005) *Overview Report in Respect of Children SW, NW, JDW, JWW and CLW.* Sheffield Area Child Protection Committee. Sheffield: Sheffield ACPC.

Children Act 1989. London: HMSO.

Cox, J.L., Holden, J.M. and Sagovsky, R. (1987) 'Detection of post-natal depression, the development of the 10 item Edinburgh post-natal depression scale.' *British Journal of Psychiatry* 150, 782–786.

Department for Education and Skills (2005) *Every Child Matters, Change for Children.* London: Stationery Office.

Department of Health (1995) *Child Protection Messages from Research.* London: HMSO.

Department of Health (2000) *Framework for Assessment of Children in Need and their Families.* London: HMSO.

Department of Health (2007) *Facing the Future, a Review of the Role of Heath Visitors.* London: Stationery Office.

Douglas, H. and Ginty, M. (2001) 'The Solihull approach: changes in health visiting practice.' *Community Practitioner* 74, 222–224.

Falkov, A. (1996) *Fatal Child Abuse and Parental Psychiatric Disorder.* London: Department of Health.

Goffman, E. (1959) 'The Presentation of Self in Everyday Life.' In C.J. Colhoun (ed.) (2007) *Contemporary Sociological Theory.* London: Blackwell.

Gordon, T.J. (2004) 'The Delphi method.' In J.C. Glenn and T.J. Gordon (eds) *AC/UNU Millennium Project*: 'Futures research technology', version 2, available at www.millennium-project.org, accessed 8 July 2008.

Hall, D. and Elliman, D. (2003) *Health for all Children*, 4th edn. Oxford: Oxford University Press.

Health Visitors Association (1994) *Protecting the Child, an HVA Guide to Practice and Procedures.* London: HVA.

Hetherington, R., Baistow, K., Katz, I. and Mesie, J. (2002) *The Welfare of Children with Mentally Ill Parents, Learning from Inter-County Comparisons.* London: Stationery Office.

Home Office (2004) *A Person Posing Risk to Children*. London: Stationery Office.

Howe, D., Brandon, M., Hinings, D. and Schofield, G. (1999) *Attachment Theory, Child Maltreatment and Family Support, a Practice and Assessment Model*. Basingstoke: Macmillan.

Human Rights Act (1998) Article 8: The right to respect for private and family life and correspondence, available at www.yourrights.org.uk, accessed 8 July 2008.

Macdonald, G. (2001) *Effective Interventions for Child Abuse and Neglect*. Chichester: Wiley.

Milner, J. (1993) 'A disappearing act: the differing career paths of fathers and mothers in child protection investigations.' *Critical Social Policy 13*, 38, 48–63.

Morrison, T. (1994) 'The emotional effects of child protection work on the worker.' *Practice 4*, 4.

Olds, D.L., Kitzman, J., Henderson, C.R. Jr. and Eckenrode, J.J. (1999) 'Pre-natal and infancy home visitation by nurses, recent findings.' *The Future of Children 9*, 1, Spring/Summer 1999. Available at www.futureofchildren.org/pubs-info2825/pubs-info_show.htm?doc_id=70386, accessed p December 2008.

Reder, P., Duncan, S. and Gray, M. (1993) *Beyond Blame*. London: Routledge.

Reder, P. and Duncan, S. (1995) 'Closure, covert warnings and escalating child abuse.' *Child Abuse and Neglect 19*, 12.

Rosenblatt, P.C. (1993) 'Grief: The Social Context of Private Feelings.' In M.S. Stroebe, W. Stroebe and R.O. Hansson *Handbook of Bereavement, Theory, Research and Intervention*. Cambridge: Cambridge University Press.

Nursing and Midwifery Council (2007) *Professional Code of Conduct*. London: NMC.

Scourfield, J. (2006) 'The challenge of engaging fathers in the child protection process.' *Critical Social Policy 26*, 2, 440–449.

Turnell, A. and Edwards, S. (1999) *Signs of Safety, a Solution and Safety Orientated Approach to Child Protection Casework*. New York: W.W. Norton.

CHAPTER 4

INFANT MENTAL HEALTH AND EARLY ATTACHMENT

DIPTI AISTROP

INFANT MENTAL HEALTH

'Health is the basis for a good quality of life and mental health is of overriding importance in this', as stated in Article 24 of the United Nations Convention on the Rights of the Child.

Bright Futures (Mental Health Education 1999), a multi-agency inquiry group, states, 'Children who are mentally healthy will have the ability to develop psychologically, emotionally, creatively, intellectually and spiritually.'

It is widely thought that at any one time, 20 per cent of children and adolescents experience psychological problems, and that the incidence may be higher in densely deprived inner city areas of the UK.

In 2006, *Reaching Out: An Action Plan on Social Exclusion* (HM Government 2006), a Government Initiative recorded that 'pregnancy and the first few years of life are crucial, and that intensive health led home visiting during pregnancy and the first two years of life can radically improve outcomes for both the mother and child, particularly in the most at risk families' (p.45). The report quotes Rutter, Giller and Hagel (1998), stating that the circumstances of early childhood can cast a long shadow, and places appropriate emphasis on the need for practitioners to be aware how important a child's early experiences are to the development of the brain. The report also refers to the work of Hoskings and Walsh (2005), asserting that the child who is nurtured and loved will develop the neural networks which mediate empathy, compassion and the capacity to form healthy relationships.

Recent research on the brain has found that, even pre-natally, a baby's brain is affected by environmental conditions, such as the kind of nourishment, care, surroundings and stimulation that the baby experiences. A lack of sensitive, critical nurturing experience and excess exposure to trauma, such as violence, will alter the developing central nervous system, predisposing the infant to becoming more impulsive and reactive with a risk of developing violent tendencies. Neglect in early childhood literally alters the physical and functional development of the brain.

Young Minds Policy: Mental Health in Infancy (Child Psychotherapy Trust 2003) states that the importance of mental health services for infants is not well understood – babies demonstrate that they are anxious and tense, distressed or fearful through, for instance, poor sleep patterns, difficulties with feeding, restlessness and gastric disturbance. These emotions need to be responded to with love and empathy by those on whom the babies depend for survival. An infant's early experiences in relation to his/her relationship with the primary caregiver affects the development of the neurobiological structure of the brain, and it is likely to be difficult to alter the 'hardwiring' when negative experiences have endured.

According to Karr-Morse and Wiley (1997), our earliest experiences become biologically rooted in our brain structure and chemistry from gestation and most profoundly, in the first months of life. Schore (2001) states that early social events are imprinted into the neurobiological structures that are maturing during the brain's growth spurt in the first two years of life, and therefore have far reaching effects. Glaser (2001) and Balbernie (2001) have led in neuroscience research, and state that we need to understand much more in this field; we are learning about serious long-term consequences of neglect, trauma and abuse on early brain development and subsequent physical, emotional and social growth.

It is predominantly the quality of a mother's sensitivity in responding appropriately to her baby's needs that is the main determinant of the baby's attachment pattern (Crittenden 1992).

The first few months of life are a sensitive period when children develop attachments and learn about emotions and social interactions in their family. This lays the foundations for future social, emotional and cognitive development. Children who do not have secure relationships early in life are at greater risk of significant mental health problems, educational difficulties or conduct disorders.

The British psychiatrist and psychoanalyst John Bowlby first developed attachment theory in the 1950s, describing it as the building blocks of development. Through a positive, reciprocal relationship the children learn to modulate affect, sooth themselves and learn to relate to others. Attachment is the base from which children explore; their early attachment experiences form their concept of self, others and the world. Mary Ainsworth *et al.* (1978) developed the classification of attachment types, using the 'strange situation' method of observing the response of toddlers when briefly separated from their mother, and left with a stranger, and their response when the mother returned. Attachment was then classified as secure, insecure-avoidant and insecure-ambivalent.

Secure attachment is a protective factor, which confers confidence and adaptability, and provides the best-known psychosocial precondition for tension free playful exploration. Children who display a secure attachment pattern are generally more enthusiastic and persistent with tasks, and are more sociable and co-operative and more resilient. It is widely thought that about 65 per cent of all infants are securely attached.

Secure child

- Is able to explore the unfamiliar environment, but frequently returns to mother
- Cries when mother leaves the room, and greets mother with pleasure when she returns
- Is easily comforted when mother returns.

Securely attached children are best able to explore when they have a sense of having a 'secure base' to return to when they might need reassurance. When they are given the reassurance through this secure base, this bolsters their sense of security and develops the child's resilience – educating the child how to cope with the same problem in the future. A child becomes securely attached when the parent is available and able to meet the needs of the child in a responsive and sensitive way – the primary caregiver, usually the mother intuitively recognises the infant's cues and identifies the needs that are expressed through the infant's behaviour and communication. Fonagy (1998) states that when the infant's mental state is anticipated and acted on, he will be secure in attachment.

Sometimes classed as anxious-avoidant insecure attachment type, this pattern of attachment is displayed by a child who avoids or ignores the parent, showing

---

Insecure-avoidant child

- Explores new environment without checking on mother's presence
- Appears not to be affected when mother leaves
- Avoids looking at or coming close to mother when she returns.

little emotion when the parent departs or returns. The child will not explore very much, regardless of who is in the room. The child would treat the stranger in this experiment no differently to the parent, as they will not express any significant emotional communication. This attachment pattern is developed from the experience of receiving a disengaged parenting style, where a child's needs are frequently unmet and based on this experience, the child believes that they have no affect on communication of need.

Insecure-ambivalent child

- Clings to mother, afraid to explore the new environment
- Extremely agitated and cries non-stop when mother leaves
- Seeks contact when mother returns
- Resists all efforts to be soothed.

This is also known as anxious-resistant insecure attachment style and a child displaying this attachment pattern is anxious of exploring and of the stranger, even when the parent is present. When the parent leaves the room the child becomes extremely distressed, and will display ambivalence when the parent returns, seeking to remain close to the parent, but resentful and resistant when the parent offers attention. This pattern of attachment may be a result of 'conditional' parenting when the parent is engaged, but on their own terms – sometimes the child's needs are not met, and at other times, attention is given through the parent's own need rather than through the child initiating a need.

Main and Solomon (1990) developed classification of the 'disorganised' attachment style:

Disorganised child

- Exhibits a diverse array of conflicted behaviours
- Rocks on hands and knees, avoids eye contact
- Moves away from parent – leans on wall when frightened
- Rises up to meet parent, but then falls.

This pattern of attachment is displayed by a lack of a coherent pattern for coping. Whilst the ambivalent and the avoidant styles are not totally effective, they are an organised way in which a child views the world and deals with it. It is suggested by Main and Solomon (1990) that children with disorganised attachment may experience their caregiver as either frightening or frightened. A frightened caregiver is alarming to the child, who uses social referencing techniques such as checking the adult's facial expression to ascertain whether a situation is safe. A frightening caregiver may be aggressive towards the child, putting the child in a situation of having 'fear without a solution': the caregiver is the source of the child's alarm as well as their haven of safety. Through parental behaviours that are frightening, the caregiver puts the child in an irresolvable paradox of approach-avoidance. This paradox may be one of the explanations for some of the 'still' and 'freezing' behaviours observed in children who are thought to have disorganised attachment. Children who display a disorganised attachment pattern are most at risk of developing severe problems, including aggression and conduct difficulties. It is also likely that these are children who might be at risk of abuse.

Attachment is the deep and long lasting emotional connection established between a child and caregiver in the first several years of life. It is not something that parents make for their child, but is a dyadic process that an infant and their primary caregiver create together in an ongoing reciprocal relationship (Levy 2000).

A secure attachment developed in the first two years of life affects the development of brain systems responsible for healthy emotional, social and cognitive development, and sets out the child's ability to establish positive relationship patterns and expectations for life. In addition, a secure attachment plays a vital role in the development of self-image, and a positive internal working model. By experiencing positive interactions with his or her primary caregiver, a child builds up the picture of the world – how s/he feels about the world and how the world feels about her or him – how things happen and how his or her actions affect what happens. A child with a positive internal working model perceives him or herself as being lovable, effective and of interest to others, and perceives others as being loving, interested and available, responsive and dependable. Through this internal model a child expects to have his or her needs met and can predict his carer's response. S/he begins to develop resilience so that s/he will be able to tolerate any minor changes or disruptions.

Neglectful, abusive and non-responsive caregivers produce children who are out of control, angry, depressed and hopeless by the time they are two or three years old (Levy 2000).

Children who have insecure attachment are more likely to develop a negative internal working model that leads to self-perception of being unlovable, uninteresting unvalued and ineffective, whilst the world is perceived as having others who are unavailable, neglectful, rejecting unresponsive and even hostile. Through a negative internal working model, a child expects that s/he cannot rely on his or her needs being attended to and cannot predict his or her carer's response. This leads to an inability to tolerate disruptions in relationships.

Children who have a secure attachment

- Learn basic trust and reciprocity

- Learn self regulation

- Develop a good sense of self-esteem and self-worth

- Have a sense of right and wrong

- Develop empathy and compassion

- Develop resilience

- Enjoy healthy brain development, leading to positive cognitive function

- Achieve academically

- Develop an ability to make and sustain long-term relationships.

PRACTICE AND ASSESSMENT STRATEGIES IN WORKING TOWARDS SUPPORTING PARENTS TO BUILD SECURE ATTACHMENTS WITH THEIR BABIES

When parents recognise their infant's communication, it enables them to reciprocate positively. New parents may need support in understanding how babies communicate, and how they might use non-verbal cues to express what they are feeling. Svanberg (2005) says:

> The idea is not to look at how people are failing at parenting, but to understand the language babies use to communicate with the world – studying the interaction between a parent and child is a powerful way of learning baby language. Families need time to read and understand their baby's unique and subtle signals.

Less than sensitive interactions tend to break down into three fairly common patterns, according to Svanberg's work based on Crittenden's CARE index protocol (1992). The most common of these is the 'inadvertently intrusive and controlling' parent, who can overwhelm an infant. The second of these patterns is that of a 'passive' parent who appears pre-occupied; this can often be a sign of postnatal depression. The third pattern is a mix of intrusive and passive, leading to unpredictable parenting. There are several studies, including Winnicott (1967) and Murray and Cooper (1997) that have identified the effect of post-natal depression on the relationship between the mother and baby. Health visitors and midwives have a key role in observing the cycle of reciprocity between a baby and mother, and to give the mother feedback on how they are responding to the baby's communication.

GOOD PRACTICE POINTS

- Encourage parents to recognise the uniqueness of their child – children have their own distinct likes and dislikes and have already begun to establish their personality at birth.

- Encourage parents to enjoy some time every day focusing just on the baby. This might be time when the parent meets the baby's daily needs, such as bathing or feeding them. It is important to ensure that the parent's focus is entirely on the baby at this time and that they are not distracted. Infant massage is an extremely beneficial way of relieving stress for both mothers and babies, and this might be incorporated into a baby's daily routine.

- When parents recognise their infant's communication, it enables them to reciprocate positively. New parents may need support in understanding how babies communicate, and how they might use non-verbal cues to express what they are feeling.

- Health visitors and midwives have a key role in observing the cycle of reciprocity between a baby and mother, and to give the mother feedback on how they are responding to the baby's communication.

ATTACHMENT, RECIPROCITY AND TEMPERAMENT

Brazelton, Koslowski and Main (1974) initially developed the concept of reciprocity through in-depth analysis of infant communication. The findings of this microanalysis of filmed interactions between infants and their mothers showed that babies are very active in their attempts to communicate, demonstrating how actively babies attempt to communicate with their mothers, and how babies and their mothers initiated contact with each other, and how each regulated contact with the other.

Reciprocity is the process through which a parent is able to respond sensitively to the infant, and the infant responds with positive reaction to the parent. It is a two-way communication, which enables the infant to form a concept of his or her own affect on their environment and on other people. Infants are active in engaging their mother in a relationship, and it is through sensitive reciprocity that a mother and baby become attuned to each other. The 'dance' of reciprocity is a process of communication described as having several components within a sequence during a typical interaction between a mother and baby:

Dance of reciprocity

- Initiation: contact is established as the baby turns his or her face and eyes towards the mother.

- Orientation: the baby moves his or her body and limbs towards the mother.

- Acceleration: the baby's interaction increases with increasing vocalisation or smile and increased movement of arms and legs.

- Peak of excitement: the baby tries to control the build up of excitement e.g. by bringing his or her hand to the mouth or by holding on to his or her hand or arm – seen as an effort to decrease the building tension.

- Deceleration: is gradual, rather than sudden – the baby may continue to hold on to a part of his or her body, and blink or yawn, and decrease the vocalisation or smiling.

- Withdrawal: the baby looks away or turns away.

Brazelton suggested that the withdrawal was an essential part of the cycle, and it helps the baby to regulate the interaction without becoming overwhelmed.

An infant's environment and the response of the primary care giver can influence the baby's personality in later years – a 'slow to warm up' infant might grow up to be a shy adolescent but a secure attachment might change the infant from being 'slow to warm up' to an 'easy' personality type who develops a strong sense of confidence and is relatively easy to please.

PARENTAL MENTAL HEALTH

Through being attuned to their baby a sensitive mother is able to understand the baby's individuality and respond to their communication appropriately and unconditionally. There is evidence from various studies, predominantly

Murray and Cooper (1997), to show that post-natal depression can have an effect on the evolving relationship between the mother and her infant. When maternal mental illness persists, it is likely that the infant becomes more passive, less content and less engaged with the mother, and more involved in self-directed activity. Stein *et al.* (1991) found a significant association between maternal depression during the first year of an infant's life and an impaired quality in the mother–child interaction at nineteen months, regardless of whether the mother had recovered from depression or not. Rutter and Quinton (1984) conducted a four-year follow-up study of children of psychiatric patients and found that a third of the children showed no emotional or behavioural difficulties, a third showed transient difficulties, and a third exhibited persistent disorders.

Emphasising the need for better interfaces between child and adult mental health services, Reder, McClure and Jolley (2000) state that childhood experiences lay the foundations for many facets of functioning in later life. The aspect of the dyadic influence is a factor through which parental behaviours and attitudes impact upon children's developmental process and conversely, children affect the emotional life of the parents. Whilst the effect of mental health on each individual in a family is complex and intertwined, most local authorities provide separate services for adults and children, and often there are limited links between the service providers.

RESILIENCE

In infancy and early childhood infants display resilience by appearing to be socially responsive with a capacity to elicit and receive attention, and appear to have determination to explore their environment. They appear to have an ability to cope with frustration and are relatively easy to soothe. In toddler years, resilient children are found to have autonomy and sociability, and can display compliance and co-operation. In pre-school years, resilient children show sensitivity and responsiveness as well as a positive sense of self-esteem.

Table 4.1: Factors that develop resilience		
Child factors	*Family factors*	*Environmental factors*
• Easy temperament • Secure attachment • Good communication skills • Positivity in approach • Ability to problem solve	• Four or fewer children in family • At least one parent available for attachment • Democratic parenting style • Presence of other significant adults, e.g. grandparents	• Support networks available within the community • Availability of good housing • Easy access to services • Lack of poverty • Facilities for parental involvement with educational services for personal development

Table 4.2: Factors that cause risk		
Child factors	*Family factors*	*Environmental factors*
• Genetic make up of the child • Likelihood of low IQ or learning difficulties • Chronic physical illness • Developmental uncertainty or delay • Communication difficulties • Temperament, e.g. 'slow to warm up' • Low self-esteem	• Poor parental mental health or post-natal depression • Overt parental discord or domestic abuse • Family breakdown and/or other losses • Bereavement • Inconsistent or unclear boundaries, with contradictory parenting styles • Hostile or rejecting relationships • Parental inability to adapt and respond to evolving change in child's needs • Parental substance/alcohol misuse that renders family lifestyle chaotic • Criminality in family • Hostile or abusive parenting style	• Homelessness • Poverty • Discrimination • Unemployment • Lack of local child-focused facilities

Mental health problems in young children may present as behavioural difficulties

- Feeding problems
- Aggression
- Sleep disturbance
- Toileting problems
- Lack of co-operation
- Attention seeking behaviour
- Poor attention span
- Longer-term problems may include emotional disorders, phobias, lack of attention and over-activity, anti-social behaviour, long-term eating disorders or sleep disorders, etc.

CASE STUDY 4.1

A young mother of a six-month-old baby has just presented herself as being homeless. She has been in a violent relationship for two years, and although she had a relatively easy pregnancy, there had been concerns about the effect of her illegal substance misuse on her unborn baby. When the baby was born, she was kept in hospital for observations in the first week, but did not require any specific treatment. When the baby was born, her parents lived together, but following an increase in the domestic abuse, the mother left. The baby feeds well, and her growth is normal, but sleeps for two hours at the most at night, and has been a very unsettled baby since birth. The mother has been attending a substance misuse support service, and is making progress in reducing her drug use. The mother is being treated by her GP for post-natal depression.

What are the implications for this baby's mental health and her attachment needs? Which services are most likely to work with this family, and how effectively will they work together to promote the baby's mental health?

In your own practice, what role do you have to promote the mental health of the baby, and what resources are available to you?

EARLY INTERVENTION AND SUPPORT

Bright Futures, (Mental Health Foundation 1999), stated that maternal stress in pregnancy appears to have an adverse effect on the development of the brain *in utero*, although the psychological mechanisms are not yet fully understood. The Parents in Partnership Parent Infant Network provided evidence to the inquiry that stress is not confined to high-risk groups. Many women and their partners experience low to moderate levels of anxiety and depression in their transition to parenthood. The report highlighted that only a small percentage of women attend ante-natal classes, and very few from families who might be considered to be 'at risk'.

The Mental Health Foundation recommended that much more should be done to prepare all parents for the emotional changes in their lives after the birth of their baby, including how to respond to their baby's emotional needs. Emphasis is placed on the need for a structured system of support (based on a home visiting model) from trained staff, for women who are identified as suffering from or at risk of postnatal depression.

In *Bonding and Parental Attachments*, one of his 'Parent, Adolescent and Child Training Skills' series, Martin Herbert (1996, p.25) gives the following criteria for measuring maternal sensitivity in responsiveness to the infant's needs:

- mother responds promptly to the infant's needs
- mother responds appropriately to the infant's needs
- mother responds consistently
- mother interacts smoothly and sensitively with the child.

And the following for measuring sensitivity in parent–infant interaction:

- parent initiates positive interactions with the infant
- parent responds to the infant's vocalisation
- parent changes voice tone when talking to the infant
- parents shows interest in face-to-face contact with the infant
- parent shows the ability to console or comfort the infant
- parent enjoys close physical contact with the infant
- parent responds to the infant's indication of distress.

Parental sensitivity is identified by Maccoby (1980) within the following dimensions of caretaking style.

Table 4.3: Parental sensitivity	
Sensitivity: The sensitive parent meshes his/her response to the infant's signals and communicates to form a cyclic turn-taking pattern of communication	**Insensitivity:** The insensitive parent intervenes arbitrarily, and the intrusions reflect parent's own wishes and moods
Acceptance: The accepting parent accepts, in general, the responsibility of child care, displaying few signs of irritation with the child	**Rejection:** The rejecting parent has feelings of anger and resentment that eclipse her affection for the child, often finding the child irritating and resorting to punitive control
Co-operation: The co-operative parent respects the child's autonomy and rarely exerts direct control	**Interference:** The interfering parent imposes his/her wishes on the child with little concern for the child's current mood or activity
Accessibility: The accessible parent is familiar with his/her child's communication and notices them at distance, and so is easily distracted by the child	**Ignoring:** The ignoring parent is pre-occupied with his/her own activities and thoughts, and often fails to notice the child's communications unless they are obvious through intensification

IDENTIFYING RISK

The Centre for Early Education and Development at University of Minnesota (Institute of Child Development 2000) has developed various training packages and parenting manuals to address infant mental health needs, focusing on early attachment, and includes the following assessment toolkit for home visitors who work with families of infants and young children:

	Table 4.4: Assessment toolkit	
Parent's mood/behaviour	*Child's appearance and/or behaviour*	*Parent–child relationship*
Parent appears significantly depressed; low energy, disinterested in the child's behaviour or progress or their welfare Parent appears extremely anxious, nervous, stressed or overwhelmed Parent appears to have a serious lack of understanding of their child's development; resulting in unrealistic expectations Parent appears to have a serious mental disorder; bipolar disorder for instance Parent appears to be misusing substances such as alcohol or drugs that may impair judgment and interfere with their ability to safely care for the child	Child's physical needs are consistently neglected – dirty or unkempt appearance, poor nutrition, lack of dental care, inadequate uptake of appropriate medical care Child is not developing as expected and developmental delay is not linked with medical condition – poor weight gain, poor language development and social skills Child is frequently emotionally upset – displays of anger and aggression, temper tantrums and inconsolable crying Child is frequently sad, anxious or worried – smiles infrequently, does not show interest in playing, reacts strongly to noise and movement Child is unresponsive to parent and/or environment; does not make eye contact with parents or others, does not engage in interactions with others and shows little awareness of surroundings	Parent and child have difficulty connecting; child does not respond to parent's presence, parent is unable to engage or play with the child or set limits Parent infrequently holds child's hand or talks to them. Parent and child have frequent miscommunications or parent says they don't know how to understand or relate to the child Parent consistently fails to protect the child, allowing child to touch eat, play with or climb on dangerous objects Parent is consistently cold or hostile to the child; parent uses hard tone or offensive words, or uses unnecessary force. Parent threatens to hit the child or call them names Parent attributes malignant motives to child's behaviour; parent may say the child deliberately makes them angry by being unco-operative

ASSESSMENT OF INFANT AND CHILD MENTAL HEALTH

Observation of children is an informed way of assessing which supports practitioners in having a raised awareness and better understanding of children's mental health. When carried out carefully and holistically, observation supports practitioners in noticing children's communication in a systematic way. Fawcett (1996, p.5) states:

> Nationally, there are persuasive arguments for increasing the emphasis on child observation in various professional and para-professional training courses…in recent years, other demanding priorities have tended to force the topic of child observation out of some courses, in particular the initial training of social workers and teachers.

Furthermore, there is little evidence of health practitioners such as paediatric nurses and health visitors receiving adequate information during their professional training on mental health of children. A holistic approach to assessing a child's mental health should incorporate all aspects of his/her life.

Assessment criteria

- Child's generic details, including name, date of birth and address.

- Family Genogram – stating a basic outline of who is in the family, and the context in which the child is part of the family. The Genogram includes a history of the parents' relationship, and includes siblings. It also includes information about the extended family, if there are significant family members involved, and in cases of separated parents, information is included about any relevant contact details. The Genogram is used routinely in family therapy, and is a structured way of gathering information that is specific to a child.

- Child's behavioural patterns – compliance and ability to respond to boundaries. Where a child is presenting with challenging behaviour, it is important to get specific information about how the child expresses emotional distress. Martin Herbert (1996) has developed a series of books, which include *ABC of Behavioural Methods*, that enables parents to develop observational skills to identify antecedents that trigger challenging behaviour, as well as exploring the consistency parents use in addressing consequences.

- Child's developmental history, including circumstances at birth and in the neonatal period.

- Temperament of the child.

- Routines of the family and child, e.g. mealtimes and bedtimes, and how the child responds to these – in young children, difficulties around feeding, sleeping and toileting are often emotionally related.

- Environmental factors need to take into consideration home circumstances as well as support networks available to the family, specifically in relation to the child's mental and emotional wellbeing, including availability of appropriate safe play spaces and the impact on the child when negative community pressures affect the family, e.g. homelessness or racism.

- Parental factors take into account parenting style as well as relevant history, such as parental discord, parental learning difficulties, domestic abuse and lifestyle implications, e.g. alcohol or substance misuse on the child's mental health. Parental mental health has a significant impact on the mental health of infants and children. It is estimated that children of depressed parents are up to five times more likely to develop behaviour problems than other children. (Cummings and Davies 1994)

CURRENT POLICY AND PRIORITY

There is significant evidence to suggest that early intervention for disadvantaged children and their families in relation to mental health support can be a sound economic investment (Barnett 2000). Babies cannot wait. If they have been adapting to emotionally compromising circumstances for any length of time, then the damage caused by inappropriate caregiving cannot be undone by a change of circumstances, as is often seen with children who are fostered or adopted; much more intensive and long-term interventions become necessary (Balbernie 2007). Sometimes, a simple change in parental understanding and attitude towards their infant's communication will enable a problem to be resolved much earlier.

The Child Health Promotion Programme (Department of Health and Department for Children, Schools and Families 2008, p. 6) states, 'Effective implementation of the policy should lead to strong parent-child attachment and positive parenting, resulting in better social and emotional well being among children.' The policy highlights that pregnancy and the first years of life are one of the most important stages in the lifecycle when the foundations of future health and wellbeing are laid down. It is a time when parents are particularly receptive to learning and making changes.

The policy places major emphasis on parenting support with the application of new information about neurological development and child development, stressing the importance of secure attachment, and identifies changed public health priorities which now highlight the need to take a proactive role in promoting the social and emotional development of children.

It outlines a 'universal progressive' model of service which addresses the need for universal provision of parenting support, as well as a progressive provision of service to target insensitive, intrusive or passive parenting interactions through assessment of parent–infant interactions, using validated tools and providing parenting support through evidenced programmes.

It is timely that government policy now has a very clear vision about the mental health needs of infants and young children. Whilst national priority is given to this crucial need, it is imperative that consideration is given locally to the development of effective infant mental health services. Midwives, health visitors and GPs provide universal health services and should play a key role in assessing and identifying vulnerable infants. They should have access to appropriate training and resources to deliver the universal/progressive service recommended in the policy, whilst local authorities ensure the commissioning of appropriate specialist services to meet the mental health needs of infants and young children.

REFERENCES

Ainsworth, M., Blehar, M., Waters, E. and Wall, S. (1978) *Patterns of Attachment*. Hillsdale, NJ: Erlbaum.

Balbernie, R. (2001) 'Circuits and circumstances: the neurobiological consequences of early relationship experiences and how they shape later behaviour.' *Journal of Child Psychotherapy* 27, 3, 237–253.

Balbernie, R. (2007) *An Infant Mental Health Service: Importance of Early Years*. London: Association for Infant Mental Health.

Barnett, W. S. (2000) 'Economics of Early Childhood Intervention.' In J.P. Shonkoff and S.J. Meisals (eds) *Handbook of Early Childhood Intervention 2000*. Cambridge: Cambridge University Press.

Bowlby, J. (1958) 'The nature of the child's tie to his mother.' *International Journal of Psychoanalysis 39*, 350–373.

Brazelton, T., Koslowski, B. and Main, M. (1974) 'The Origins of Reciprocity: the Early Mother–Infant Interaction.' In M. Lewis and L. Rosenblum (eds) *The Effect of the Infant on its Caregiver*. New York: Wiley.

Child Psychotherapy Trust (2003) *Young Minds Policy; Mental Health in Infancy*. London: Child Psychotherapy Trust Publications.

Crittenden P.M. (1992) 'Children's strategies for coping with adverse home environments; an interpretation using attachment theory.' *Child Abuse and Neglect 16*, 3, 329–343.

Cummings, E.M. and Davies, P.T. (1994) 'Maternal depression and child development.' *Journal of Child Psychology and Psychiatry 35*, 1, 73–112.

Department of Health and Department for Children, Schools and Families (2008) *The Child Health Promotion Programme*. London: Department of Health and Department for Children, Schools and Families.

Fawcett, M. (1996) *Learning through Child Observation*. London: Jessica Kingsley Publishers.

Fonagy, P. (1998) 'Prevention, the appropriate target of infant psychotherapy.' *Infant Mental Health Journal 19*, 2, 124–150.

Glaser, D. (2001) 'Child abuse and neglect and the brain; a review.' *Journal of Child Psychology and Psychiatry and Allied Disciplines 41*, 1, 97–116.

Herbert, M. (1996) *Bonding and Parental Attachments*, PACTS series. London: British Psychological Society.

HM Government (2006) *Reaching Out; an Action Plan on Social Exclusion*. London: published for the Cabinet Office by COI.

Hoskings, G. and Walsh, I. (2005) *The WAVE Report 2005: Violence and What to Do About It*. Croydon: WAVE Trust.

Institute of Child Development (2000). *Centre for Early Education and Development*. Minneapolis, MN: University Of Minnesota, Center for Early Education and Development (CEED)

Karr-Morse, R. and Wiley, M.S. (1997) *Ghosts From the Nursery, Tracing the Roots of Violence*. New York: Atlantic Monthly Press.

Levy, T.M. (ed.) (2000) *Handbook of Attachment Interventions*. New York: Academic Press.

Maccoby, E.E. (1980) *Social Development: Psychology, Growth and the Parent–Child Relationship*. New York: Harcourt Brace Jovanovich.

Main, M. and Solomon, J. (1990) 'Procedures for Identifying Infants as Disorganised/Disoriented during the Ainsworth *Strange Situation*.' In M.T. Greenberg, D. Cicchetti and E.M. Cummings (eds) *Attachment in the Pre-School Years: Theory, Research and Intervention*. Chicago: University of Chicago Press.

Mental Health Foundation (1999) *Bright Futures; Promoting Children and Young People's Mental Health*. London: Mental Health Foundation Publications.

Murray, L. and Cooper, P.J. (1997) *Post Partum Depression and Child Development*. New York: Guildford Press.

Reder, P., McClure, M. and Jolley, A. (eds) (2000) *Family Matters, Interfaces between Child and Adult Mental Health*. London: Routledge.

Rutter, M., Giller, H. and Hagel, A. (1998) *Antisocial Behaviour by Young People*. Cambridge: Cambridge University Press.

Rutter, M. and Quinton, D. (1984) 'Parental psychiatric disorder; effects on children.' *Psychological Medicine 14*, 853–880.

Schore, A.N. (2001) 'Effects of a secure attachment relationship on right brain development, affect regulation and infant mental health.' *Infant Mental Health Journal 22*, 1–2, 7–66.

Stein, A., Gath, D.H., Bucher, J., Bond, A., Day, A. and Cooper, P.J. (1991) 'The relationship between post natal depression and mother-child interactions.' *British Journal of Psychiatry 148*, 46–52.

Svanberg, P.O. (2005) *Early Screening and Primary Prevention*. The Sunderland Infant Programme. Sunderland: Surestart Report.

Winnicott, D. (1967) 'Mirror Role of Mother and Family in Child Development.' In D. Winnicott *Playing and Reality*. London: Tavistock Publications.

Young Minds (2003) *Tuning into our Babies: the Importance of the Relationship Between Parents and their Babies and Toddlers*. London: Young Minds.

FURTHER READING

Child Psychotherapy Trust in association with the Association for Infant Mental Health (UK) (1999) *Promoting Infant Mental Health: A Framework for Developing Policies and Services to Ensure the Healthy Development of Young Children*. London: Child Psychotherapy Trust Publications.

Department for Children, Schools and Families (2007) *The Children's Plan; Building Brighter Futures*. London: Department for Children, Schools and Families.

Department of Health (2004) *NSF for Children, Young People and Maternity Services*. London: Department of Health.

Heads Up Scotland, A National Project for Children and Young People's Mental Health (2007) *Infant Mental Health, a Guide for Practitioners*. Edinburgh: Scottish Development Centre.

Perry, B. (2002) 'Childhood experience and the expression of genetic potential; what childhood neglect tells us about nature and nurture.' *Brain and Mind 3*, 79–100. In K. Hilyard and D. Wolfe (2002) 'Child neglect; developmental issues and outcomes.' *Child Abuse and Neglect 26.*

Solihull PCT (2001) *Solihull Approach Resource Pack.* Birmingham: School of Primary Health Care, University of Central England.

CHAPTER 5

WORKING WITH UNCO-OPERATIVE OR HOSTILE FAMILIES

RUTH PEARSON

INTRODUCTION

This chapter will cover the possible impact of unco-operative or hostile families on the wellbeing of their children, on the assessment process and on workers who are involved with them. It will consider some factors affecting parents' reaction to agencies and some techniques for effective working. Issues of confidence, clarity, recording and multi-agency working will be addressed. The chapter will finish with a discussion on some aspects of the personal safety and emotional wellbeing of workers, some helpful responses and the role of workers themselves, managers and organisations.

The chapter is written against a background of attempts to meet the needs of children through early intervention and supportive working in partnership with parents, characterised by the move from 'Child Protection' to 'Safeguarding'. The importance of supporting families whilst working in partnership with parents was enshrined in the Children Act 1989 and expounded in later 'Messages from Research' guidance which stated that 'supporting families, when necessary, to bring up their children and working in partnership with parents whose circumstances may be difficult is at the heart of our Children Act' (Department of Health 1995a, p.1). A long lasting impact of this guidance has been the concept of 'refocusing' or 'rebalancing' of work with children and families. The 'Challenge of Partnership in Child Protection' (Department of Health 1995b) also set the tone and framework for 'partnership' working with families. The Every Child Matters agenda encourages the development of early intervention and support by a variety of agencies not just those involved with child protection work.

Not only are notions of support and partnership working based on the practice of effective support for children, but they are also very much key to personal, professional and even political values in working with service users and carers. Most of those in the caring professions and agencies will have some basis for their work in the ethics of individual rights and welfare, the promotion of equality and challenge of oppression as well as some under-standing of how the professional role may relate to this ethical base (Banks 2006). Work with children and families tends to attract those who view them-selves as caring and able to relate to other people. Those involved in interview-ing potential students for training courses, such as the social work degree, will have heard many times the statement that candidates consider themselves suitable for the task as they 'are a good listener', 'like helping people', 'like caring for those less fortunate than myself'. Whilst these attributes and aspira-tions are all laudable and, of course, necessary for this work, they are not suffi-cient. Few are attracted to the work because they want to be shouted at or because they want to 'lay down the law' (one would hope!). However, there are situations where families do not welcome what they see as intrusion into their lives and this may not sit well with workers' initial motivation to enter the caring professions.

We know too that, despite the early intervention and support agendas, pressures on resources and capacity can mean that many children's services are perceived to have high thresholds for allocation of work and becoming involved in child in need or safeguarding issues. Difficulties and attitudes may have become entrenched within families entering the statutory arena (Pearson 2005), making initial contact particularly contentious. Families may have had little or no support for 'non-acute' problems for some time, even when they have requested it but then get 'an overwhelming amount of support when problems become so bad that they meet service thresholds' (HM Treasury/Department for Education and Skills 2007, p.85). Issues of partner-ship may be purely aspirational when working with some families in the current child protection system (Bell 1999). There are, unfortunately, adults who, for a variety of reasons, demonstrate a history of meeting any instance of challenge throughout their lives with hostility, aggression, or false compliance.

The increased importance of multi-agency working, a key to good practice in safeguarding children, may also draw professionals from a wide range of caring agencies into the arena of complex work with families, some of whom will have had little or no training or professional expectation of working with conflictual child protection situations. Contracting of support services from other agencies, largely from the voluntary sector, can mean that these workers are now becoming involved with some of the most troubled families, who may not view the services offered, and the staff offering them, as welcome in their lives.

So here we have the dilemma: a workforce from many different agencies with a core value base of helping and empowering parents, working within a system which espouses support and early intervention, who nevertheless will need to work with families who are at the very least reluctant to receive services, in order to promote the wellbeing of the children in those families.

Parental hostility and non-co-operation can increase the risks to their children to a dangerous degree. There have been a number of high-profile child deaths where workers from a variety of agencies withdrew from the family due to overt or covert threats of violence or intimidation and many instances where non-compliance with plans has gone unchallenged. The report into the death of Ainlee Labonte in 2002 details a catalogue of instances of non-co-operation, manipulation and aggression by her parents, having the effect that the 'fear with which the family are regarded leads to almost paralysis in terms of action' (Newham Area Child Protection Committee 2002, p.20). This situation is reflected in a number of other Serious Case Reviews where authors of these reviews also noted that where parents were hostile there was evidence that 'workers often became frozen and this hampered their ability to reflect, make judgements and act clearly, and to follow through with referrals, assessments or plans' (Brandon *et al.* 2008, p.96). Research has also shown that where particular families with long-term entrenched problems showed lack of acceptance of agencies' concerns, they were responded to with a lower level of both support and authoritative working (Pearson 2005). There are voices who are clear that the current investigative system militates against partnership working (Bell 1999) and those who call for an approach to child care that considers the social and political context in which families find themselves (Parton 1997).

However, there will still exist a situation where families may be reluctant to engage with services and whilst training for professionals, particularly social workers, emphasises anti-oppressive practice and empowerment of service users, it is sometimes possible to forget that the main service user is the child and possible also to get enmeshed in looking solely at issues for parents and carers. This may be particularly relevant when parents feign co-operation (Haringey 2008). The previous limited reference to dealing with hostility or non-co-operation in the literature and in professional training may add to workers' difficulties in addressing conflict or non-co-operation. This issue has been taken up by those considering the issues of staff assaulted or threatened by service users (Littlechild 2005) and also by those considering the report into the death of Victoria Climbié (Laming 2003). In considering this report, Rustin speaks of workers engaging in behaviour that avoids the 'mental pain' of child protection work and linking that behaviour with the infant-like behaviour of Victoria herself. This mental pain can relate both to considering the experiences of the child and to working with hostility from parents, engendering feelings of anxiety and helplessness. Rustin also feels that 'the kind of training and support made available to staff does not seem to have helped them mobilise more adult mental capacities to cope with the unavoidable emotional disturbance of this difficult work' (Rustin 2005, p.13).

At this point it is important to be clear about what level of behaviour the parents are displaying and, therefore, what level of risk this poses to both children and workers. Unco-operative responses may include:

a)   **Ambivalence** which may, understandably, be present in many parents in the safeguarding arena. This may be seen when people miss a number of appointments or avoid discussing difficult areas.

b)   **Avoidance** which is also very common and will include such behaviours as regular avoiding of appointments, visits and meetings; using distracting techniques to avoid discussing difficult areas.

c)   **Confrontation** includes direct challenge to workers, either based on verbal, sometimes written, exchange or extreme avoidance (such as not answering the door as opposed to not being in). Some comments can be covertly intimidating over a period of time.

d)   **Violence** which includes either threatened or actual violence. Threats may be explicit or implicit and may involve threats of actual violence, use of threatening dogs or other adults. This represents the minority of unco-operative behaviour but can be the most difficult for workers to engage with and presents the highest risk to both children, the non-violent parent, and workers. (Based on Sheffield Safeguarding Children Board 2007)

Responses may change due to circumstances and may improve or deteriorate with time, therefore the assessment of risk to children and workers posed by families must be a continuous process. When examining parental reaction to engagement, a good place to start is with workers' own reactions to criticism,

---

Exercise: Your reaction to criticism

1.   Think of a specific situation where you were criticised unjustly:

   a)   How did you feel?

   b)   How did you react?

2.   Think of a specific situation where you were criticised justly:

   a)   How did you feel?

   b)   How did you react?

   Be honest!

3.   If there was any difference in your answers to 1 and 2, consider why.

which is what, after all, parents may experience wher[...] capacity to meet their children's needs.

Many people undertaking this exercise are surprise[...] that despite thinking that they would respond positi[...] criticism, many of their feelings and reactions are simi[...] they felt unjustly criticised. It is worth remembering from this [...] is often an instinctive reaction to greet any form of criticism with antagonism. If there is a more positive response, this is often connected with how the criticism was worded, who the other person was, and the severity of the comment and the nature of the consequences. The range of responses to criticism is also mirrored in the range of responses to intervention displayed by families. Many of the families who come into the safeguarding arena may well not perceive their behaviour as detrimental to the needs of their children, or if they do, feel unable to respond positively for a variety of reasons. Each parent and their history will be different and it is essential that at the earliest stage of any engagement factors are identified that may contribute to initial and, possibly, ongoing lack of co-operation.

Reasons for lack of co-operation

List some possible reasons for each parent not co-operating.

Examples could include:

- History of dislike or fear of authority figures?

- Parents' own childhood characterised by hostility and conflict?

- Poor previous experience of agencies/your particular agency?

- Concerns that agencies may lack understanding of cultural issues or be racist if family from a minority ethnic group?

- Lack of understanding about what is expected?

- Doubts over ability to change problematic behaviour?

- Non-acceptance of the definition of the problem?

- Fear of being judged to be poor parents because of substance misuse, mental health problems, disability?

- Perceptions impaired by mental health problems, substance misuse, learning difficulty?

- Current relationship characterised by abuse of power?

- Attempts, either by the perpetrator or the victim, to hide domestic abuse?

- Fear that the children may be taken away?

- Issues connected with the individual worker – i.e. issues of race, gender, attitude?

- In-built power differences in relationship between worker and family?

- Other suggestions – based on knowledge of the family?

Once some of the possible origins of lack of co-operation are identified, it is helpful to consider what role the worker themselves may be able to play in the early stages of intervention. When looking at problems of partnership in child protection and safeguarding work and the inequality of power relationships, some have identified that 'what is often lacking is attention to the basic requirements for ensuring working relationships' including 'basic human decencies of human relationships' (Pinkerton 2002, p.103). Consider the importance of personal style, empathetic and anti-discriminatory practice that should characterise relationships with any family. Supervision, peer support or joint working can be used to identify workers' own personal style and how this assists or impairs effective working. As with the development of any skill or learning, it is vital to continue to reflect on effective practice and experience. It is useful to be aware of the concept of 'reflection-before-action; reflection-in-action and reflection-on-action' (Knott and Scragg 2007, p.81). Any incident can be a point of learning and development about our own style and skills.

A useful mental image can be used when encountering parents or carers who are, understandably, reacting to feelings related to challenge (as with the 'criticism' exercise).

First encounters

Imagine walking into the sea when the waves are quite rough. The time to walk forward is when the waves are receding, not when they are crashing about your knees!

Wait for parents' initial reaction to reduce and accept that this may well be the response you expected. Battling with strong feelings will only exacerbate the situation.

But remember – some seas are too dangerous to swim in alone – if at all!

Lishman (1994) identifies several key factors in avoiding a clash of perspective. This clash is less likely to occur when there has been not only positive engagement, empathy and attentive listening but also a clear explanation of the purpose of the contact. It is easy for workers to lapse into professional jargon or refer to terms and processes that are simply not understood by many people, so it is important to develop methods of ensuring that there is genuine understanding by parents of what the concerns are and what is expected. Clarity of expression of the worker's involvement may not always be apparent to the parent and, in some cases, to the worker themselves. Some may have a clear remit for contact, for example a health visitor or a representative of the housing department, but it is still important to be clear about identifying the nature of the problem and possible strategies for intervention. A recent local authority inspection identified that a significant number of parents whose children's names were on the Child Protection Register had no idea what they had to do in order for their children's names to be removed. It is perfectly possible for workers, particularly those new to an organisation, to be unsure, themselves, about such things as level of risk, process of assessment, practical or specialist support available, roles and responsibilities of their and other's agency. Lack of clarity on the part of the worker may well transfer to insecurity and anxiety on the part of the parent.

It is quite common to speak to workers involved in complex family problems who, when asked, are actually unclear about their specific remit, why they are visiting and what they hope to achieve from their intervention. It is important, through supervision, case discussion and sound multi-agency working, to ensure that any risks have corresponding clear and realistic goals present in plans and that parents are given clear messages about the expectations of the agencies. Workers can ask themselves:

- Do I know why I am seeing this family?

- Does this family know why I am seeing them?

- If this contact is part of an assessment, am I clear what I am trying to find out?

- Am I using a clear framework for my assessment?

- If there is ongoing involvement, does my contact relate to a plan?

- Are the parents truly clear about what is expected of them?

- Is this realistic, reasonable and achievable?

- Are parents, workers and others in the inter-agency network, clear of the consequences of non-adherence to parts of any plan?

- How involved has the family been in the drawing up of the plan?

In recent research, it was identified that many of the families with long-term problems who demonstrated very low levels of co-operation were those who were presented with unclear plans and a poor level of inter-agency collaboration (Pearson 2005). Often, when families feel that they have no choice in the nature of intervention and planning, co-operation is understandably hard to establish. Even if agreement is reached this may be characterised by an 'atmosphere of sullen acquiescence' (Turnell and Edwards 1999, p.147) and it is then extremely hard to gain real progress. Turnell and Edwards, in their work on working with families in a solution and safety-oriented approach to child protection work, are clear that in order for the family to feel engaged and for agencies to be able to gauge the likelihood of a positive outcome, it is vital that the perspective of the family members is sought prior to the finalising of the plan. However, constant professional curiosity is required to avoid workers being involved in colluding with parents' own avoidance or re-framing of concerns.

Other issues that workers may need to consider before they begin work with a potentially hostile or unco-operative family are those personal to workers themselves and which may impact on both their confidence in themselves and their relationship with the parents they work with. The process of articulating these concerns can be helpful in itself, but rehearsing and accumulating a repertoire of useful responses is the beginning of a lifetime of skills development. This also links well to issues of reflective practice referred to previously.

Exercise: Rehearsing responses

In supervision, team meeting, peer support session, use 'mini-role play' questions to issues that you are most concerned about (again, be honest!). Rehearse responses that others have found useful and that you may comfortably make your own.
  For example:

- So, have you got kids then?

- What do you know? You're only young.

- What do you know about my culture?

- I'm not having a male/female/black worker!

- You haven't been doing this long have you?

- You must be pretty out of touch.

- Why should I listen to you? You're just a student/new to this job.

- What's it got to do with you? You're a teacher, not a social worker.

All safeguarding work should take place on an inter-agency basis. As well as the many benefits for the child and family, a strong network of other professionals can provide both support and learning opportunities for workers. Sharing both concerns and effective approaches with other professionals can reduce isolation and also foster the development of effective responses to particular families and to safeguarding work in general. Good, open communication between agencies can avoid parents misleading workers or making some workers feel isolated if they feel that they are the only ones singled out for aggression.

Techniques of assertiveness were important in the empowerment of women in the 1980s. Social care workers have a good deal to learn from these techniques, as they can assist in the development of a clear and fair relationship with service users and parents by 'having appropriate behaviour that is halfway between aggressive and passive' (McBride 1998, p.15). An assertive worker is one who can respect themselves and others; who can maintain a clear stance, regardless of diversions, and who also has the confidence in themselves to be able to voice their own doubts or uncertainties. It is important to recognise that the ability to express doubts is a strength born of confidence rather than weakness. Being assertive is not adopting a bullying approach or failing to listen to others' views, neither is it avoiding situations or responding in a sarcastic or indirect manner. For McBride the key to an assertive approach is our core beliefs in ourselves and about others and she links these with four forms of behaviour:

An assertive approach	
Assertive Behaviour *'I'm OK, you're OK'* (underlying belief about self is that they are OK)	**Aggressive Behaviour** *'I'm OK you're not OK'* (underlying belief about self is that they are not OK)
Passive Behaviour *'I'm not OK, you're OK'* (underlying belief about self is that they are not OK)	**Indirectly Aggressive Behaviour** *'I'm OK, you're not OK, but I won't tell you I think that'* (underlying belief about self is that they are not OK)
	(McBride 1998, p.5)

In order to be clearer about these different stances, consider an example from your own or a colleague's practice that has troubled you, or consider the following situation:

Exercise

A young mother, who has been very difficult to engage in the provision of services for her child, Jane, tells you that she did not attend Jane's open day because she had run out of milk and went to the shops.

What would you say?

Passive response

- Oh, fair enough.

- Ignore.

Aggressive response

- You're kidding! Have you no idea how that child feels?

- You really are going to have to sort yourself out.

Indirectly aggressive response

- Well, another triumph of organisational skills!

Assertive response

- I'm sorry to hear that. I really don't think that's the best thing for Jane. How do you think she might be feeling?

- We can work on planning your day, but it is important that you prioritise Jane's needs.

- I need to remind you of the contract we made about being more involved in Jane's education. What arrangements will you make to go into school to speak to her teachers?

Any other suggestions?

Whilst some of these responses could be considered to be extreme, most workers will have heard colleagues speak to parents in ways similar to those described. Consider:

- Why do workers respond to parents in a passive way?

- Why do workers respond to parents in an aggressive way?

- Why do workers respond to parents in an indirectly aggressive way?

- What gets in the way of us responding in a clear, respectful assertive way?

- Are you clear about your own style?

- Have you sought honest feedback from colleagues and service users?

It is often possible to work with ambivalence and avoidance by considering factors that might be influencing this and by creating clarity of expectation and giving the message that it is important that plans are adhered to. It is also important to mirror good parenting by giving positive reinforcement when parents do comply with plans. It is very easy, particularly with families where there are long-term concerns and those who are not easy to engage with, to only attend to them when things are going wrong. We need to continue to reinforce the message that elements in plans are there for the welfare of the children and that all agencies will be constantly vigilant around compliance, whilst offering appropriate support.

When confronted with behaviour ranging from ambivalent to violent, the focus needs always to remain on the child or children in the family. Parental behaviours towards the workers involved should not be seen as separate from their parenting behaviours, but need to be considered as an element in the assessment. For full information about a child's life to be collected or observed, access to areas identified in any plan of assessment must gained. Ideally this would involve working in partnership with parents and carers and in a way that is appropriate to the needs of the child. If there are restrictions placed on this by adults denying reasonable access to the home, the child or whatever has been outlined in any plan, this must be recorded and brought to the attention of the parents and to the multi-agency network and must be included in the assessment of their ability to meet the needs of their children. Workers need to examine their behaviour and check that their assessment is not being limited by decisions, either conscious or unconscious, that have the effect of withdrawing from contact with the family. Ask yourself:

- Am I spending less time with this family compared to others of equal concern?

- If my remit is to spend time with the child, have I been able to do this in the way that I should?

- Am I relieved when they fail to be in or keep an appointment?

- How rigorous am I in making further attempts to make contact?

- When I do see the family, am I sure that I have covered all the points that I was intending to, or was I distracted or did I avoid contentious areas?

- Am I able to challenge accounts from parents that do not tally with my perception?

The concept of 'professional dangerousness' is a useful one here (Calder 2008; Morrison 1986). Amongst a number of factors involved in workers practising in a manner and context which allows for risks to children to continue, can be the collusion of workers with the family 'to avoid the "real" issues and to avoid having to raise concerns with the parents' (Calder 2008, p.65).

Should parents be aggressive, hostile or intimidating, particularly if this occurs when the child is present, clear links must be made with the effect that this behaviour could have on the child. Workers must ask themselves if they, as professional adults, are made to feel intimidated and frightened by a parent's behaviour, what is the experience of a child living with parents who respond in such a way? If a parent's response to stressful situation is one that is aggressive and lacks control, are there parallels to be drawn with the stressful challenges of parenting? If implicit or explicit threats have involved aggressive dogs or adult contacts with a history of violence, how well are the children protected from any potential risk posed? Do the parent/s have a personal or criminal history of violence, and, if so, how has this been incorporated into any assessment of risks to the child?

As well as these factors becoming integral to the assessment of risks to children, there also needs to be clear identification and clarification of what behaviour is unacceptable. A useful way to make explicit the impact on child, worker and assessment of parental behaviour is to draw up a contract.

Contract of expectation

Written contract specifying:

a) Exactly what behaviour is not acceptable, e.g. raising of voice, swearing, pointing, threatening, etc.

b) Being clear that this will be taken into account in any risk assessment of the child

c) Clearly explaining the consequences of continued hostile or unco-operative behaviour.

(Based on Sheffield Safeguarding Children Board 2007, p.10)

The very fact of making explicit the concerns both to the family and within the inter-agency setting will indicate that the worker has been able to identify fears and relate these fears to their own safety and to that of the child. Workers also need to bear in mind that a clear statement on behaviour that is not acceptable will also send a strong message to other vulnerable adults in the family. Those subject to domestic abuse and oppression need also to have their wellbeing and safety identified and made explicit in a safe manner.

In every case, good recording is essential. Patterns of poor co-operation need to be recorded, fed back to the family and shared within the multi-agency network. The report into the death of Ainlee Labonte recorded that 'most of the records do not acknowledge that the family was frightening' (Newham 2002, p.53). In his research into violence and aggression towards social workers, Littlechild found that 'the most common forms of violence…were verbal abuse and threats, but these were rarely reported or recorded unless clear threats were attached to them' (Littlechild 2005, p.394). A very powerful tool in all safeguarding work is a clear chronology. In many cases where children died as a result of parental abuse, instances can be identified where information was treated discretely either by individual workers or within the inter-agency network (Brandon *et al.* 2008; Reder, Duncan and Gray 1993). A parent can minimise their behaviour or the inter-agency network can underplay the exact nature of avoidance or hostility if each incident is viewed individually. A clear account of exactly what happened, the impact on the worker and/or child and the dates, will serve to make explicit concerns and may highlight risks. A key message here is that whilst acts may be minimised by a parent, the impact on the worker must be noted, recorded and reported, i.e. raising of the voice; standing too close; veiled or overt threats.

There are, however, some situations which cannot be tolerated and which pose grave risks to workers, family members and children. These situations would be those characterised as extremely confrontational or violent behaviour, either actual or threatened. There should be no expectation that workers should stay in a situation where they feel physically threatened. Should any such situation arise and there is a potential for violence or assault, workers should leave in the safest way possible and then make immediate contact with the manager and, if necessary, the police, especially if children remain in the situation. Workers need to take account of personal safety issues and policies within their own workplace. It is not safe for workers to make a guess about whether or not a threat will be carried out. It is sufficient and reasonable that they experience it as a likely risk. Wild (2007) gives a powerful example of a parent responding to a home visit by a worker by placing a carving knife on the table. Whilst not exactly explicit, this action should be enough for the worker not to continue the visit and to seek further support. Contact with families known to pose a risk must be carefully planned, although as it is never possible to predict which parent may suddenly become aggressive, safe practice must be adhered to in all circumstances. Key considerations for worker and organisation may need to be the development of an accepted safety policy and culture which could include:

- ensuring colleagues are clear of your whereabouts at all times, including estimated return time

- clear procedures in place for what should be done if a worker does not return within this time

- information for who family members should contact about a worker's non-return

- use of mobile phones to check staff safety, contact manager and, if necessary, summon help

- consideration of joint visits or joint interviewing

- taking precautions such as having ex-directory phone number

- workers not expected to visit or park in dark and threatening situations unprotected. (Based on Sheffield Safeguarding Children Board 2007, p.26)

Each organisation should have their own in-house arrangements informed by safe practice guidance for staff (Suzy Lamplugh Trust 2008). However, workers need also to take responsibility for raising issues of safety if they feel threatened or that there is an expectation that they will work in a situation in which they feel frightened. Whilst all these are sensible precautions when working with any family, questions must be raised about the wellbeing of children living with parents who can only be worked with by staff using stringent safety procedures on each occasion.

Unfortunately, however, we do know that many workers are not able to voice their own fears about the families they are working with. Tony Morrison proposes a model, based on Roland Summit's Sexual Abuse Accommodation Syndrome (Summit 1983). In his Professional Accommodation Model, Morrison (1997) considers workers coping with anxiety in child protection scenarios. He takes Summit's description of children unable to disclose sexual abuse and relates this to the experiences of some workers coping with risk and dangerousness. Workers may feel that their organisational culture does not give them permission to reveal their fearful thoughts. Morrison takes the pre-disclosure stages of secrecy, helplessness, entrapment and accommodation and locates some of the factors within both staff and organisations that can result in workers feeling that their concerns are not valid. Workers and organisations need to consider what circumstances may lead to staff not feeling safe to talk about their fears and anxieties and need to consider their response when workers do express concerns.

Consider

- Are issues of personal feelings, staff safety and lack of confidence on the agenda as acceptable and, indeed, anticipated by managers or supervisors?

- Are workers provided with good training and skills development opportunities to develop their assessment skills and increase confidence?

- Are staff regularly asked if there is a family who is causing them to feel frightened or personally challenged?

- Is regular staff supervision or support part of the organisation's responsibility to their staff and service users?

- Are supervision/support arrangements given a high priority by the organisation, managers and staff?

- Is it a routine expectation that supervision sessions or case discussions are able to consider the emotional impact of the work as well as the procedural aspects of case management?

- Are there clear and meaningful procedures for monitoring staff safety at all times?

- Are staff made aware of the organisation's policies and procedures for staff safety and staff support?

- Does the organisation, or the professional body, have a staff support and counselling scheme?

As well as structural and procedural commitment to staff support and safety, the organisational culture can play a key part in encouraging workers to feel helpless: 'Myths exist that trained staff should act logically, rationally and objectively' (Morrison 1997, p.204).

Workplace stereotypes of workers

Consider these questions:

- Are there some who almost wear difficult cases as 'badges'?

- Is it truly acceptable to be seen to be distressed or anxious?

- What is the underlying view of those who are upset by frightening families? Is it that the difficulty is with the worker rather than the family or the organisation?

> - Would it be acceptable for a worker to express distress, particularly those who may be expected to cope better with difficult families, e.g. more experienced workers; male workers; workers from the same ethnic background as the family in question?

If workers have felt unable to share their concerns about how they are feeling, by the time it becomes apparent that they are distressed by their work it may be that it is this distress that is noted rather than the underlying causes. This may then cloud the issue of the dangerous nature of the family and the worker themselves could be considered, or consider themselves, to be at fault. Remember again, the delayed or unconvincing disclosure from an abused child and how this is often responded to with lack of attention to the abuse.

- Are organisations able to provide an environment where time and thought can be given to clear and sensitive discussion of the origins of workers' feelings and how this relates to the family and risks to children?

- Are workers able to distinguish between what is their responsibility, what is not and what steps need to be taken to ensure safe practice?

- Is the organisation able to make clear plans that maintain staff safety, yet still protects the wellbeing of the child and family?

In some circumstances workers can withdraw through sickness or resignation and many organisations are suffering from staff leaving early after working, unsupported, with caseloads of some of the most challenging family situations. A clear goal for agencies is to challenge cultures that accept that aggression and intimidation is somehow 'part of the job' and requires no additional support. When working with the complexities presented by some of the most troubled and troubling families workers need support in recognising when they are being 'drawn into a family's disempowering power/control dynamics' (Littlechild 2005, p.398).

It is hoped that it has been shown that, whilst all efforts need to be made to work in partnership with families, we cannot divorce the impact of hostile or unco-operative behaviour of parents from the assessment of the needs of their children: children who, in turn, depend on workers to remain clear, effective and well supported in order to safeguard their wellbeing.

REFERENCES

Banks, S. (2006) *Ethics and Values in Social Work*. Basingstoke: Palgrave.

Bell, M. (1999) 'Working in partnership in child protection: the conflicts.' *British Journal of Social Work* 29, 437–455.

Brandon, M., Belderson, P., Warren, C., Howe, D., Gardner, R., Dodsworth, J. and Black, J. (2008) *Analysing Child Deaths and Serious Injury Through Abuse and Neglect: What Can We Learn?* London: Department for Children, Schools and Families.

Calder, M. (2008) *Contemporary Risk Assessment in Safeguarding Children.* Lyme Regis: Russell House Publishing.

Department of Health (1995a) *Child Protection: Messages from Research.* London: HMSO.

Department of Health (1995b) *The Challenge of Partnership in Child Protection: Practice Guidance.* London: HMSO.

Haringey Safeguarding Children Board (2008) 'Serious Case Review "Child A".' Haringey: Haringey Local Safeguarding Children Board.

HM Treasury/Department for Education and Skills (2007) *Policy Review of Children and Young People: A Discussion Paper.* London: Stationery Office.

Knott, C. and Scragg, T. (2007) *Reflective Practice in Social Work.* London: Learning Matters.

Laming, H. (2003) *The Victoria Climbié Inquiry: The Report.* London: Stationery Office.

Lishman, J. (1994) *Communication in Social Work.* Birmingham: BASW Macmillan.

Littlechild, B. (2005) 'The nature and effects of violence against child protection social workers: providing effective support.' *British Journal of Social Work 35*, 387–401.

McBride, P. (1998) *The Assertive Social Worker.* Aldershot: Arena.

Morrison, T. (1986) 'Proffesional Dangerousness.' In P. Dale and T. Morrison (eds) *Dangerous Families.* London: NSPCC.

Morrison, T. (1997) 'The Staff Dimension: Emotionally Competent Child Protection Organizations: Fallacy, Fiction or Necessity?' In J. Bates, R. Pugh and N. Thompson *Protecting Children: Challenges & Changes.* Aldershot: Arena.

Newham Area Child Protection Committee (2002) *Ainlee: Chapter 8 Review.* London: Newham Area Child Protection Committee.

Parton, N. (ed.) (1997) *Child Protection and Family Support: Tensions, Contradictions and Possibilities.* London: Routledge.

Pearson, R. (2005) 'Factors affecting retention of children's names on the Child Protection Register for a period of two years or over.' Unpublished MA Dissertation, Huddersfield University.

Pinkerton, J. (2002) 'Child Prootection.' In R. Adams, L. Dominelli and M. Payne *Critical Practice in Social Work.* Basingstoke: Palgrave.

Reder, P., Duncan, S. and Gray, M. (1993) *Beyond Blame: Child Abuse Tragedies Revisited.* London: Routledge.

Rustin, M. (2005) 'Conceptual analysis of critical moments in Victoria Climbié's life.' *Child and Family Social Work 10*, 11–19.

Sheffield Safeguarding Children Board (2007) 'Uncooperative families protocol.' Available at www.safeguardingsheffieldchildren.org.uk, accessed 7 December 2008.

Summit, R. (1983) 'The child sexual abuse accommodation syndrome.' *Child Abuse and Neglect 7*, 2, 177–193.

Suzy Lamplugh Trust (2008) 'Personal safety at work: A guide for everyone.' Available at www.suzylamplugh.org, accessed 7 December 2008.

Turnell, A. and Edwards, S. (1999) *Signs of Safety: A Solution and Safety Oriented Approach to Child Protection Casework.* New York and London: Norton.

Wild, J. (2007) 'Dealing with violent service users.' *Community Care*, 12 April.

CHAPTER 6

NEGLECT AND PARENTAL LEARNING DISABILITY

ROSIE JAKOB AND GAIL GUMBRELL

INTRODUCTION

Historically, people with learning disabilities in England lived in long-stay institutions on the edges of communities. They were viewed as being outside of the communities and, at different times, have been considered as dangerous or as people to be pitied (Mencap 2007). The National Assistance Act 1948 and the Chronically Sick and Disabled Person's Act 1970 reflected the view that people with learning disabilities were not individuals who could make choices, but were there to be 'helped' (Oliver 1990).

The theory of 'normalisation' which developed in the 1980s 'argued that stigma could only be overcome if people were able to live "an ordinary life" in the community and to adopt socially valued roles and this was a major influence on policies to close segregated institutions' (Curtice 2007, p.2). In 1993 the NHS and Community Care Act 1990 came into force. This led to the dismantling of these institutions with the aim of people with learning disabilities becoming active members of their community. The reality for many of those discharged from hospital was that they became isolated in communities that did not welcome them. Responsibility for their care was often placed on individual families instead of it being seen as a collective, societal or community responsibility. There was some recognition of the need for people coming out of institutions to be re-educated and offered training in independent living skills such as budgeting, cooking, self-care, etc. but it was not even considered that people with learning disabilities might become parents.

In 1998 the Human Rights Act came into force. Article 8 requires the right to respect for private and family life, home and correspondence. This Act recognised that *all* people had a right to form sexual relationships and the right to a family life. Coupled with the Children Act 1989, whose philosophy is that children should remain within their families if at all possible, there has been a gradual recognition that these rights extend to all people, including those with learning disabilities. As an increasing number of adults with learning disabilities have begun to form sexual relationships, and subsequently have children, issues regarding their ability to care for their children have become a significant item on the social care agenda.

The government produced a white paper, *Valuing People*, in 2001, which considered the needs of people with learning disabilities and ways in which they could be further included within today's society. It considered directly the needs of parents with learning disabilities and their children and recognised the importance of 'supporting parents with learning disabilities in order to help them, wherever possible, to ensure their children gain maximum life chance benefits' (Department of Health 2001, Sub-objective 7.4, p.127).

For the purposes of this chapter it is important to define what is meant by the terms 'learning disability and neglect'. *Valuing People* states that a learning disability is 'A significantly reduced ability to understand new or complex information, to learn new skills (impaired intelligence); with a reduced ability to cope independently (impaired social functioning); which started before adulthood, with a lasting effect on development' (Department of Health 2001, p.14).

We are using the *Working Together to Safeguard Children* (Department of Health, Home Office, Department of Education and Employment 1999) definition of neglect, which is as follows:

> Neglect is the persistent failure to meet a child's basic physical and/or psychological needs, likely to result in the serious impairment of the child's health or development. It may involve a parent or carer failing to provide adequate food, shelter and clothing, failing to protect a child from a physical harm or danger, or the failure to ensure access to appropriate medical care treatment. It may also include neglect of, or unresponsiveness to a child's basic emotional needs. (p.6, 2.7)

Neglect is considered the most common reason for the children of learning disabled parents coming to the attention of professionals (Cleaver and Nicholson 2005). It is important, however, to recognise that parents with learning disabilities are as capable as any other parent of harming children in any other way.

In all work with children and their families the child's needs are paramount. It is important, however, that work with families is approached from a holistic stance. The Assessment Framework for working with children in need and their families (Department of Health 2000) is a common and useful tool in beginning to look at the needs of all families and can be used positively in considering the needs of children where a parent has a learning disability.

SAFEGUARDING CHILDREN

Although each individual situation is different, it is undeniable that having a parent with a learning disability adds another dimension to a child's experience of being parented. This may not be a positive experience; if a parent is targeted in the community, for example, this is quite likely to affect the child too (Booth and Booth 1997). Often parents with learning disabilities are not able to parent without support (McGaw and Newman 2005). They may struggle with basic care tasks and/or understanding the changing developmental needs of their child. If they have more than one child, they may struggle with multi-tasking and meeting the differing demands made upon them by their children. As vulnerable adults, they may not be able to identify dangerous situations or people themselves and therefore their ability to safeguard and protect their children becomes questionable.

Many children of learning disabled parents become frustrated as their intellect begins to surpass that of their parents (Woodhouse, Green and Davies 2001). They can find themselves in the position of role reversal, where they become the parent and their parent the child. They may be the person who makes sure the doors are locked at night or that the gas ring is turned off, for example. If they are the oldest of several children, the onus can fall upon them to do much of the caring for their younger siblings. In this position they may not have anyone to turn to in order to have their own needs met and may become isolated. They may begin missing out on schooling and other social activities.

If a child is living within a family where they are dependent on a parent or carer with a learning disability, then they may well be at risk of harm. If that parent or carer is well supported however, their children may have the opportunity to grow up feeling loved and having a positive self-image (McGaw and Newman 2005). Parents with learning disabilities are as likely or unlikely to harm their child as any other parent (Tymchuck 1992). There is, however, an assumption of incompetence with this particular group of parents which has led to a higher number of their children entering the care system (Tarleton, Ward and Howarth 2006). The children are therefore disadvantaged by the state as well as any other parenting difficulties they may encounter.

Children whose parents do have learning disabilities are likely to benefit from some level of direct support. This could be through Young Carers support groups, where they are introduced to other young carers and are offered opportunities to socialise and participate in age appropriate activities (Barnardo's 2007). Ensuring children attend nursery or school and developing a level of home–school communication (the use of learning mentors can be particularly effective here) can be a positive benefit. Direct work with children in respect of building self-esteem is valuable. If children can develop an awareness of why their parent has a learning disability, this can be used to help develop an improved self image and a more positive sense of identity (Booth and Booth 1997).

DIRECT WORK WITH PARENTS WITH LEARNING DISABILITIES
Communication

The baseline of any work with parents with learning disabilities is how professionals communicate with them effectively. Whilst communication is always a key area for professionals working with people, the needs of learning disabled people can be more specific and require a more considered approach (Affleck and Baker 2004). An important starting point is that the professional accepts that it is their responsibility to ensure that the service user understands what has been communicated. Professionals often make assumptions that someone has understood what they have said or written when they tell them that they have. With parents with learning disabilities it is particularly important that workers do not make this assumption. The following is a list of helpful factors to consider when working with parents with learning disabilities:

- Can they read for meaning?

- Can they tell the time?

- Think about language, e.g. avoid using jargon, 'good enough parenting', etc.

- Always check that they have understood – ask them to relay the information back.

- Simplify language in written reports/agreements, etc.

- Provide a copy of reports to parents so that they have time to read them before going into meetings.

- Check language for sense, e.g. advising a parent not to put hot drinks on a coffee table only to find they put them on the floor.

Exercise in communication

Purpose of exercise: To allow participants to explore assumptions that are made about communication and understanding and to think about how they can communicate more effectively.

Participants: Exercise to be done in pairs.

Equipment: Paper, pencils and copy of Figure 6.1 for each pair.

Task: One of each pair is given a copy of the diagram from Figure 6.1 and asked not to show it to the other person. The other person is given a blank piece of paper and a pencil. The person with the diagram must describe the drawing to the other person who must then attempt to redraw the diagram on their blank sheet.

Time: Allow ten minutes for the pair exercise – followed by ten minutes feedback in large group.

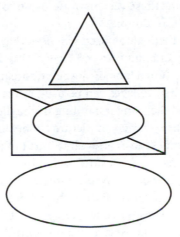

Figure 6.1 Turn this into words

VISUAL AIDS

It is quite possible that a parent with a learning disability may not read or may struggle with reading or the interpretation of words. The use of visual aids can be particularly useful in this circumstance.

Although cartoon representations can be used as visual aids, photographs can be far more effective as a tool. The use of photographs to portray a sequence of actions or activities that the parent is required to do, can be a positive way of supporting a family. An example of this is in teaching a parent to follow a morning routine. This can be particularly helpful if the parent and child themselves are used for such photographs, for example making breakfast, brushing teeth, etc. If a parent struggles with telling the time, photographs of a clock set at various times can be useful (it is important that the clock is one that the parent can then have in their home to refer to).

Often, families in this situation have many different professional visitors. Using a timeline of seven days with photographs of the workers stuck on can also be helpful. Timelines using photographs can also be of assistance for specific tasks parents need to carry out, for example photographs showing each stage of making a meal can be placed in order and be removed by the parent as they complete each stage of the recipe.

When assisting parents in managing diaries and appointments, it is always important that the worker explores what feels most comfortable for that individual. They may prefer to have a diary sheet that uses vertical or horizontal columns for days of the week. Colour coding can also be used, for example a different colour for each professional. It is essential that professionals take responsibility for keeping these various systems up to date and do not expect the parent to remember to do this.

Other visual tools that can be used when working with families where a parent has a learning disability are collages. This is a particularly useful method for assessment. When looking at specific areas of concern, such as the food a parent is providing, collages can be used to record their views on what children should eat and their understanding of the dietary needs of children. In order to do this, gather a variety of pictures of healthy and unhealthy foods and drinks from magazines, etc. Use a large sheet of paper and divide it into seven columns, one for each day. Ask the parent to choose pictures of the food and drink they give to their children throughout the day. Stick these onto the sheet of paper. It is important to discuss the choices made by the parent in order to explore their reasons for choosing specific foods. The collage can be brought back to further sessions as a visual prompt and to facilitate further discussion.

MODELLING

Modelling can be a great help to parents with learning disabilities, if done correctly. Often workers will go into a home and demonstrate a task and then make the assumption that the parent will have understood and remembered the instructions given. For someone with a learning disability, this is unlikely to be successful. In these situations, it is likely to be far more productive to complete tasks alongside the parent, and to repeat the task on a regular basis (Tarleton, Ward and Howarth 2006).

Modelling example

A worker shows a parent how to make the bed. Later she insists, 'I've shown her how to make the bed, so I know she knows how to do it.' An alternative would have been to make the bed with the parent, repeating this task regularly until the parent is completing the task on their own initiative.

Another area where modelling can be useful is in stimulating the child. Often parents with learning disabilities can spend a small fortune on buying toys for their children but never use them. If the worker gets down on the floor alongside the parent and child and encourages interaction, it can ensure that the child is being stimulated and can lead to the parent developing their own play skills.

CASE STUDY 6.1: DIRECT WORK IN PRACTICE

Tina is 31. She has a learning disability. She is the single parent of three children: David, aged six; Jenny, aged three and Sam, who is two months old. There are concerns for various professionals about Tina's ability to cope with the demands of her three children.

The school has expressed concern that David is often late and usually tired. He has been coming to school with no coat, and wearing just t-shirts on top even though it is November. Other children have begun teasing him about smelling unpleasant. The health visitor describes Jenny as developmentally delayed. Her speech is limited and she has referred her to the speech and language therapist. The health visitor is also working with Tina regarding Jenny's toilet training but has had no success to date. She is concerned that there are few toys or activities for the children in the home and is worried that they are being under stimulated. The health visitor has made a referral to Social Services because the home environment has deteriorated dramatically since Tina gave birth to Sam.

Issues to address:

- Ensuring the children are safe.

- Assessing the individual needs of the children.

- Assessing Tina's strengths and areas where she struggles.

CASE STUDY 6.2: POSSIBLE INTERVENTIONS

Daily support from workers who are familiar with the needs of learning disabled people. Support targeted at significant times of day, e.g. morning and evening routines.

- Identifying nursery placement for Jenny.

- Modelling to help improve conditions in the home.

- Using photographs to assist in establishing routines.

- Modelling behaviour with regard to improving stimulation of the children.

- Using collage to help Tina to identify age appropriate toys for each child.

- Supporting Tina to attend appointments, e.g. speech and language therapist, clinic.

- Supporting Tina to think about meals, make a shopping list and go shopping.

- Supporting Tina regarding clothing, e.g. daily sets of clothes for each child.

MULTI-AGENCY WORKING

The document *Working Together to Safeguard Children* (Department for Education and Skills 2006) focuses strongly on the fact that safeguarding children is a shared responsibility:

> Safeguarding and promoting the welfare of children – and in particular protecting them from significant harm – depends on effective joint working between agencies and professionals that have different roles and expertise. Individual children, especially some of the most vulnerable children and those at greatest risk of social exclusion, will need co-ordinated help from health, education, children's social care, and quite possibly the voluntary sector and other agencies, including youth justice services. (p.33, para 1.14)

Multi-agency working is essential in safeguarding children, no matter what their circumstances. It is a significant issue when working with parents with learning disabilities because of the need to draw together professionals from both adult and children's services. The importance of communication has already been highlighted when working with this group of service users. The same issues apply in developing more effective communication skills and systems between agencies.

The Baring Foundation produced a report in 2006 called *Finding the Right Support?* (Tarleton *et al.* 2006). One of its key findings was the need to develop multi-professional and multi-agency support for parents with learning disabilities and their families. It 'highlights the need for children's and adult services to work together in a pro-active and preventative way to meet the needs of the whole family' (Morris, in Tarleton *et al.* 2006, p.92). The report's findings have contributed to the most recent guidance provided by the

Department for Education and Skills and the Department of Health (2007), *Good Practice Guidance on Working with Parents with a Learning Disability*. The guidance recommends that joint protocols are developed between the different agencies, providing 'a valuable opportunity for the different services involved to get a better understanding of each other's roles and responsibilities' (p.10). Although the guidance is not legislation and cannot be enforced, it clearly reiterates the need for developing strategies that will ensure a smoother and more effective service for these families. Local safeguarding boards would be in an ideal position to develop multi-agency training regarding the needs of these service users and promote a more cohesive service.

There are a number of different professionals who come into contact with families where a parent has a learning disability. For a successful service there is a need for clear communication guidelines. Each professional will require an understanding of who to make referrals to and how to go about this. As soon as the pregnancy is confirmed, services need to begin to fall into place. A system could be developed in which the midwife contacts both adult and children services. The parent needs to be involved in this process as much as possible. Professionals should be looking at the best possible way of supporting a family to stay together. This may be a useful point for an advocate to step in and begin supporting the parent if necessary.

Historically there have been tensions between adult and children services (McGaw and Newman 2005). Children's services are, quite correctly, concerned with safeguarding children and meeting their needs. Their focus when working with parents with learning disabilities can often be on the deficits that a parent has in meeting a child's needs, rather than a holistic approach. This can lead to short-term solutions which only remedy the situation temporarily, with the consequence being a higher number of children of learning disabled parents coming into care (Booth, Booth and McConnell 2005). Adult services are focused on the rights and needs of adults, often having little understanding of the safeguarding issues surrounding the child or children of a parent with a learning disability. The gulf between adult and children services is currently being further reinforced by the structural changes in local authorities. Children's services are being aligned with education, whilst adult services are aligned with health (Department for Education and Skills 2003; Department of Health 2005).

The separation between adult workers and child-care workers begins within their training as professionals. In social work, students are asked to specialise early on in one field or the other. Although there is some generic training, the fact that it is not used on a daily basis means that it is often forgotten. Once practising, the professional's expertise develops in their chosen areas and there are currently few policies within local authorities that encourage training outside an individual's current practice areas. To provide effective services to families where a parent has a learning disability, training needs to be developed for practitioners in order that they can address their own learning deficits (Department for Education and Skills and Department of Health 2007, p.11, para 1.2.2).

The need to understand how different professionals work is essential in multi-agency practice and in providing a united and successful service.

Multi-agency practice

Traditionally in social services, children's services provide support to families from within their own resources, e.g. family centres. This is usually time-limited and restricted to a weekday service only. Practitioners within these settings may not have the knowledge required to work with learning disabled adults. Adult services assess the needs of the adult and then provide or buy in services (as necessary) to meet those needs in the form of a care package. These services can be more flexible but adult workers are not necessarily experienced in identifying the needs of children and safeguarding issues.

If a parent with a learning disability needs support during the weekend or late at night, it will be necessary for the workers involved to work together to find a way to provide appropriate support to meet the needs of the whole family. In order to meet holistically the needs of families where a parent has a learning disability it is important to combine the valuable assets of all services.

One of the essential factors of working with families where a parent has a learning disability is that support is necessary on a long-term basis. It is important to acknowledge that someone with a learning disability will have that disability for life – there is no cure. Just as parents with a physical disability may require certain services to care for their children long-term, the same is true for those with a learning disability. Although the needs of the children may differ as they grow, the parent will continue to require support and guidance to address those changing needs. Thus, support packages for such a family are not fixed and may vary over time. The family will require continuous reviewing and reassessment as circumstances change. It is essential, therefore, that the worker recognises that a generic approach cannot be used:

> Service providers need to be wary of the argument that all parents should be treated alike and offered the same services as the mainstream population. Empirical research and clinical practice indicate that the majority of services are

as yet inadequate in meeting the needs of families that may need extra, specialised help. (McGaw and Newman 2005, p.14)

Whilst excellent support can be devised by professionals when working with an immediate crisis, this is so often then withdrawn once the crisis has passed. With families where a parent has a learning disability, the long-term neglect of their children is often a key factor (Tarleton *et al.* 2006). To withdraw support when a certain standard of care has been achieved does not recognise that these parents will not be equipped to retain their learning or translate that learning to new situations and will need the committed support of professionals throughout their child's upbringing. It is this factor that is crucial when examining the reasons why children of parents with learning disabilities are more likely to come into the care of social services.

There is an aim in social work practice that work with families should be time-limited, with the hope that the families will become largely independent and no longer require services. This is often a positive goal but disadvantages these particular families who are unable to achieve such a level of independence. Intensive short-term interventions are unlikely to be successful with them; they require a regular, drip, drip approach to learning and maintaining good-enough parenting.

Given the need for such a long-term commitment, the requirement for joined-up thinking becomes even more apparent. A holistic approach recognises that the best way to meet the needs of children is to look at the needs of the parents and therefore the whole family. In order to do this a holistic service needs to be created, where issues of policy, protocol and funding can all be addressed (Department for Education and Skills and Department of Health 2007)

GOOD PRACTICE POINTS

WORKING TOGETHER:

- Early identification and appropriate referrals
- Clarity about the role of each professional involved
- Recognition that each professional has a duty of care
- Ensuring that professionals are all giving the same message
- Respecting each other's area of expertise and not being afraid to ask questions
- Clear lines of communication within and between agencies
- Ensure that a lead professional is identified

- Acceptance of the need for long-term support
- Regular reviews of the family's progress and of the support package
- Developing a shared funding policy
- Appropriate training being available
- Parenting groups specifically targeted at people with learning disabilities
- Co-ordinated assessment procedures
- Appropriate advocacy, especially during any court proceedings
- Provision of easy to understand information, especially at meetings and reviews
- Recognition that meetings and visits will take longer
- Flexible support to meet changing needs
- Developing multi-agency networking and support
- Working in partnership with parents
- Consistency regarding expectations
- Positive feedback to parents – praise and encouragement
- Establishing a pool of regular support workers
- Prompting the parent rather than doing the parenting.

One of the concerns expressed by professionals about the use of an ongoing support package is that the child or children will begin looking towards workers for their needs to be met and may become confused about who their parent is. In practice, often the most successful approach to managing this concern is the provision of a small team of support workers who visit on a rotational basis. The workers' role is to assist and prompt the parent, not to take over the role of parenting. This can help to clarify who is the parent, thus ensuring that a bond remains between child and parent. It also allows for the possibility of workers becoming sick or going on holiday, etc. The child is then not exposed to so many different professionals that s/he becomes immune to the possibility of dangerous strangers. A parent with a learning disability also needs some consistency in workers in order that a level of trust can be built, but it is as important that they do not become reliant on a particular worker and are able to work with some degree of flexibility.

CASE STUDY 6.3: GOOD PRACTICE
IN WORKING TOGETHER

Aisha is a 24-year-old Asian woman with limited understanding of English. She is married to Aman, who is 28 and works full time as a security guard. They have two children, Mohammed, aged three, and Sajna, aged three months. The family has an allocated children and family social worker due to concerns from the health visitors that Mohammed was developmentally delayed and that Aisha was struggling with his care.

Sajna was born very prematurely and has been in hospital since birth. She has a naso-gastric tube for feeding and is hearing and visually impaired. It is not yet clear whether she is learning disabled too. Sajna is now ready to be discharged from hospital but the staff are concerned that the parents do not seem to be able to cope with the tube feeding. The nurses have been trying to teach Aisha how to use the tube with the support of an interpreter. During their demonstrations the interpreter has questioned Aisha's level of understanding and the staff now wonder whether she has a learning disability.

The social worker has made a referral to the learning disability team and requested an assessment of Aisha. The social worker from the learning disability team speaks the same language as Aisha and during an initial assessment, establishes that Aisha does in fact have a significant learning disability and is eligible for their support.

The social worker from children's services and the social worker from adult services have met and agreed to undertake a joint assessment of the family. They spend time establishing what the family's strengths are and the areas where they are struggling, referring to the *Assessment Framework for Children in Need and their Families* (Department of Health 2000).

It is discovered that the family manages well in the mornings when Aman returns from his night shift. He is able to prompt Aisha and supports her with preparing breakfast and dressing Mohammed. Once Aman goes to bed however, Aisha begins to struggle. She is unsure of how to set boundaries for Mohammed and leaves him strapped in his push chair for long periods of time.

A multi-agency meeting is called, involving the hospital staff, the health visitor, the social workers from both teams, the parents and an interpreter. It is decided to put together a support package involving workers going into the family home at lunchtimes and bedtimes Monday to Friday. Where possible, the workers will speak the same language as Aisha. The same interpreter has agreed to attend at other times. This support is to be provided by the family centre and adult services have agreed to fund an outside agency who specialise in working with parents with learning disabilities to go shopping with Aisha once a week and to help her establish household routines. All workers will use a book of photographs that has been made to prompt Aisha regarding daily tasks.

A programme of teaching is set up by the learning disability social worker in conjunction with the nursing staff around feeding Sajna. Photographs of each stage of the process are taken and Aisha is now able to use these visual aids to successfully feed Sajna.

The children's social worker makes a referral to the local nursery for Mohammed and has managed to identify a worker from a parenting programme to teach Aisha some play skills.

It is agreed that regular monthly meetings will be held to review the family's needs once Sajna is discharged home.

WHEN CHILDREN HAVE TO BE REMOVED

There are situations in which no amount of preventative support can ensure that children are not at risk of or likely to suffer significant harm. In these circumstances the child or children may need to be accommodated by the local authority, either on a voluntary basis or through the instigation of care proceedings under section 37 of the Children Act 1989. As with any family, this can be a traumatic experience for the children and the parents. For children, the unexpected separation from their primary caregivers can be devastating. It is to be hoped that they will be supported appropriately by their social worker and temporary carers, whether foster carers or residential workers, in coping with their loss and making sense of what is happening in their lives.

Children who have a parent with a learning disability need appropriate guidance and support in understanding the learning disability and recognising that the possible lack of care they have received from their parent(s) is not necessarily a deliberate act but as a consequence of their disability. It is also important that carers are able to reinforce a positive view of the parent(s) to the children. Again, this is quite likely to involve specific training of carers around the difficulties learning disabled people experience. The Commission for Social Care Inspection (2006) found that young people 'had strong views about the importance of helping parents, both in their own right and in relation to children's needs. They recognised that parents need clear messages about what needs to change, and help to do so' (p.44).

With all parents it is important that a working relationship is maintained. When working with parents with learning disabilities, their ability to understand the concerns may be limited and it is important to ensure that a worker is allocated specifically to support them through the confusion of care proceedings and what is happening to their children. The court process is bewildering for any parent – when the parent has a learning disability it may be helpful to identify an advocate for that parent to assist them in understanding the process (Skills for People 2004).

One of the key factors for children being separated from their parents is the role of contact. Contact is essential in maintaining a relationship between the child and parent. It is also a useful opportunity for workers to observe how parents and children relate to each other and possibly offer alternative guidance in order to develop their relationship more positively. In arranging contact when there is a parent with a learning disability it is essential that a worker makes clear what the purpose of the contact is. The supervision of contact is often facilitated by workers based at family centres. Again, they may not have an understanding of the different approach required when working with people with learning disabilities and may require further training or consultation.

If there is recognition by workers that a learning disabled parent requires additional support, it is likely that contact will be a more positive experience for all involved. It may be appropriate that the contact supervisor offers ideas about age appropriate toys and games, and models play with the children. The expectation that a parent will be able to accept this guidance and repeat this interaction without prompting during subsequent contact sessions would be misguided (McGaw and Newman 2005). Contact has to be organised with the awareness that any learning by the parent will take much longer than with other parents. A useful approach may be to involve the parent and child, if appropriate, in planning the contact ahead of time and choosing activities which they may enjoy together.

During care proceedings there is likely to be an ongoing assessment of the parents. This will incorporate the contact, assessments by social workers and possibly specialist assessment. Often, one of the first tasks is to establish whether the parent has the capacity to instruct a solicitor. If they are found not to have capacity then the official solicitor is appointed. This can be difficult to explain to the parent as it will mean that any decisions made about whether to agree or disagree with other parties will not be made by them but by someone they are unlikely to ever meet. Regardless of this, an advocate is essential in order that the parent does feel involved and included in the future plans for their children.

There are various assessments that the parent may be required to undertake. A psychologist may become involved. If so, they may well be able to offer a further insight into the parent's intellectual functioning and advise about methods of working with them. A parent may be required to attend a family assessment centre with their child. This could be on a day basis, through outreach or residentially. There is some evidence that home-based interventions are most successful with parents with learning disabilities (Social Care Institute for Excellence 2005) although this is not always practicable. It is important that any workers involved are experienced in assessing families, including those in which a parent has a learning disability.

The statistics suggest that parents with learning disabilities who have their children removed often do not have them returned (Booth *et al.* 2005). Their children may remain in the care system or they may be adopted. If they remain in the care system then direct contact at a reduced level is likely to continue. It is important that a parent is supported in understanding why the contact is being reduced and in coming to terms with the likelihood that their children are not going to be returned to them. This may involve direct work with the parent by a social worker from adult services. It may be appropriate to develop a life story book (Shah and Argent 2006) for the parent to assist them in making sense of what has happened.

When children are placed for adoption there is an option for direct or indirect contact to be arranged. Although uncommon in England and Wales, direct contact can be a positive option for some children but research suggests that this is dependent on the approach of the agencies involved (Neil 2002). Indirect contact is usually arranged for once or twice a year and can involve the exchange of letters and photographs via an intermediary. In either situation parents with learning disabilities may need particular support in participating in the contact. There may, for example, be a difficulty with writing and reading and they may need support to write letters to their child. They may need help to take photographs or prompting when it is the relevant planned time of year for the contact to take place. They may also need specialist counselling by someone who can work with people with learning disabilities in coming to terms with their loss.

Children have a right to grow up with their birth families if at all possible (UN Convention of the Rights of the Child 1990, Articles 8 and 9). It is increasingly clear that people with learning disabilities are going to have children and they should therefore have an equal opportunity to raise their children. The challenge for professionals is to join together different areas of expertise and work in a holistic way. The fact that a learning disability is not always visible leaves this group of people even more vulnerable to unrealistic expectations and the dangers of professionals making assumptions. In order that these families are given an equal opportunity to remain together there is a need for early identification of the learning disability and the appropriate services being brought in from the beginning. There is a need for every local authority to establish clear protocols and to establish a cohesive service to meet the needs of these families.

REFERENCES

Affleck, F. and Baker, S. (2004) *You and Your Baby*. Leeds: CHANGE.

Barnardo's (2007) *Barnardo's Work with Young Carers*. Ilford, Essex: Barnardo's. Available at www.barnardos.org.uk/what_we_do/working_with_children_and_young_people, accessed 11 August 2008.

Booth, T. and Booth, W. (1997) *Exceptional Childhoods, Unexceptional Children*. London: Family Policy Studies Centre.

Booth, T., Booth, W. and McConnell, D. (2005) 'Care proceedings and parents with learning difficulties: Comparative prevalence and outcomes in an English and Australian court sample.' *Child and Family Social Work 10*, 4, 353–360.

Cleaver, H. and Nicholson, D. (2005) 'Children Living with Learning Disabled Parents.' Report submitted to the Department for Education and Skills.

Commission for Social Care Inspection (2006) *Supporting Parents, Safeguarding Children: Meeting the Needs of Parents with Children on the Child Protection Register*. London: Commission for Social Care Inspection.

Curtice, L. (2007) 'The Social and Spiritual Inclusion of People with Learning Disabilities: A Liberating Challenge?' Glasgow: Craighead Institute. Available at www.contactpracticaltheology.org/downloads/sample_article1.php, accessed 11 August 2008.

Department for Education and Skills (2003) *Every Child Matters*. London: Stationery Office.

Department for Education and Skills (2006) *Working Together to Safeguard Children*. London: Stationery Office.

Department for Education and Skills and Department of Health (2007) *Good Practice Guidance on Working with Parents with a Learning Disability*. London: Stationery Office.

Department of Health (2000) *Framework for the Assessment of Children in Need and their Families*. London: Stationery Office.

Department of Health (2001) *Valuing People: A New Strategy for Learning Disability for the 21st Century*. London: Stationery Office.

Department of Health (2005) *Independence, Well-being and Choice (Green Paper on Adult Social Care)*. London: DoH.

Department of Health, Home Office and Department of Education and Employment (1999) *Working Together to Safeguard Children*. London: Stationery Office.

McGaw, S. and Newman, T. (2005) *What Works for Parents with Learning Disabilities?* Ilford, Essex: Barnardo's.

Mencap (2007) *Changing Attitudes to People with a Learning Disability*. London: Mencap. Available at www.mencap.org.uk/html/about_mencap/changing_attitudes.asp, accessed 11 August 2008.

Neil, E. (2002) 'Contact after adoption: The role of agencies in making and supporting plans.' *Adoption and Fostering 26*, 1.

Oliver, M. (1990) *The Politics of Disablement*. London: Macmillan.

Shah, S. and Argent, H. (2006) *Life Story Work: What it is and What it Means*. London: BAAF.

Skills for People (2004) *Working with Parents with Learning Disabilities. A Guide to Child Protection Conferences*. Newcastle upon Tyne: Skills for People.

Social Care Institute for Excellent (2005) *Helping Parents with Learning Disabilities in their Role as Parents*. London: SCARE. Available at www.scie.org.uk, accessed 11 August 2008.

Tarleton, B., Ward, L. and Howarth J. (2006) *Finding the Right Support?* Bristol: Baring Foundation.

Tymchuck, A. (1992) 'Predicting adequacy of parenting by people with mental retardation.' *Child Abuse and Neglect 16*, 165–178.

Woodhouse, A., Green, G. and Davies, S. (2001) 'Parents with learning disabilities: Service audit and development.' *British Journal of Learning Disabilities 29*, 4, 128–132.

STATUTES

Children Act (1989) London: HMSO.

Chronically Sick and Disabled Person's Act (1970) London: HMSO.

Human Rights Act (1998) London: HMSO.

National Assistance Act (1948) London: HMSO.

NHS and Community Care Act (1990) London: HMSO.

The United Nations Convention on the Rights of the Child (1990). Geneva: Office of the United Nations High Commissioner for Human Rights. Available at http://www.unhchr.ch/html/menu3/b/k2crc.htm, accessed 11 August 2008.

CHAPTER 7

SAFEGUARDING CHILDREN WHO LIVE WITH PARENTAL SUBSTANCE MISUSE

MANDY CRAIG

Parental substance misuse is a significant factor when considering safeguarding children and promoting their wellbeing. It presents a wide spectrum of challenges to all services; both those working with children and their families (Bates *et al.* 1999; Forrester 2000; Harwin and Forrester 2002; Kroll and Taylor 2000, 2003) as well as those that primarily focus on the adult (Weir and Douglas 1999). However, it is important to acknowledge that the ability to provide a safe and nurturing environment for children does not have to be compromised by parental substance misuse and many parents who misuse substances are able to provide 'good enough parenting' for their children.

It is estimated that over a million children in the UK are living with parents who misuse alcohol (Turning Point 2006) and that between 250,000 and 350,000 are in the care of parents who misuse drugs (ACMD 2003), equating to 'one in ten of Britain's child population' (Harbin and Murphy 2006, p.2).

Throughout this chapter the generic term 'substance' is used to encompass alcohol, illicit drugs and misused prescribed medication. The term 'misuse' means: 'use which leads to social, physical and psychological harm' (SCODA 1997, p.36).

The aim of this chapter is to improve the outcomes for children whose parents/carers misuse substances by suggesting holistic approaches that support the family. At its core is the promotion of early recognition and appropriate intervention, good communication between all agencies and the family, accurate and multi-agency assessment that engages the parent and keeps the child as the primary focus. The chapter offers a straightforward approach that encompasses the key findings from relevant legislation, guidance and research. Exercises and training examples are included which are designed to enable practitioners to develop the skills necessary to meet the needs of this often 'hidden' population.

Through consultation with parents and children, the chapter also reflects the benefits of providing the parent with information relating to how their substance misuse has the potential to 'cause serious harm to children at every age from conception to adulthood' (ACMD 2003, p.3) and what it is like for their child to live with the day-to-day unpredictability of substance misuse.

As a primary source of information, this chapter will draw on the findings and experience of a Sheffield Safeguarding Children Board (SSCB) Substance Misuse Development project. This was set up in 1999 to specifically look at ways to improve the outcomes for families where substance misuse was an issue, by developing a whole systems approach, involving both adult and child care services in the solution.

SSCB Substance Misuse Development Project

Main objectives:

- To consult with substance misusing parents and their children about how to improve service provision.

- To produce appropriate literature for the substance misusing community regarding potential impact on children.

- To ensure national legislation is translated into a local working procedure.

- To ensure all substance misuse agencies have up-to-date, workable child protection policies.

- To audit substance misuse agency case files regularly, thereby ensuring the agencies address the subject of the potential impact on parenting and childcare.

- To develop and deliver multi-agency training on safeguarding children and substance misuse.

- To develop and manage early intervention screening systems for pregnancy.

- To provide advice and consultation to all agencies across the city to ensure consistency when working with parental substance misuse.

SETTING THE SCENE: SUBSTANCE MISUSE AND SAFEGUARDING CHILDREN – THE PATHWAY TO INTEGRATED PRACTICE

To understand how current models of good practice have taken shape, some of the key findings, developments and recommendations from recent legislation and research relating to substance misuse and safeguarding children need to be revisited briefly:

Drug Using Parents: Policy Guidelines for Inter-Agency Working (SCODA (Standing Conference on Drug Abuse) 1997)

These guidelines specifically addressed drug using parents and their children, and reiterated what the contemporary research indicated: not all substance misusing parents mistreated their offspring, and that to ensure that the children needing additional support were identified, it was important for parents with drug problems to be treated in the same way as other parents whose personal difficulties affect their ability to provide good parenting. SCODA hoped that this would encourage parents to seek advice and help from appropriate agencies and to work collaboratively to safeguard their children.

The guidelines highlighted good practice for both statutory and non-statutory agencies and demonstrated the importance of working together to provide an effective response for children whose parents misuse substances.

Tackling Drugs to Build a Better Britain (Drugs Strategy Directorate 1998, updated in 2002 and 2004)

In the Government's ten-year drug strategy, little reference was made to the needs of children living with substance misusing parents. The strategy primarily focused on four key aims: to help young people resist drug misuse; to protect communities from drug related anti-social and criminal behaviour; to enable people with drug problems to overcome them and to minimise the availability of illegal drugs on the street.

When the drugs strategy was updated in 2002, and again in 2004, its agenda became more targeted, with a strongly preventative aim, but still ignored the children of substance misusers. The then Home Secretary, David Blunkett, however, acknowledged the vulnerability of the children in the foreword to the strategy: 'Very often jobs and homes are lost; friendships and family ties are broken. When children are involved there is the danger of aban-donment and neglect' (Home Office *et al.* 2002).

Working Together to Safeguard Children (Department of Health 1999)

This government publication highlighted that there are occasions when the difficulties parents are experiencing such as substance misuse, domestic abuse and/or problems with their mental health, can impact on their capacity to meet the developmental needs of their children (Cleaver, Unell and Aldgate 1999).

Hidden Harm – Responding to the Needs of Children of Problem Drug Users (Advisory Council on the Misuse of Drugs 2003)

The main aims of this inquiry were to estimate the number of children living in the UK in households with parental drug use; to examine the immediate and long-term consequences of parental drug use for these children from conception through to adolescence; and to make policy and practice recommendations. The inquiry resulted in 48 recommendations and the following six key findings:

- We estimate there are between 250,000 and 350,000 children of problem drug users in the UK.

- Parental problem drug use can and does cause serious harm to children at every age from conception to adulthood.

- Reducing the harm to children from parental problem drug use should become a main objective of policy and practice.

- Effective treatment of the parent can have major benefits for the child.

- By working together, services can take many practical steps to protect and improve the health and wellbeing of affected children.

- The number of affected children is only likely to decrease when the number of problem drug users decreases. (ACMD 2003)

The Children Act (2004)

Section 11 places a statutory duty on all agencies, including those working with the adult regarding substance misuse and mental health issues, to safeguard and promote the welfare of children.

Every Child Matters (2003)

Five key outcomes for all children were identified that practitioners should promote through their work with families; be healthy; stay safe; enjoy and achieve; make a positive contribution and achieve economic wellbeing. This constitutes a significant challenge when working with children whose parents misuse substances.

Government response to Hidden Harm 2005

In March 2005 the government published its response to the *Hidden Harm* report (ACMD 2003) – acknowledging the work that had been done and accepting 42 of the 48 recommendations across children's services, primary health care and maternity services, drug and alcohol treatment services and criminal justice agencies.

Working Together to Safeguard Children (2006)

The profile of children of substance misusers was highlighted as a key area for action in this revised government guidance, published in April 2006, which sets out how individuals and organisations should cooperate to safeguard and promote the welfare of children. It makes clear that services for substance misuse 'have a responsibility in safeguarding children when they become aware of, or identify, a child at risk of harm' (HM Government 2006, p.59, paragraph 2.92). Parental substance misuse is also clearly referenced in the Common Assessment Framework (CAF).

Adult Drug Problems, Children's Needs (Hart and Powell 2006)

The Department of Health funded the National Children's Bureau published toolkit for practitioners as a next step in supporting local areas in their work with families where parents misuse substances and concerns exist about the child's welfare.

Hidden Harm Three Years On: Realities, Challenges and Opportunities (Advisory Council on the Misuse of Drugs February 2007)

When the ACDM revisited their Hidden Harm inquiry in 2007 there was a certain air of disappointment that the changes it contributed to were not as far reaching as they had hoped. However, it provided evidence that change had started and that services were beginning to focus on the lives of children living with substance misusing parents. Unfortunately, the lack of any strategic response still remained and therefore mounting problems relating to the lack of mainstream funding for resources to support the children and families.

Drugs: Protecting Families and Communities (The 2008 Drugs Strategy)

Children and families affected by drug misuse is the theme at the core of the government's new ten-year drugs strategy. It recognises that the impact of substance misuse on children and families can be significant and long term, and has been underestimated in previous drug strategies.

It does not address all the recommendations of the Hidden Harm Report (ACMD 2003, 2007) but it does not ignore them either. It recognises that substance misuse can limit effective parenting which in turn can lead to children growing up and being involved in youth crime and low educational attainment and that the most effective way forward is to become family focused in the whole approach to drug treatment. It talks about prioritising efforts to identify children and families at risk from substance misuse and provide appropriate interventions to address the challenges they face.

RESEARCH

There is a considerable body of research that shows children who grow up in families where there is parental substance misuse are at an increased risk of significant harm (see for example: Barnard 2007; Cleaver *et al.* 1999; Harbin and Murphy 2000; Kroll and Taylor 2003; Kearney *et al.* 2005; Klee, Jackson and Lewis 2002; Tunnard 2002; Velleman and Orford 2001). Whatever the primary cause of the parent's difficulties in caring adequately for their child, substance misuse will add to these challenges.

The short and long-term impact on children will depend on a multitude of factors including their age, level of understanding, personality, circumstances, coping strategies and degree of external support. Additionally, children's responses can alter over time as circumstances change and children adopt alternative coping strategies (Cleaver *et al.* 1999).

Summary

The findings from research have highlighted the vulnerability of children who live with parental substance misuse by illustrating how these issues impact negatively on all aspects of children's lives. To ensure these children are safe and their welfare promoted, input from both the agencies working with the child and those working with the adult is required. Recent policy documents produced by the government have acknowledged the importance of inter-agency working, and it is to be hoped that the new drugs strategy will also emphasise and support this way of working.

WHAT HINDERS EFFECTIVE PRACTICE?

Nobody would deny that with parenting and substance misuse being activities that predominantly take place within the private domain of the house, the assessment of when substance misuse starts to have a negative impact on parenting is extremely hard. The following are some examples of why practitioners may find it difficult to intervene.

The hidden nature of parental substance misuse leading to denial and secrecy

The public image of a substance misusing parent is one that often provokes anger, disgust and condemnation. As a result, it is not surprising that the parents, and the children who live with them, prefer to keep their day-to-day lives hidden from the public and professional eye, concealing or minimising their substance misuse and any suggestion that it may impact on their parenting ability.

Tessa Jowell, the then Minister of State for Public Health, acknowledged the challenges for society in the foreword to the SCODA guidelines:

> How we as a society deal with the problem of parents who misuse drugs is one of the most difficult and sensitive aspects of the drug problem. In general, society disapproves of drug misusers who have, or want to have children. (1997, p.1)

In 2000 the SSCB Substance Misuse Development Project consulted with groups of substance misusing parents on the subject of secrecy and denial. The parents reported being reluctant to access treatment relating to their substance misuse due to likelihood it would result in their use entering the public domain; something they resisted not only because of the impact on their own lives (how they would be viewed by relatives, neighbours) but also due to the perceived 'knock-on effect' on their families. Concerns included the teasing and bullying of their children in school because their parent misused drugs or alcohol, and the local community ostracising their children.

As a consequence of these fears the parents would not seek help as they held a strong belief that their status as substance misusers would override any fair consideration of their parenting abilities.

Lack of insight into life from the child's point of view

An increasing number of publications have focused on the voices of children and adults with direct experience of growing up with drug and alcohol misusing parents. They provide a picture of compromised care and inadequate emotional support. These messages are particularly challenging for practitioners, who share responsibility for safeguarding and promoting the welfare of children whatever agency they work for.

Practitioners need to consider what it is like for the child to wake up in the morning, go to school and go to bed at night, all with the uncertainty of something happening in their home that involves their parents, but nobody wants to talk about or listen to how they feel about the situation and what bits they may want to change. 'It is argued that a focus on the "elephant" often leads to children remaining "invisible" to those whose role it is to ensure their welfare' (Kroll 2004, p.129).

Things to consider from the child's point of view

What is day-to-day life like? The good bits? The bad bits? How do they feel waking up in the morning? If they are at home when their parent is misusing substances what changes do they see in their parents' character? How do they feel about this? What does substance misuse mean to them? What would they like to see change and why? Is there anyone they like to talk to? Do they like having friends come and play?

Too much emphasis is often focused on parents achieving abstinence from substances without consideration as to whether first, this is realistic and second, whether it would actually benefit the child and the family functioning. There appears to be a belief that if the parent's needs are addressed the child will automatically benefit. One example of this is the parent entering treatment for their drug or alcohol misuse. Due to the necessary emphasis on parental change and engagement with the substance misuse services it is seen as a positive step for the whole family. However, often for children there is generally a feeling of acceptance of and familiarity with their parents' substance misuse in the pre-change state. However risky it appeared to the outsider, it was the norm to those living in the household. This familiar way of life is shattered when the change process begins and an emotional roller coaster of unpredictability, underpinned with self-blame, broken promises and uncertainty becomes the norm instead.

The complexity of multi-agency working

The multi-layered nature of the problems experienced when you add substance misuse together with parenting difficulties, and maybe also elements of mental health issues, criminal activity, poverty, threat of eviction, and domestic abuse, clearly make decisions about both how to and when to intervene very problematic. Practitioners become confused as to which agency is supposed to be doing what and with whom, and about who is the actual client.

However to ensure that children are supported in reaching the five key outcomes from *Every Child Matters* (2005); be healthy, stay safe, enjoy and achieve, make a positive contribution and achieve economic wellbeing, it is not acceptable for substance misuse practitioners to say that the child is not their client and that they have a duty of care to the adult only, or for the child-care practitioners to say they do not have sufficient knowledge to be able to understand the effects of substances on the parent's behaviour.

Key to addressing these issues is the development of appropriate multi-agency training which leads to a greater understanding of each others' roles, the development of basic skills in each others' fields and joint policies being developed to cross the barrier of inter-agency working.

Training example

Objective: To encourage discussion of what constitutes risk for each agency/individual and why?

    Split the participants into groups of four.

1. Ask the participants to rank the following scenarios from 1–9, with 1 equalling the most risky in terms of child protection and 9 equalling least risky.

2. Ask the participants to look at the four scenarios they consider to be the most risk invoking and think of some strengths they may be able to develop in the family to reduce the current risk.

A. Dad drives his three children to school in the morning after drinking ten pints of Carlsberg Special Brew the night before.

B. Dad comes home drunk from a night out with colleagues, he is physically aggressive towards his partner, and their children are in the house. He doesn't remember coming home.

C. Mum is lying intoxicated on the sofa whilst her two-year-old daughter is playing on the floor.

D. A seven-year-old girl and her nine-year-old brother are locked out of the house when they come home from school as mum has gone to score. She's left a note saying she won't be long.

E. Eleven-year-old girl sent to buy cannabis from their local dealer for her mother.

F. Mum and dad inject three £10 bags of heroin each a day. They have three children in the house – 12 months old, two years old and four years old.

G. Mum has been substance free for six months, it's her birthday and she feels she deserves a treat. She takes five-year-old Jack to buy a £10 bag of heroin, takes it home and injects it.

H. Mum is pregnant and is being prescribed 35mls of methadone but is still using occasional heroin as well.

I. Mum has decided to do a home self-detox. She uses £50 heroin a day. Four-year-old Bradley lives with her.

IMPROVING PRACTICE AND OUTCOMES FOR CHILDREN WITH SUBSTANCE MISUSING PARENTS AND CARERS: EVIDENCE-BASED PRACTICE

When asked, parents reply the way to improve children and families outcomes is for all services to focus on improving the following: 'Communicating with families; attitudes to families; listening to families; access to services; longer term service provision; and improved coordination of services' (Cleaver *et al.* 2007).

To enable this to happen effectively there needs to be an integrated strategic response, with all agencies recognising that under The Children Act 2004, Section 11 they have a statutory duty to safeguard and promote the welfare of children, 'the effective safeguarding of children and provision of support for families requires all professionals and agencies to work together on both the strategic and operational levels' (SCODA 1997, p.5).

Focusing on safeguarding children and promoting their welfare when their parents are misusing substances, we must consider the following as being essential parts of improving practice.

Listening to children and their parents

Listening to what children and parents tell us about what they need, what would help, and the way services could be organised is an important part of working together. It is also important that information is provided for parents which explains the services available and the support they offer the family. Services should address family needs rather than just those of the drug or alcohol user. Appreciating the totality of their lives rather than simply dealing with the perceived 'problem' will help achieve a number of aims. It will identify strengths as well as shortcomings.

Voices of children!

Children report the impact substance misuse has on the functioning of their home and family life.

Family conflict

They describe high levels of tension, threats and aggressive conflict between parents. They say they are often confused by the sheer variety of moods that parents can go through, from affection and warmth to withdrawn, moody and aggressive behaviour. It is difficult for the children to predict their parents' behaviour and therefore they feel responsible for protecting and taking care of their younger siblings.

Fear and anxiety

Through the media and lessons at school children come to understand, often from a relatively young age, that the use of substances can be harmful, and does not happen in everyone's house. Those living with a substance misusing parent are often fearful of parental death, abandonment and the constant uncertainty over what might happen next. Children report having seen their parents unconscious, injured and bleeding, vomiting and incontinent and find this a great source of anxiety. Children also say that having people they do not know coming in and out of their home promotes a feeling of powerlessness in the whole situation.

Role reversal

Where parents are pre-occupied with their own activities and problems it often falls to their children to take on responsibility for meeting their own needs as well as those of the other children and sometimes even the parent by encouraging them to eat, to attend appointments, providing them with emotional support, etc. Becoming responsible for parents and siblings can mean that the child's developmental and social needs are ignored: a 'lost childhood'.

Keeping the family's secret

Children say they understand from an early age, often with the help of parents that what goes on in the home must not be spoken about outside of it. This is reinforced by the child's loyalty to their parents as well as their own shame once they come to an understanding that their family life is not 'normal'. The stigma associated with substance misuse serves to further isolate children from others, condemning them to a world of secrecy and shame. (Barnard and Barlow 2003)

The Scottish Executive (2006) stresses the importance of including the child's perspective: 'What does the child think? What do other family members think? How do you know?' (Scottish Executive 2006, p.10).

Listening to the child

Objective: To encourage participants to think how the substance misusing world may appear to the child in the family.

Split into groups of four participants. Give each participant a copy of Jane's story.

1. Ask them to think about what are the safeguarding issues in this situation and what they as agencies could do to support this family?

My name is Jane.

When the kids' dad went I was just left with debts and coping with both kids on my own the last four years. If it weren't for some friends in the pub I would have gone under. The worst thing is being on my own all the time with Davey and Tom. One or two drinks in the evening help me feel better in myself, not so frightened. And then I can relax. Sometimes I pop out for a quick drink, only when the kids are asleep though. It's not like I can't do without a drink, but I wouldn't want to. It's my only pleasure really, and anyway I play a lot more with the kids when I'm a bit merry, so they love it. I shout a lot when I'm tired, but underneath I'm a big softy. Davey and Tom know that. They know I love them. I'm not saying I'm the best mum in the world but they're OK. I'm a lot more loving than my mum was! Davey seems to manage fine on his own anyway; he's my little helper. You'd never believe he was only six, always fussing round Tom, like a little daddy! He has a really quizzical look on his face sometimes, makes me laugh he does.

Invite feedback from each group.

Split participants into pairs and give them Davey's story to read.

My name is Davey and I am six. It was my birthday a few weeks ago but I didn't have a party. I live with my mum and Tom my little brother. He's three and half. My mum is tired a lot so I look after Tom. I get him a drink and some toys when my mum is in bed. I get my mum a drink too; it's a special drink she says, that makes her feel better. But I think it makes her act funny. When she goes out to get some of her drink she doesn't come back for a long time. Once she was out so long it was dark when she got back. Tom had been crying a lot. I told him I loved him so he would stop.

Sometimes my mum is good fun, she laughs a lot and plays with us and lets us play outside in our pyjamas. But sometimes she forgets to get us anything for our tea so we have cornflakes. When she's not fun she gets cross with us a lot, and we have to be quiet.

Sometimes mum's friends come round for a party. They are a bit scary and some of them sleep at our house. After a party my mum can't get up in the morning so I don't go to school. My best friend at school is Dan. I wonder if his mum is like mine.

2. How do you think Davey feels?

How does it make you feel as the worker?

(Alcohol Concern 2007)

In addition to listening to the child it is also important to provide parents with the necessary tools to help them improve their parenting. These may include:

- developing literature that explains some of the ways that parental substance misuse can impact on parenting and provides ways to reduce this impact. If parents recognise the impact their substance misuse has on their children they are more likely to develop safeguarding strategies

- providing 'safer storage boxes' for parents, where they can keep their medication, out of reach and sight of their child. This may also act as a prompt for workers to address the serious issue of the child ingesting illicit drugs, prescribed medication or alcohol.

Questions to ask the parent to consider

- What do you think your child understands about your drug/alcohol use?
- How do you think your drug/alcohol use affects your child?
- How do you explain your use to your child?
- Are there any things you would like to change to reduce the effect on your child?
- Is there any support you feel you and your child need?
- Is there anyone you can turn to for help?

A multi-agency response/practice guidance/assessment

Various models have been developed to help professionals to undertake assessments where there are concerns about parental substance use (Kroll and Taylor 2003; Murphy and Harbin 2003; NTA 2005; SCODA 1997). These offer suggestions about the information that may be particularly relevant in these circumstances. For example, Kroll and Taylor (2003) state that the assessment should look at the quality and 'feel' of the home environment; the patterns and effects of the substance misuse; whether it is the central preoccupation of the parent and what this means for the child.

Murphy and Harbin (2003) point out that the picture will not be static: the needs of children will change over time, as will parents' capacity to look after them. Forrester (2004) suggests four key principles for undertaking assessments:

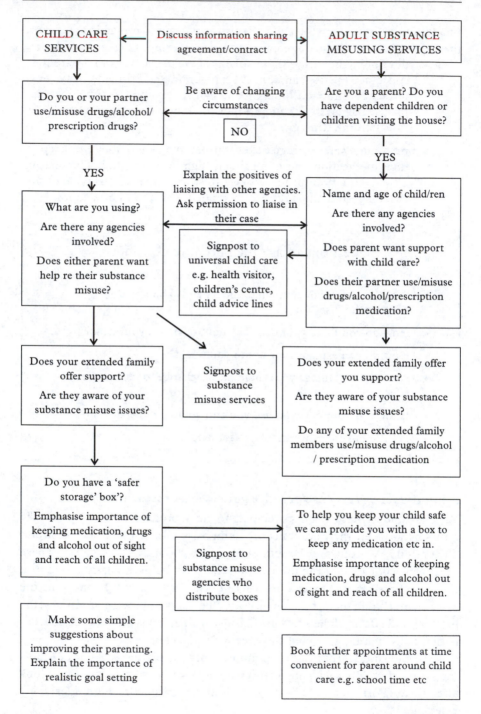

Figure 7.1 Addressing the issue of parental substance misuse – initial contact

1.   Focus on the child's life.

2.   Recognise that the parent's management of their own life is a good indicator of their ability to look after the child.

3.   The best predictor of future behaviour is past behaviour.

4.   Information from a variety of sources is better than information from one.

Ensuring early identification of children with unmet need requires all parents with substance misuse problems to be identified. Routine questioning regarding whether a parent misuses drugs and or alcohol, or has ever misused them, needs to be built into all universal assessments. All substance misuse agencies must also ask all their clients whether they have children and whether those children live with them.

Following the initial contact with the substance-misusing parent it is important that child-care services do not concentrate solely on the parent's substance misuse. Their focus needs to remain on how to improve the parenting skills; however, they should ask the parent regularly regarding any changes in the substance misuse, happening or planned, as this is likely to impact on parenting and therefore the child. Regular liaison with the substance misuse services will help increase understanding regarding how certain aspects of the parent's substance misuse may impact on child care.

Integrated practice requires a common understanding across all services of what constitutes strengths and what constitutes difficulties in the family.

Difficulties/risk factors

The following is not a checklist but examples of what might be considered as risk factors.

- Both parents being poly drug/alcohol misusers, and misusing substances together at the same time

- Parents using illicit drugs or drinking alcohol in addition to their prescribed medication

- Drug/alcohol misuse taking place in the home

- Exposure to and awareness of criminal activity

- Presence of the child (though not necessarily in the same room) when substances are being used

- Witnessing someone inject drugs and the dangers associated with the drug using paraphernalia

- Material deprivation and neglect
- The absence of a stable adult figure (such as a non-using parent or another family member)
- The absence of extended family support
- Inconsistent, ambivalent or neglectful parenting
- High levels of family disharmony, including general disruption to family life, routines and the presence of domestic abuse
- The family not engaging with services, not attending for appointments
- Mental health issues
- Parental or child illness
- School holidays.

There is a cumulative effect of these risk factors, i.e. the more that are present, the higher the risk of negative outcomes.

This enables agencies to work together to build on the strengths and where possible reduce the difficulties.

However, all the major risk factors are amenable to intervention, even if the parental alcohol/drug misuse is not at this time. This means that practitioners engaged with families where parents have drug and/or alcohol misuse problems can focus on: family violence; parental conflict; parental separation and loss; inconsistent and ambivalent parenting; daily supervised consumption of prescribed medication and safer storage; safer drug and alcohol use; parents using separately and not to the point of intoxication; planning substance misuse around reducing and stopping illicit drug use/alcohol misuse; the child's routine; making safe child care arrangements.

Strengths/protective factors

- Parents recognising the possible effect of their substance misuse on their family life and wanting to make changes
- Parents engaged with services and complying with treatment
- Honesty from both the parent and practitioner and an understanding that risks that develop will be discussed

- Extended family to be fully aware of the substance misuse problem and to offer support to the children

- For the child to develop a close positive bond with at least one adult in a caring role (including parents, siblings and grandparents) who can provide them with consistent attention and support and ensure that family activities are maintained

- The family to nurture a good support network outside of the nuclear family

- The family to maintain contact with the universal services that can provide support

- For the child to be engaged in a wide range of activities, within which they can recognise that they are separate from their parent's problems and therefore develop their own sense of self and self-esteem.

At the same time as recognising the potential risk factors, it is important to identify what protective factors are present in the home environment and how to build on these strengths.

The framework for the assessment of children in need and their families (Department of Health 2000) was developed to offer a holistic, multi-agency approach in considering the 'full range of children's and family's strengths as well as needs and difficulties, including the wider environment and circumstances in which they live' (Cleaver and Walker 2004, p.82).

Harbin and Murphy (2000) proposed the idea of adding a fourth domain to the Assessment Framework, one that focuses on the use of substances by the parent (taking into account such factors as what substance, how much is taken, how is it taken, where and with whom, what is the pattern of use and what are the implications for lifestyle). This additional domain therefore integrates in one process the work of both substance misuse and child and social care practitioners, which aids information sharing processes.

Hart and Powell (2006) developed this framework even further by adding substance misuse into each of the existing domains of the Framework. Both these methods of assessment help agencies keep the focus on the child and at the same time, work collaboratively to support the family. With specific groups where there is the potential for the children to be at risk of significant harm, for example pregnant women disclosing that they are misusing substances, another way to improve communication between agencies is to set up a multi-agency group which assesses and screens all cases.

Multi-Agency Pregnancy Liaison and Assessment Group (MAPLAG)

The following pathway is to ensure effective multi-agency collaboration to safeguard the babies whose mothers disclose substance misuse during pregnancy.

- The community midwife must routinely ask all pregnant women about their use of prescribed and non-prescribed drugs (both legal and illicit) and alcohol.

- All women that disclose any drug or problematic alcohol use during their current pregnancy are discussed in a multi-agency meeting.

- The meeting comprises of named representatives from the agencies which the woman is likely to have contact with during her pregnancy, e.g. specialist midwife in drug and alcohol use, specialist social worker in drug and alcohol use, specialist GP in drug and alcohol use, liaison health visitor in drug and alcohol use and senior practitioner from social care work department.

- The woman's situation will be discussed for the first time at approximately 24 weeks' gestation.

- The following topics are covered: details of the referral to the specialist midwife in drug and alcohol use; the woman's social, medical, psychological and forensic history; the health and care of the pregnant woman and unborn baby; progress in managing any drug and/or alcohol misuse and details of the treatment plan; attendance at appointments and co-operation, or non-compliance, with support services; the care of any existing children and any relevant information about previous pregnancies; whether any family/friends support network is available; whether the woman and/or partner, or any of their children have ever been known to Children's Social Care and why; information about the pregnant woman's partner, including any available details of the partner's treatment plan, if they are a drug and/or alcohol misuser; preparation for the baby's birth and the woman and her partner's perception of the situation, and, if necessary, commitment to change.

- Details of all workers involved with the family who provide up-to-date information to the group need to be noted on the minutes.

- A risk assessment, birth plan and action plan is written based on the above information to provide co-ordinated support for the woman, stating who will action certain points.

- The minutes are circulated to all members of the group, the woman's GP, prescriber, significant workers and any social workers involved.

- The group identifies which professional will make the contents of the minutes known to the woman and her partner, and will bring back any update from them to the meeting.

- The risk assessment indicates the following:

  ○ Low risk (Tier 1) – monitoring through normal universal pathways

  ○ Medium risk (Tier 2) – family support approach: multi-agency meeting with mother/partner to look at CAF. Lead professionals identified by MAPLAG

  ○ High risk (Tier 3) – child protection issues identified – social work assessment

- Following the completion of any assessment undertaken, a multi-agency meeting is convened to ensure all parties, including the parents, are clear of the expectations and outcome (e.g. child protection conference, children in need meeting, multi-agency meeting). This must happen prior to the birth of the baby. A birth plan is then completed.

By working together, attending multi-agency training events and using joint assessment tools, practitioners will gain the necessary skills and knowledge to be competent and confident in dealing with the multitude of issues that may arise when addressing the needs of children living with parents who misuse substances.

CONCLUSION – GOOD PRACTICE RECOMMENDATIONS

To reiterate, the task to improve outcomes for children and their families' outcomes requires the following equally important ingredients:

1. A strategic approach to be adopted by the government, local Drug and Alcohol Action Teams and commissioners to support the work that frontline workers are engaged in and help develop family focused services.

2. Recognition that 'safeguarding is everybody's business'.

3. A multi-agency approach to parental substance misuse and safeguarding:

   - universal screening

- shared policies and vision for outcomes

- understanding of each others roles

- joined up assessments

- peer group supervision – offering opportunities for dialogue, reflection and review.

4. Confident and competent practitioners who ask the questions that have to be asked in a way that engages parents.

- substance misuse workers who understand children's needs

- child-care workers who understand substance misuse

- ongoing discussion and consultation between services with practitioners recognising their part in the jigsaw.

5. Insightful parents and family members.

REFERENCES

ACMD (Advisory Council on the Misuse of Drugs) (2003) *Hidden Harm: Responding to the Needs of Children of Problem Drug Users; The Report of an Inquiry by the Advisory Council on the Misuse of Drugs*. London: Home Office.

ACMD (Advisory Council on the Misuse of Drugs) (2007) *Hiden Harm: Three Years On*. London: Home Office.

Alcohol Concern (2007) 'Supporting Children Affected by Parental Alcohol Missuse: A Toolkit.' Available at http://www.alcoholandfamilies.org.uk/toolkits.htm, accessed 19 November 2008.

Barnard, M. (2007) *Drug Addiction and Families*. London: Jessica Kingsley Publishers.

Barnard, M. and Barlow, J. (2003) 'Discovering parental drug dependence: silence and disclosure.' *Children and Society 17*, 45–56.

Bates, T., Buchanan, J., Corby, B. and Young, L. (1999) *Drug Use, Parenting and Child Protection; Towards an Effective Interagency Response*. Liverpool: University of Central Lancashire.

Cleaver, H., Nicholson, D., Tarr, S. and Cleaver, D. (2007) *Domestic Violence and Parental Substance Misuse – Family Experiences and Effective Practice*. London: Jessica Kingsley Publishers.

Cleaver, H., Unell, I. and Aldgate, J. (1999) *Children's Needs – Parenting Capacity; The Impact of Parental Mental Illness, Problem Alcohol and Drug Use, and Domestic Violence on Children's Development*. London: Stationery Office.

Cleaver, H. and Walker, S. (2004) 'From policy to practice: the implementation of a new framework for social work assessments of children and families.' *Child and Family Social Work 9*, 81–90.

Department for Education and Skills (2003) *Every Child Matters*. Available at www.everychildmatters.gov.uk, accessed 9 December 2008.

Department for Education and Skills (2005) *Government Response to Hidden Harm*. London: Department for Education and Skills.

Department of Health, Home Office and Department for Education and Employment (1999) *Working Together to Safeguard Children: A Guide to Inter-Agency Working to Safeguard and Promote the Welfare of Children*. London: Stationery Office.

Department of Health, Department for Education and Employment, and Home Office (2000) *Framework for the Assessment of Children in Need and Their Families*. London: Stationery Office.

Drugs Strategy Directorate (1998) *Tackling Drugs to Build a Better Britain*. Available at http://drug.homeoffice.gov.uk/drug-strategy/overview/, accessed 19 November 2008.

Forrester, D. (2000) 'Parental substance misuse and child protection in a British sample: A survey of children on the child protection register in an inner London district office.'*Child Abuse Review 9*, 235–246.

Forrester, D. (2004) 'Social Work Assessments with Parents who Misuse Drugs or Alcohol.' In R. Phillips (ed.) *Children Exposed to Parental Substance Misuse: Implications for Family Placement*. London: BAAF.

Harbin, F. and Murphy. M. (eds) (2000) *Substance Misuse and Childcare: How to Understand, Assist and Intervene when Drugs Affect Parenting*. Lyme Regis: Russell House Publishing.

Harbin, F. and Murphy, M. (eds) (2006) *Secret Lives: Growing with Substance: Working with Children and Young People Affected by Familial Substance Misuse*. Lyme Regis: Russell House Publishing.

Hart, D. and Powell, J (2006) *Adult Drug Problems, Children's Needs – Assessing the Impact of Parental Drug Use*. London: National Children's Bureau.

Harwin, J. and Forrester, D. (2002) *Parental Substance Misuse and Child Welfare: A Study of Social Work with Families in which Parents Misuse Drugs and Alcohol*. Interim Report. London: Nuffield Foundation.

HM Government (2006) Working Together to Safeguarding Children: A Guide to Inter-agency Working to Safeguard and Promote the Welfare of Children. Norwich: Stationery Office.

Home Office (2008) *Drugs: Protecting Families and Communities*. London: Home Office.

Home Office, HM Customs and Excise, Office of the Deputy Prime Minister, DFES, DoH, DWP and Foreign and Commomwealth Office (2002) *Updated Drug Strategy*. London: Stationery Office.

Kearney, J., Harbin, F., Murphy, M., Wheeler, E. and Whittle, J. (2005) *The Highs and Lows of Family Life: Familial Substance Misuse from a Child's Perspective*. Bolton: Bolton ACPC Research Report.

Klee, H., Jackson, M. and Lewis, S. (2002) *Drug Misuse and Motherhood*. London: Routledge.

Kroll, B. (2004) 'Living with an elephant: Growing up with parental substance misuse.' *Child and Family Social Work 9*, 129–140.

Kroll, B. and Taylor, A. (2000) 'Invisible Children? Parental Substance Abuse and Child Protection: Dilemmas for Practice.' *Probation Journal 47*, 2, 91–100.

Kroll, B. and Taylor, A. (2003) *Parental Substance Misuse and Child Welfare*. London: Jessica Kingsley Publishers.

Murphy M. and Harbin, F. (2003) 'The Assessment of Parental Substance Misuse and its Impact on Childcare.' In M. Calder and S. Hackett (eds) *Assessment in Child Care: Using and Developing Framework for Practice*. Lyme Regis: Russell House Publishing.

NTA (National Treatment Agency for Substance Misuse) (2005) *Working with Drug Using Parent: Training Manual. Competency Based Training Module SD19*. Available at www.nta.nhs.uk/areas/workforce/docs/SD19_Drug_using_parents.doc, accessed on 19 November 2008.

SCODA (Standing Conference on Drug Abuse) (1997) *Drug Using Parents: Policy Guidelines for Interagency Working*. London: Local Government Association Publications.

Scottish Executive (2006) *Hidden Harm: Next Steps. Supporting Children – Working with Parents*. Edinburgh: Scottish Executive.

Tunnard, J. (2002) *Parental Drug Misuse – A Review of Impact and Intervention Studies*. Dartington: Research into Practice.

Turning Point (2006) *Bottling it Up: The Effects of Alcohol Misuse on Children, Parents and Families*. London: Turning Point.

Velleman, R. and Orford, J. (2001) *Risk and Resilience: Adults Who were the Children of Problem Drinkers*. Amsterdam: Harwood Academic Publishers.

Weir, A. and Douglas, A. (eds) (1999) *Child Protection and Adult Mental Health: Conflict of Interests?* Oxford: Butterworth Heinemann.

STATUTE

Children Act (2004) London: Stationery Office.

CHAPTER 8

DOMESTIC ABUSE AND SAFEGUARDING CHILDREN

SUE PECKOVER

INTRODUCTION

Safeguarding children affected by domestic abuse is a key responsibility for all those whose work brings them into contact with children and their families. This chapter discusses how domestic abuse impacts upon children, the policy and legislative frameworks around domestic abuse, and some essential elements for developing safeguarding practice in this area.

THE EXTENT AND NATURE OF DOMESTIC ABUSE

Before examining the issues involved in safeguarding children from domestic abuse, it is important to establish the extent and nature of the problem. One of the difficulties lies with the terminology. Although both the terms 'domestic abuse' and 'domestic violence' are widely used, neither adequately captures the full range of experiences and contexts that may be involved. The government use the following definition: 'Any incident of threatening behaviour, violence or abuse (psychological, physical, sexual, financial or emotional) between adults who are or have been, intimate partners or family members, regardless of gender or sexuality' (Home Office 2005, p.7). This highlights the different types of abuses that may be involved, it acknowledges it can occur within same sex relationships, and can involve female as well as male perpetrators. However as feminists have pointed out, the overwhelming majority of domestic violence is perpetrated by men against women, making it a particularly gendered issue. They argue it occurs as a result of unequal power and control within a relationship, and is intentional behaviour that usually escalates in frequency and severity (Dobash and Dobash 1992; Hester, Kelly and Radford 1996; Kelly 1988; Mullender 1996). In the United Kingdom one in four women have experienced domestic violence at some time in their lives, and two women are killed each week by their partners or ex-partners

(Mirlees-Black 1999; Walby and Allen 2004). Whilst all women are vulnerable to domestic violence, there is a higher incidence amongst younger women and those with children (Radford and Hester 2006), making it a key safeguarding issue.

CHILDREN AND DOMESTIC ABUSE

There are difficulties in establishing with accuracy the numbers of children and young people who are affected by domestic abuse. A recent report has suggested that one million children in the United Kingdom are affected (UNICEF 2006). It is now well established that the majority of children living in households where domestic abuse is occurring will witness or overhear it. Parents frequently underestimate the extent this happens, often considering they have managed to keep the domestic abuse hidden from their children. Hughes (1992) has suggested that 90 per cent of children are in the same or next room to a domestic violence incident, whilst research undertaken with children has found they are generally aware of domestic violence much earlier than their parents realise (Gorin 2004). Estimates suggest at least 750,000 children witness domestic violence each year (Department of Health 2002).

Children and young people living with domestic violence can also experience direct abuse themselves. Research studies have found between 30 to 66 per cent of children who had been physically abused were also living with domestic violence (Edelson 1999). However a large prevalence study of 2,869 adults undertaken in the United Kingdom found eight out of ten young people who had experienced serious physical abuse also reported living with domestic violence (Cawson et al. 2000). Such abuse is frequently deliberate and is part of the overall pattern of power and control that the perpetrator has over family members. In addition many children and young people become 'caught in the crossfire' of domestic violence, receiving injuries and abuse directed at their mother/carer. For younger children this is usually because they are physically close to their mothers during a violent incident, whilst older children frequently attempt to intervene to stop the violence. There are very real dangers for children who are physically abused by the perpetrator, particularly as domestic violence has featured in a high number of child death inquiries (O'Hara 1994). Children living with domestic abuse can also be sexually abused by the perpetrator.

Whilst many mothers living with domestic abuse are able to provide good levels of care for their children, it does make the task of parenting more challenging (Radford and Hester 2006). Often women's emotional and physical health is impaired as a result of the domestic violence, leading to exhaustion and loss of self-confidence and this can add to the difficulties of caring for children, in some cases leading to 'neglect' (Abrahams 1994; Radford and

Hester 2006). Children may respond to the domestic abuse in ways that aggravate the situation, through, for example, negative emotional and behavioural responses. Whilst there has been less emphasis upon domestically violent men as fathers/carers (Featherstone and Peckover 2007; Harne 2004) research suggests they may exert a controlling influence upon parenting style, often undermining the mother–child relationship (Hooper and Humphreys 1997).

Exerting control over household finances can be a feature of domestic abuse, and children and young people living in such circumstances often experience additional hardships and isolations. This may occur because the perpetrator places restrictions upon their mother about household spending and activities, restricting 'treats' and access to social worlds. Leaving the abusive relationship frequently leads to poorer socio-economic circumstances, and many women and children find themselves living in poverty and poor housing. There may also be severe disruptions to children's lives impacting, for example, upon their contact with friends, social networks, school and other services such as health care. At the same time leaving domestic violence can be dangerous for both women and children. Post-separation violence is common and can be extremely serious and child contact can provide opportunities for the perpetrator to continue to abuse both women and children (Humphreys and Harrison 2003; Humphreys and Thiara 2003; Radford, Sayer and AMICA 1999).

Children may also be affected by domestic abuse even before they are born. Many women experience domestic abuse during pregnancy; this is a time when domestic violence often commences or increases in frequency, and is associated with an increased risk of miscarriage, stillbirth, pre-term and low birth weight babies (Mezey and Bewley 1997). This can be a direct result of the physical violence but contextual factors arising as a result of being abused such as poorer maternal health, substance use and non-engagement with maternity services, are also important.

A wide range of physical, emotional, social and behavioural problems are associated with experiencing domestic abuse as a child. These include physical injuries, weight loss, developmental delays, headaches, stomach aches and diarrhoea. Emotional and behavioural impacts include, for example, anxiety, panic attacks, fear, anger, insecurity, depression, running away, sleep disturbances, nightmares, bed-wetting, eating difficulties and increased risks of self-harm, drug and alcohol misuse. The social impacts include difficulties at school, poor or highly developed social skills, social isolation and difficulties with trusting others (see for example Hester *et al.* 2006; Mullender and Morley 1994; Royal College of Psychiatrists 2004).

Although the overall picture is disturbing, individual children react very differently to experiencing or witnessing domestic abuse. Some children are more resilient than others (Gewirtz and Edelson 2007; Mullender *et al.* 2002). Factors influencing resilience include the child's developmental age, their particular experience of abuse, what they know of their mother's abuse, their understanding about what is happening, what support they receive, and their relationships with adults outside the family (Mullender *et al.* 2002). The extent to which their mother is able to maintain her parenting abilities is also positively associated with children's resilience. There is also evidence to suggest the provision of a safe and secure environment, free from post-separation violence, enables many children to recover their competence and behavioural functioning (Mullender *et al.* 2002).

THE POLICY AND LEGISLATIVE CONTEXT

Recent years have seen considerable developments in policy and legislation designed to address domestic violence. Of particular relevance for safeguarding children is the Working Together guidance which acknowledges the impact of domestic violence upon children and states:

> Where there is evidence of domestic violence, the implications for any children in the household should be considered, including the possibility that the children may themselves be subject to violence, or may be harmed by witnessing or overhearing the violence.

(Extract from *Working Together*
Department for Education and Skills 2006a, 11.45)

The definition of 'significant harm' has now been extended to include 'witnessing or hearing the ill-treatment of another' (introduced in the Adoption and Children Act 2002 s120). This provides legal recognition of the serious impact living with domestic abuse can pose for children and young people. There have been a number of other legislative developments designed to improve the safety of women and children, and to exclude men. These include the Domestic Violence, Crime and Victims' Act (2004) implemented in 2005, which provides non-molestation, occupation and restraining orders, including powers of arrest for breach of non-molestation orders and an associated widening of the groups of people to whom it is applicable, including co-habiting and same sex couples. As an amendment to the Children Act 1989, there are also additional powers for the local authority to exclude a person who poses a risk to a child. The Protection from Harassment Act (1997) has established the criminal offences of criminal harassment (s.2) and fear of violence (s.4) and provides restraining orders and injunctions for prevention of harassment.

An overall strengthening of police and criminal justice responses to domestic violence, such as using powers of arrest, court orders and prosecution of offenders, aim to provide better protection to victims. Other developments include the establishment of Specialist Domestic Violence Courts which aim to avoid delays and ensure higher conviction rates for domestic violence cases, the provision of an advocacy service to ensure women are fully supported during this process, and multi-agency risk assessment conferences (MARACS) focusing upon cases involving high risk domestic violence offenders (Cook *et al.* 2004; Robinson 2004). The police are also now required to make referrals or notifications to children's social care services in relation to domestic violence incidents where there are children in the household (Department for Education and Skills 2006a). This latter has been a significant development, not only because it has revealed high numbers of children living with domestic violence, but also because it has illustrated some of the complexities in ensuring that children and young people are appropriately safeguarded.

The Every Child Matters agenda provides an important framework for safeguarding children and young people affected by domestic abuse. All of the five outcomes: be healthy, stay safe, enjoy and achieve, make a positive contribution, and achieve economic wellbeing, are of relevance to children and young people affected by domestic abuse (Department for Education and Skills 2003). Importantly within the Outcomes Framework one of the standards by which children's services will be inspected directly addresses this issue, requiring that 'children affected by domestic violence are identified, supported and protected' (Department for Education and Skills 2005, 2.2.5). The National Service Framework for Children, Young People and Maternity Services (Department of Health 2004a, 2004b), which provides service standards for health professionals and agencies specifically addresses domestic violence.

The last few years have also seen a wide range of policy and practice guidance produced to help practitioners fulfil their roles and responsibilities in relation to their work with children and families affected by domestic abuse. This includes for example guidance for health care professionals (Department of Health 2005), court welfare workers (CAFCASS 2007), and police and criminal justice agencies (Association of Chief Police Officers 2004; Crown Prosecution Service 2005).

SAFEGUARDING PRACTICE

Safeguarding children affected by domestic abuse is a key responsibility for those whose work brings them into contact with women and children. Ensuring individual children and young people receive the most appropriate, effective and timely response, however, remains a complex task. Some children affected by domestic abuse will be in need of protection and will

---

Extract from the *National Service Framework for Children, Young People and Maternity Services*

All staff working with women and children are alert to the relationship between domestic violence and the abuse and neglect of children, and that witnessing domestic violence also constitutes harm to a child or young person. (*Children Act 1989*)

All staff are aware of and supported by a local multi-agency agreement on the thresholds for referral to social services in cases where there is domestic violence.

All practitioners are trained and equipped to include routine questions about domestic violence in all assessments, including ante-natal care. (*See Standard 11*)

(Department of Health 2004a, p.166)

---

require immediate and sometimes long-term statutory child-care involvement. Others will require a package of support as 'children in need'. Other children and young people affected by domestic abuse may have 'additional needs' that can be met by universal or targeted service providers such as Sure Start or the voluntary sector (see Department for Education and Skills 2007). Determining the most appropriate practice response towards children and young people affected by domestic abuse is further complicated by the increased numbers being recognised and reported to agencies.

The rest of the chapter describes some important elements for practitioners concerned with safeguarding children and young people affected by domestic abuse. These key points are illustrated within the two case studies below, describing different domestic violence scenarios.

CASE STUDY 8.1: MANDY

Mandy is a 33-year-old mother who has four children. Sarah is now six months old and reported to cry quite a lot. She has been slow to gain weight. Aimee is four years old and has just started at school. She has had difficulty settling and frequently wets herself. Maria is ten years old, and is reported to be withdrawn at school and has a poor attendance record. Steven is 13 years old and attends local secondary school. He enjoys football. Earlier this year he ran away but returned after a few hours.

Mandy and her partner Kevin have been together for five years. He is the father of Aimee and Sarah. Maria and Steven see their own father Michael in the school holidays only as he lives in a different area of the country.

Mandy and Kevin have a turbulent relationship. They argue quite a lot, and Kevin can be very aggressive. He has hit Mandy on several occasions and the police have been called to the house a number of times. Mandy is worried about what will happen in the future as she is becoming very scared of him. Her mood is low, and she is not coping very well with caring for the children. She has previously been to stay in a women's refuge on two occasions taking all four children with her but returned after a few days. Kevin has threatened to kill her if she leaves again.

On Saturday night the police were called to the house following a severe domestic violence incident. Kevin had attempted to strangle Mandy. She was holding Sarah in her arms at the time. Steven attempted to intervene and received a blow to his head from Kevin as a result.

Key issues:
The first priority is to ensure the immediate *safety* of the children and Mandy. The police arrested Kevin at the scene. He was later charged with assault and bailed to a different address; an Occupation Order was granted excluding him from living at the family home. These measures ensured he was *held responsible* for the domestic violence.

Social services were immediately involved and Section 47 Inquiries commenced. A medical examination was undertaken to assess the injuries sustained by Steven and Mandy. The *assessment process* involved clearly establishing what had been happening, and how the children were affected. Network discussions with other agencies including school and health visiting services revealed a number of worrying concerns about their overall welfare. A child protection conference was held; all four children were considered to be at risk of *significant harm* and in need of child protection plans.

Work was undertaken within school and by the social worker to *talk directly* with the older three *children* to ensure their views and fears were heard during this process. The children's needs were assessed separately and support and recovery work was provided. This involved making referrals to specialist service such as CAMHS, as well as providing opportunities in school (through individual sessions and as part of an ongoing schools Domestic Violence Programme) and the home situation for the children to address their experiences. The website (www.thehideout.org) proved very useful and was popular with Steven and Maria.

Mandy was offered support from a women's voluntary sector domestic violence service who advised her about legal measures and benefits. The housing department were able to supply her with security alarms. Throughout this process she was supported to take measures to *increase her safety*, and this enabled her to become more confident overall and in relation to parenting.

CASE STUDY 8.2: PHILIPA

Philipa is 23 years old and expecting her second baby. She is married to Jonathan who works as a computer programmer. The couple have a two-year-old son called Oliver. Philipa and Jonathan have known each other for four years and although they started off with a very a happy relationship, it has become more strained since Oliver was born. Jonathan is very jealous of the time Philipa spends with Oliver. He is verbally abusive towards her, saying she is 'fat' and 'useless', and not a good mother. Jonathan is very stressed at work and likes to relax at home with a drink, but recently he has become quite aggressive and has threatened to hit Philipa. She has never spoken to anyone about her situation as she is embarrassed and worried about what will happen if she tells someone.

Key issues
Philipa is pregnant and visits her GP surgery for ante-natal care. Here she usually sees the same midwife who she feels confident talking to. It is a great surprise when the midwife asks Philipa if she has ever experienced domestic violence. Philipa denies this and quickly changes the subject. Afterwards she thinks it would be a good idea to talk to someone about what is happening at home and decides to disclose to the midwife at the next ante-natal appointment.

Philipa is pleased that she has the opportunity to talk about what is happening, and surprised when she realises how many other women are also experiencing domestic abuse. The midwife informs Philipa about local and national support services that can help her. There are leaflets, phone numbers and details of a website and Philipa is able to put these safely in her handbag where

Jonathan will not find them. The midwife also discusses with Philipa about how Jonathan's behaviour may impact upon Oliver and the risks to her unborn baby.

Philipa makes contact with a local women's domestic abuse support service and meets a women's outreach adviser who helps her think about ways to increase her safety and explores her options in terms of staying with Jonathan, and/or leaving the relationship.

Philipa agrees for her midwife to share the information she has disclosed with her health visitor and GP. This has made it much easier when she sees her GP and health visitor as she feels they better understand why she has been feeling so low. The health visitor is particularly supportive and offers her extra visits to enable her to talk through her options and plans for living with and/or leaving Jonathan.

When Philipa is eight months pregnant and feeling very tired all the time, Jonathan finally carries out the threat of violence and during an argument he slaps Philipa across the face. Although drunk at the time he is quite surprised by what happens next. Philipa calls the police who arrest him, and he finds he is blamed for what happened. Philipa says she wants a separation and engages a solicitor. She appears to have a lot of support from family and friends. Jonathan realises his marriage is over and he will have limited contact with Oliver and his new daughter Emily who is born a couple of weeks later.

SAFETY CONSIDERATIONS

The first priority when responding to a child affected by domestic abuse is to determine their immediate safety. Depending upon their individual circumstances this may require the immediate involvement of police and/or social care agencies. Where possible it is always preferable for the perpetrator of the domestic violence to be removed from the household; this can be achieved through police powers of arrest, and through legal measures such as exclusion of the perpetrator from the family home, restraining orders and/or court injunctions. Often the only safe option for women and children is for them to leave the household and go to a safe place such as a women's refuge. If it is considered that children/young people are at immediate risk of suffering significant harm it may be necessary to pursue immediate legal procedures to ensure their protection, for example police protection and/or a care order. Good safeguarding practice requires that it is always necessary to consider children's likelihood of suffering significant harm and if this is the case formal child protection proceedings should be followed.

Supporting the non-abusive parent (usually the mother) to increase their safety is an effective means to ensure the safety and welfare of the child (Department for Education and Skills 2006a). The term 'safety planning' refers to work undertaken with women to establish their personal plans for improving their safety and responding to risk (Radford and Hester 2006). This may include practical measures such as ensuring key documents and essentials such as medicines are available in case they need to leave quickly, having available emergency telephone numbers, and helping women think through whom they can call on for help. It can also be useful for women to take opportunities to plan with their children how they can be safe when violence occurs. Providing women with additional information about accessing help and support from for example local organisations, refuges and advice lines also contributes to improved safety (Department of Health 2005).

Other measures to improve women's safety include schemes that focus upon home security such as Sanctuary schemes and the provision of alarms, which are developing in some parts of the United Kingdom. Whilst these are designed to make women feel safer at home, their usefulness and effectiveness also requires ongoing police involvement to ensure their resources are directed at the known perpetrator. Separation from a perpetrator often represents a highly dangerous time for women and children. For many it places them at the highest risk and every step should be taken to ensure their safety and security. In these circumstances it is particularly important to maintain the highest standards of confidentiality to avoid any risk of a perpetrator finding out the relocation details of their former partner and children.

CAREFUL ASSESSMENT

One of the most important steps in ensuring children affected by domestic abuse are appropriately safeguarded is through careful assessment (Calder, Harold and Howarth 2004; Humphreys 2007; Radford and Hester 2006; Rivett and Kelly 2006). This should aim to establish the extent and nature of the domestic abuse, ascertaining details about both the perpetrator and the victim, what type of abuse/behaviour is involved, how long it has been occurring, and establish how those involved are being affected by the abuse. Such assessment aims to establish the overall picture about what is happening, rather than focusing upon a single incident. In undertaking assessment it is important to be aware that many victims may minimise their experiences, particularly mothers who fear that telling workers what is happening will lead to them losing their children (Kelly 1994).

For those using the Common Assessment Framework (Department for Education and Skills 2006b) or other tools based upon the Framework for Assessment of Children in Need (Department of Health 2000), it is important the assessment considers separately the different roles and contributions to parenting of the abusing and non-abusing parent. The generic focus upon 'parenting capacity' is a particular shortcoming of these assessment tools when used in situations where domestic violence is a feature (Radford, Blacklock and Iwi 2006; Women's Aid Federation of England 2005).

There have been a number of developments, used mainly within social care and specialist services, which aim to assess severity and risk (see for example Calder *et al.* 2004; Healey and Bell 2005; Humphreys 2007; Radford *et al.* 2006). For example, the model developed by Barnardo's in Northern Ireland (Healey and Bell 2005) aims to identify and differentiate between those children exposed to domestic violence who are at risk of significant harm, and those who should be considered as 'children in need'. Using a risk scoring system, this model focuses upon nine assessment areas: nature of abuse; risks to child posed by perpetrator; risks of lethality; perpetrator's pattern of assault and coercive behaviours; impact of abuse on woman; impact of abuse on children; impact of abuse on parenting roles; protective factors; and the outcome of woman's past help-seeking.

Perpetrator risk assessments, which are widely used by the police, aim to determine the risks posed by domestic abuse perpetrators and focus upon known risk factors for domestic homicide and risk of re-offending. A widely used perpetrator risk assessment tool, referred to as SPECCS, identifies the following key risk factors for domestic homicides: separation/violation of contact; non-contact and protective orders; pregnancy/new birth; escalation; community issues/isolation; stalking; and sexual assault (Association of Chief Police Officers 2004; Richards 2003). In some areas of the country perpetrator risk assessments are being shared with children's social care to help with their decision-making when receiving referrals, enabling them to focus attention on those children in families facing the highest risks. They also provide important information that may contribute to establishing a cumulative cause for concern where children are repeatedly exposed to domestic abuse. However, as Humphreys (2007) points out, they are preventive rather than predictive tools and cannot act as a substitute for careful assessment and judgement.

CHILD-FOCUSED PRACTICE

Children and young people affected by domestic violence require support and protection. Whilst these needs are often interlinked with those of their mothers, it is important to ensure they are considered separately. This means practitioners involved in safeguarding children affected by domestic abuse must adopt a child-centred focus to their assessment and interventions. This is particularly important given the research findings, which suggest many children affected by domestic violence are not offered help from practitioners such as police officers and social workers who are working with their mothers (Mullender *et al.* 2002). This study also found few professionals, apart from refuge workers, talked directly with children about the domestic violence. Children consistently report they want to be safe, to have somebody to talk to, and to be actively involved in decision-making, both by their mothers, and any professionals involved with the families (McGee 2000; Mullender *et al.* 2002). Children can also be involved in safety planning. This may include helping them to establish how they can hide and/or summon help when there is a domestic violence incident, although as Humphreys *et al.* (2000) explain this process should also help them understand it is not their responsibility to intervene in the domestic violence.

All practitioners should consider the opportunities they have for working directly with children. This will vary depending upon skills and role, but remains an important means to support children affected by domestic violence. It can be undertaken on an individual basis or as part of a more formal group work setting and can involve counselling, play therapy, life story work, crisis work and safety planning. Direct work with children gives them permission to talk about their experiences, to express their feelings about this and to receive reassurance that the violence is not their fault (Mullender 2004).

HOLDING PERPETRATORS RESPONSIBLE

It is particularly important that perpetrators of domestic abuse are identified and held responsible for their behaviour (Radford *et al.* 2006). This is increasingly recognised by the government and there is now a wide range of legal measures designed to ensure that perpetrators are held accountable. These include police powers of arrest, specific orders such as restraining orders and non-molestation orders (see Domestic Violence, Crime and Victims Act, above) and new criminal charges (see Protection from Harrassment Act, above). The majority of existing programmes for perpetrators of domestic violence are court mandated; many are based upon the Duluth model of 'power and control' (Pence and Paymar 1993; Shepard and Pence 1999) and provide support for women as well as challenging male perpetrators (see for example Burton, Regan and Kelly 1998b; Respect 2004; Skyner and Waters 1999). However as Featherstone and Peckover (2007) have noted, whilst male perpetrators of domestic violence are drawn into the criminal justice system as 'offenders', there is generally a paucity of engagement with them by services at an earlier level of intervention, which acknowledges them as 'domestically violent' fathers/carers (for discussion see Radford *et al.* 2006; Rakil 2006).

MULTI-AGENCY WORKING

Domestic violence is a complex issue and usually requires a multi-agency response. This may involve professionals from statutory and voluntary sector agencies, including those who work with adults as well as children; for example workers from health, social care, education, housing, women's advocacy, and criminal justice agencies (police, probation and legal services). Ensuring effective inter-professional working in the context of domestic abuse can be highly challenging not least because of the complexity of the issues being addressed, the conflicting and overlapping imperatives and the limited resources that are available to fully address what may often be a problem that may have long-term consequences for all those involved. There are also important requirements to maintain client confidentiality and agencies must ensure information sharing does not further compromise the safety of family members or workers (Douglas *et al.* 2004).

It is also important for local agencies to work together at a strategic level to ensure appropriate services are developed to support women and children affected by domestic abuse. Here domestic violence fora have a key role in bringing together representatives from local agencies to co-ordinate the development of local policy and practice across organisations, although they have developed with varying degrees of success across the country (Harwin, Hague and Malos 1999; Humphreys *et al.* 2000). Recognition of the need to develop services at all levels for children affected by domestic abuse has led to the publication of a recent document which aims to inform the commissioning process (Local Government Association 2005). Based upon the tiered model of need and intervention (Department of Health 2000) it identifies the range of services and responses that should be available on a local basis in order to support and protect children affected by domestic abuse.

TAKING A LONGER-TERM VIEW: AVOID A 'QUICK FIX'

The tiered model of need and intervention provides a useful approach for developing a broader understanding of how children affected by domestic abuse can be supported and protected. For women and children affected by domestic abuse there is always a need to address the immediate situation, particularly safety considerations. However it is important to avoid a purely incident or event based focus and address the longer-term impacts and contexts of living with domestic abuse for women and children. Indeed supporting and protecting woman and children affected by domestic abuse is a process rather than a single event (Department of Health 2005; Humphreys and Stanley 2006). For example, women often make several attempts at leaving violent partners and understanding this as a process is important. For children whose mothers have left violent relationships there is often a need for both short and long-term work to support the recovery process. For professionals responding to women and children affected by domestic abuse there is therefore a need to adopt both an immediate and longer-term perspective, ensuring that appropriate services are available that are able to provide longer-term support as required.

PREVENTION AND EARLY INTERVENTION

Preventative work is an important aspect of safeguarding children from domestic violence. One of the ways this has been undertaken has been by increasing public awareness of the problem and changing public perceptions so it is no longer condoned as a normal part of gendered relationships. This is by nature a long-term strategy and, as with many chronic social problems, the effectiveness of preventative work is often difficult to evaluate. Significant developments have been 'Zero Tolerance' and other poster campaigns run in many parts of the country, as well as heightened awareness of domestic violence within the media.

Early identification is important to ensure that women and children are offered appropriate support and protection at the earliest opportunity. An important development is the introduction of routine or selective enquiry within health care settings, particularly with women who are pregnant or with very young children (Department of Health 2005). Research suggests such initiatives can increase levels of recognition and disclosure (Bacchus, Mezey and Bewley 2002) although it is important to ensure that staff involved in such developments receive adequate training and support (Department of Health 2005). Taking such opportunities to raise the issue of domestic abuse with women, acknowledging their experiences, and providing information sources and/or suggesting referral to another agency can provide a valuable contribution to women's help seeking, and one that contributes to their child/unborn baby's safety and welfare.

There are now a number of initiatives, usually within educational settings, that aim to raise awareness and support children and young people about domestic abuse (Alexander, Macdonald and Paton 2005; Bell and Stanley 2006). Such schools-based programmes are accessible and non-stigmatising (Statham 2004) and provide important opportunities for children and young people to increase their understanding and awareness of domestic violence, and address issues such as disclosure, and seeking help (Alexander *et al.* 2005; Bell and Stanley 2006). Some programmes focus upon healthy relationship issues and these represent an important element of preventative work in relation to domestic abuse. These are particularly important given the worrying attitudes that appear to be held by some young people. For example, almost half the young men and a third of the young women who participated in a survey of 2,039 (14–21-year-olds) in UK could envisage circumstances where they thought it would be acceptable for a man to hit his female partner (Burton *et al.* 1998a).

SUMMARY

This chapter has provided an overview of some of the key debates and developments associated with safeguarding children and young people affected by domestic abuse. Drawing upon a range of research evidence it has examined both how children can be affected by domestic abuse and how they can be safeguarded.

The case studies have provided an opportunity to illustrate some of the key elements of practice in relation to different scenarios. Safeguarding children affected by domestic abuse is an important but challenging area and different situations require different responses. The chapter has discussed some of the important elements that always need to be considered when working with children affected by domestic abuse. These are safety issues, careful assessment, child-centred practice, holding perpetrators responsible, multi-agency working, and the importance of adopting a long-term view. Finally early intervention and preventive work are important elements of safeguarding children from domestic abuse.

Domestic abuse is a complex issue and requires a careful and knowledgeable response. It often means that practitioners are facing difficult and challenging situations that may be emotionally as well as professionally demanding. It is therefore important for all practitioners involved in safeguarding children and young people from domestic abuse to be appropriately trained, supported and supervised to ensure they are able to effectively and safely fulfil their roles and responsibilities.

GOOD PRACTICE POINTS

- Protecting the non-abusing parent – usually the mother – helps protect the children.

- Assessing the situation carefully to establish exactly what is happening, who is being affected, and how the domestic abuse is impacting on those involved.

- Talking with children and young people and ensuring their views and experiences are heard and considered.

- Engaging in multi-agency working.

- Holding the perpetrator responsible for the abusive behaviour.

- Adopting a long-term view; understanding that domestic abuse is a process and not a single event.

- Always consider opportunities for early intervention and preventive work.

REFERENCES

Abrahams, C. (1994) *The Hidden Victims: Children and Domestic Violence.* London: NCH Action for Children.

Alexander, H., Macdonald, E. and Paton, S. (2005) 'Raising the issue of domestic abuse in school.' *Children and Society 19*, 187–198.

Association of Chief Police Officers (2004) *Guidance on Investigating Domestic Violence 2004.* Bramshill, Hampshire: National Centre for Policing Excellence. Available at www.acpo.police.uk/asp/policies/Data/Guidance%20on%20DV.pdf, accessed 11 August 2008.

Bacchus, L., Mezey, G. and Bewley, S. (2002) 'Women's perceptions and experiences of routine enquiry for domestic violence in a maternity service.' *BJOG: An International Journal of Obstetrics and Gynaecology 109*, 1, 9–16.

Bell, J. and Stanley, N. (2006) 'Learning about domestic violence: young people's responses to a Healthy Relationships programme.' *Sex Education: Sexuality, Society and Learning 6*, 3, 237–250.

Burton, S., Kitzinger, J., Kelly, L. and Regan, L (1998a) *Young People's Attitudes Towards Violence, Sex and Relationships: A Survey and Focus Group Study*, Research Report 2. Edinburgh: Zero Tolerance Charitable Trust.

Burton, S., Regan, L. and Kelly, L. (1998b) *Supporting Women and Challenging Men: Lessons from the Domestic Violence Intervention Project.* Bristol: Policy Press.

CAFCASS (2007) *Domestic Violence Toolkit.* Available at www.cafcass.gov.uk/publications/policies.aspx, accessed 12 August 2008.

Calder, M., Harold, G. and Howarth, E. (2004) *Children Living with Domestic Violence: Towards a Framework for Assessment and Intervention.* Lyme Regis: Russell House Publishing.

Cawson, P., Wattam, C., Brooker, S. and Kelly, G. (2000) *Child Maltreatment in the United Kingdom: A Study of the Prevalence of Child Abuse and Neglect.* London: NSPCC.

Cook, D., Burton, M., Robinson, A. and Vallely, C. (2004) *Evaluation of Specialist Domestic Violence Courts/Fast Track Systems.* London: Department of Constitutional Affairs.

Crown Prosecution Service (2005) *Good Practice Guidance.* London: DV Project Team. Available at http://publications.everychildmatters.gov.uk/default.aspx?PageFunction=productdetails&ProductId=DCSF-00331-2008, accessed 9 December 2008.

Department for Children, Schools and Families (2008) *Every Child Matters Outcomes Framework.* Available at http://publications.everychildmatters.gov.uk/default.aspx?PageFunction=productdetails&PageMode=publications&ProductId=DCSF-00331-2008, accessed 9 December 2008.

Department for Education and Skills (2003) *Every Child Matters: Change for Children.* London: DfES.

Department for Education and Skills (2006a) *Working Together to Safeguard Children.* London: DfES.

Department for Education and Skills (2006b) *Common Assessment Framework for Children and Young People: Practitioners' Guide*. London: DfES.

Department for Education and Skills (2007) *Sure Start Local Programmes and Domestic Abuse*. Research Report 025. London: HMSO.

Department of Health (2000) *Framework for the Assessment of Children in Need and their Families*. London: Stationery Office.

Department of Health (2002) *Women's Mental Health: Into the Mainstream*. London: HMSO.

Department of Health (2004a) *National Service Framework for Children, Young People and Maternity Services. Core Standards*. London: Department of Health.

Department of Health (2004b) *National Service Framework for Children, Young People and Maternity Services. Standard 11: Maternity Services*. London: Department of Health.

Department of Health (2005) *Responding to Domestic Abuse: A Handbook for Health Professionals*. London: Stationery Office.

Dobash, R.E. and Dobash, R.P. (1992) *Women, Violence and Social Change*. London: Routledge.

Douglas, N., Lilley, S.J., Kooper, L. and Diamond A. (2004) *Safety and Justice: Sharing Personal Information in the Context of Domestic Violence – an Overview*. Home Office Development and Practice Report. London: Home Office.

Edelson, J. (1999) 'Children's witnessing of adult domestic violence.' *Journal of Interpersonal Violence 14*, 839–870.

Featherstone, B. and Peckover, S. (2007) 'Letting them get away with it: Fathers, domestic violence and child welfare.' *Critical Social Policy 27*, 2, 181–202.

Gewirtz, A. and Edelson, J. (2007) 'Young children's exposure to intimate partner violence: Towards a developmental risk and resilience framework for research and intervention.' *Journal of Family Violence 22*, 3, 151–163.

Gorin, S. (2004) *Understanding What Children Say: Children's Experiences of Domestic Violence, Parental Substance Misuse and Parental Health Problems*. York: National Children's Bureau in association with the Joseph Rowntree Foundation.

Harne, L. (2004) 'Childcare Violence and Fathering – Are Violent Fathers Who Look After their Children Likely to be Less Abusive?' In R. Klein and B. Wallner (eds) *Gender, Conflict and Violence*. Vienna: Studien-Verlag.

Harwin, N., Hague, G. and Malos, E. (1999) *The Multi-Agency Approach to Domestic Violence: New Opportunities, Old Challenges?* London: Whiting and Birch.

Healey, J. and Bell, M. (2005) 'Assessing the Risks to Children from Domestic Violence.' *Barnardo's Policy & Practice Briefing No. 7*. Belfast: Barnardo's.

Hester, M., Kelly, L. and Radford, J. (eds) (1996) *Women, Violence and Male Power*. Buckingham: Open University Press.

Hester, M., Pearson, C., Harwin, N. and Abrahams, H. (2006) *Making an Impact: A Reader*, 2nd edn. London: Jessica Kingsley Publishers.

Home Office (2005) *Domestic Violence. A National Report*. London: Home Office. Available at www.crimereduction.homeoffice.gov.uk/domesticviolence/domesticviolence51.pdf, accessed 12 August 2008.

Hooper, C.A. and Humphreys, C. (1997) 'What's in a name? Reflections on the term non-abusing parent.' *Child Abuse Review 11*, 298–303.

Hughes, H. (1992) 'Impact of spouse abuse on children of battered women. Implications for practice.' *Violence Update (August) 1*, 9–11.

Humphreys, C. (2007) 'Domestic violence and child protection: exploring the role of perpetrator risk assessments.' *Child & Family Social Work 12*, 4, 360–369.

Humphreys, C. and Harrison, C. (2003) 'Focusing on safety: Domestic violence and the role of child contact centres.' *Child and Family Law Quarterly 15*, 3, 237–253.

Humphreys, C., Hester, M., Hague, G., Mullender, A., Abrahams, H. and Lowe, P. (2000) *From Good Intentions to Good Practice: Mapping Services with Families Where There is Domestic Violence*. Bristol: Policy Press.

Humphreys, S. and Stanley, N. (eds) (2006) *Domestic Violence and Child Protection: Directions for Good Practice*. London: Jessica Kingsley Publishers.

Humphreys, C. and Thiara, R.K. (2003) 'Neither justice nor protection: Women's experiences of post-separation violence.' *Journal of Social Welfare and Family Law 25*, 3, 195–214.

Kelly, L. (1988) *Surviving Sexual Violence*. Cambridge: Polity Press.

Kelly, L. (1994) 'The Interconnectedness of Domestic Violence and Child Abuse: Challenges for Research, Policy and Practice.' In A. Mullender and R. Morley (eds) *Children Living with Domestic Violence: Putting Men's Abuse of Women on the Child Care Agenda*. London: Whiting and Birch.

Local Government Association (2005) *Vision for Services for Children and Young People Affected by Domestic Violence. Guidance to Local Commissioners of Children's Services*. Produced in association with CAFCASS, Women's Aid, and Association of Directors of Social Services. London: Local Government Association.

McGee, C. (2000) *Childhood Experiences of Domestic Violence*. London: Jessica Kingsley Publishers.

Mezey, G.C. and Bewley, S. (1997) 'Domestic violence and pregnancy.' *British Medical Journal 314*, 1295.

Mirlees-Black, C. (1999) *Domestic Violence: Findings from a New British Crime Survey Self-Completion Questionnaire*. London: Home Office.

Mullender, A. (1996) *Rethinking Domestic Violence. The Social Work and Probation Response*. London: Routledge.

Mullender, A. (2004) *Tackling Domestic Violence: Providing Support for Children Who Have Witnessed Domestic Violence*. Home Office Development and Practice Report 33. London: Home Office.

Mullender, A., Kelly, L., Hague, G., Malos, E. and Iman, U. (2002) *Children's Perspectives on Domestic Violence*. London: Routledge.

Mullender, A. and Morley, R. (eds) (1994) *Children Living with Domestic Violence: Putting Men's Abuse of Women on the Child Care Agenda*. London: Whiting and Birch.

O'Hara, M. (1994) 'Child Deaths in Contexts of Domestic Violence: Implications for Professional Practice.' In A. Mullender and R. Morley (eds) *Children Living with Domestic Violence: Putting Men's Abuse of Women on the Child Care Agenda*. London: Whiting and Birch.

Pence, E. and Paymar, M. (1993) *Educational Programmes for Men Who Batter*. New York: Springer.

Radford, L., Blacklock, N. and Iwi, K. (2006) 'Domestic Abuse Risk Assessment and Safety Planning in Child Protection – Assessing Perpetrators.' In C. Humphreys and N. Stanley (eds) *Domestic Violence and Child Protection: Directions for Good Practice*. London: Jessica Kingsley Publishers.

Radford, L. and Hester, M. (2006) *Mothering through Domestic Violence*. London: Jessica Kingsley Publishers.

Radford, L., Sayer, S. and AMICA (1999) *Unreasonable Fears? Child Contact in the Context of Domestic Violence: A Survey of Mother's Perceptions of Harm*. Bristol: Women's Aid Federation of England.

Rakil, M. (2006) 'Are Men Who Use Violence against their Partners and Children Good Enough Fathers? The Need for an Integrated Child Perspective in Treatment Work with Men.' In C. Humphreys and N. Stanley (eds) *Domestic Violence and Child Protection: Directions for Good Practice*. London: Jessica Kingsley Publishers.

Respect (2004) *Statement of Principles and Minimum Standards of Practice for Domestic Violence Perpetrator Programmes and Associated Women's Services*. London: Respect.

Richards, L. (2003) *Findings from the Multi-agency Domestic Violence Murder Reviews in London*. Prepared for the ACPO Homicide Working Group. London: Metropolitan Police.

Rivett, M. and Kelly, S. (2006) 'From awareness to practice: children, domestic violence and child welfare.' *Child Abuse Review 15*, 4, 224–242.

Robinson, A. (2004) *Domestic Violence MARACs for Very High Risk Victims in Cardiff: A Process and Outcome Evaluation*. Cardiff: Cardiff University Press.

Royal College of Psychiatrists (2004) *Domestic Violence: Its Effects on Children*. Mental Health and Growing Up Factsheet 17. London: Royal College of Psychiatrists.

Shepard, M. and Pence, E. (1999) *Coordinating Community Responses to Domestic Violence.* Thousand Oaks, CA: Sage Publications.

Skyner, D.R. and Waters, J. (1999) 'Working with perpetrators of domestic violence to protect women and children: a partnership between Cheshire Probation Service and the NSPCC.' *Child Abuse Review 8*, 1, 46–54.

Statham J. (2004) 'Effective services to support children in special circumstances.' *Child: Care Health & Development 30*, 6, 589–598.

UNICEF (2006) *Behind Closed Doors. The Impact of Domestic Violence on Children.* Littlehampton and New York: Body Shop International and UNICEF. Available at www.unicef.ca/portal/Secure/Community/502/WCM/WHATWEDO/ChildProtection/pdf/ bodyshop/UNReport_en.pdf, accessed 9 December 2008.

Walby, S. and Allen, J. (2004) *Domestic Violence, Sexual Assault and Stalking: Findings from the British Crime Survey.* Research Study 276. London: Home Office.

Women's Aid Federation of England (2005) *Every Child Matters – Common Assessment Framework.* Briefing Paper 4. Bristol: Women's Aid Federation of England. Available at www.womensaid.org.uk/page.asp?section=00010001000900050005&search=every+ child+matters+briefing, accessed 12 August 2008.

FURTHER READING

Department of Health (2005) *Responding to Domestic Abuse: A Handbook for Health Professionals.* London: Stationery Office.

Hester, M., Pearson, C., Harwin, N. and Abrahams, H. (2006) *Making an Impact, A Reader*, 2nd edn. London: Jessica Kingsley Publishers.

Humphreys, C. and Mullender, A. (2000) *Children and Domestic Violence: A Research Overview of the Impact on Children.* Dartington: Research in Practice.

Humphreys, C. and Stanley, N. (eds) (2006) *Domestic Violence and Child Protection: Directions for Good Practice.* London: Jessica Kingsley Publishers.

Local Government Association (2005) *Vision for Services for Children and Young People Affected by Domestic Violence. Guidance to Local Commissioners of Children's Services.* Produced in association with CAFCASS, Women's Aid, and Association of Directors of Social Services. London: Local Government Association.

Mullender, A. (1996) *Rethinking Domestic Violence. The Social Work and Probation Response.* London: Routledge.

Radford, L. and Hester, M. (2006) *Mothering through Domestic Violence.* London: Jessica Kingsley Publishers.

STATUTES

Adoption and Children Act (2002)

Children Act (1989)

Domestic Violence, Crime and Victims' Act (2004)

Protection from Harassment Act (1997)

RESOURCES

Humphreys, C., Thiara, R.K., Skamballis, A. and Mullender, A. (2006) *Talking About Domestic Abuse: A Photo Activity Workbook to Develop Communication Between Mothers and Young People.* London: Jessica Kingsley Publishers.

Humphreys, C., Thiara, R.K., Skamballis, A. and Mullender, A. (2006) *Talking to My Mum: A Picture Workbook for Workers, Mothers and Children Affected by Domestic Violence.* London: Jessica Kingsley Publishers.

USEFUL WEBSITES

www.womensaid.org.uk
Women's Aid is a national charity working to end domestic violence against women and children. Women's Aid support a network of over 500 domestic and sexual violence services across the UK. The website provides a range of information about services, campaigns and topics relating to domestic violence.

www.thehideout.org.uk
This award winning website developed by Women's Aid provides a valuable resource for children and young people affected by domestic abuse.

www.zerotolerance.org.uk
The website of Zero Tolerance Charitable Trust, an organisation that raises awareness about male violence against women and children through educational and poster campaigns and activities.

www.dvip.org.uk
The Domestic Violence Intervention Project is a London-based voluntary sector project that provides a range of services to those affected by domestic violence, including a Violence Prevention Programme for men who are abusive to their partners or ex-partners.

CHAPTER 9

SAFEGUARDING CHILDREN AND MENTAL HEALTH PRACTICE: EXPERIENCING THE FIELD

KAREN JOHNSON

INTRODUCTION

Nowadays, professionals are expected to work in areas not yet provided for in their preparatory training for example, safeguarding children for adult mental health professionals, and likewise mental health training for generic professionals. Both subjects can provoke anxiety as they are often associated with fear and demand a great deal of the workforce, not only an ability to detect concerns but also an ability not to scare too easily. That being said, professionals in the course of their work can and do absorb and manage frightening and tragic events.

Many people work from the heart, have a passion for their work, shaped by their own experiences and observations made throughout their own working and private lives. This may result in an attraction or focus in a particular direction, towards working with children or towards working with adults. This is often consonant with employment, and people tend towards work with children or with adults. Increasingly however, health and social policy is focused on the family, and agencies are being encouraged towards working with whole families; see *Think Family: Improving the Chances of Families at Risk* (Social Exclusion Task Force 2008) or mandated through Section 11, Children Act, in the direction of working with both children and adults. What this can mean in practice is that workers find themselves straddling two worlds. Child, maternity and family workers are faced with challenges relative to adults with mental health difficulties and adult mental health professionals are faced with challenges relative to the needs of the children of their clients. This has resulted in a significant change in the way in which agencies are expected to work. Pre-registration training courses have yet to update course content in order to relate these new health and social policy drivers to professional practice.

All helping relationships require skills in communication. In each circumstance, it is necessary that relationships develop, either with a client and/or with other professionals. The interpersonal and inter-professional field can be complex especially in the areas of mental health and safeguarding children and not all that is communicated can be clearly understood. Additionally, at the heart of a complex case lies a group of professionals and each professional is likely to have their own subjective sense of their client or fellow professionals. This often leads to differences of opinion. The question is how can professionals work more constructively with differences?

COMMUNICATION

Policies and guidance addressing the issue of communication mostly refer to conscious communication. Limited in the literature and training is information about different forms of communication, particularly unconscious communication and its impact upon the helping relationship. Some people are difficult, they may frighten you and make you feel incompetent, or fill you with confusing and unwanted feelings. Hawkins and Shohet (1989, p.3) state 'We have often seen very competent workers reduced to severe doubts about themselves and their abilities to function in their work through absorbing disturbance from clients'.

People with difficult lives often have difficult relationships with themselves as well as with others, and this will include those who try to help. For professionals engaged with people now sometimes referred to as 'hard to reach', learning to think, talk and work with a greater range of difficult experiences is essential to remaining productive and healthy at work. It is beyond the scope of this chapter to address the huge topic of supervision, however, I want to emphasise the use of supervision or supervisory conversations to include important elements of case work that may normally be left out.

LEARNING TO BE BOTH A PARTICIPANT AND AN OBSERVER

In every helping situation there is participation in some kind of relationship. Most professionals enter the workforce with a range of skills about building relationships with clients. What is less explicit is the usefulness of examining the interpersonal dynamic field of the helping relationship itself. All relationships carry obscure and hidden communications. In learning about hidden communications development of skills in participant observation may help, that is learning how to be both a participant and an observer of a relationship. Being a participant observer involves a willingness to examine sensitive responses to encounters with others.

Reflecting on how people make you feel and then learning how to talk to each other about those feelings can be hugely important for processing difficult feelings absorbed in the course of case work. Being able to reflect and then put into words confusing and frightening experiences is at the heart of understanding why participation in a particular relationship is problematic or perplexing. Speaking about difficult feelings generated in case work is to be encouraged through any kind of supervisory conversation or helping encounter.

WORKING WITH DIFFERENCE

It is likely that different professionals will carry different perceptions of the same person. It is also likely that only when information is collated, for example at a child protection case conference, does it become clear *how* differently those professionals perceive the same person. Those differences of perception often serve to impede the workforce, rather than inform it, as the case study that follows attempts to highlight. I want to propose a useful means of working with differences and suggest that exploring those differences might helpfully inform the multi-professional group. If an understanding of the differences can be acknowledged, then this may constitute a shared formulation about the nature of the problem, and the way in which the workforce can come together to help to contain it.

In the following case study I want to illustrate some of the factors that might explain why different professionals perceive the same person differently and how a professional's own characteristics may shape or impede judgement. I will argue the importance of professionals meeting together and attempting to reach a common understanding of the interpersonal (client and helper) and inter-professional field (the multi-agency group). I will argue that it is through reflection on the experience of helping itself that professionals might begin to recognise the kind of obscured communication indicative of psychological difficulties identified in many parents and carers who harm or kill children.

The tragic case of Victoria Climbié, like other high profile child deaths, brings into focus many things, not least the role of deception or obscured communication as an indication of disturbance in child abuse perpetrators. Bower (2005) states, 'The Climbié case is an extreme and tragic example of the failure to recognise severe psychological disturbance in a parent or carer (p.6)' Parton (2004) attributes difficulties in the workforce to lack of supervision and reasons about the role of deception and lack of analysis, 'considerable deceit on behalf of the key primary carers and insufficient critical analysis and scepticism on behalf of the professionals as to what was being told and being presented to them; and the severe lack of consistent and rigorous supervision' (p.82). It is likely that a range of difficult feelings were projected into people in contact (or not) with Victoria's carers and that a good deal of fear surrounded the case.

The following case material conveys something of the way in which distorted communication patterns (conscious and unconscious) develop in early relationships. The case study will aim to demonstrate how early relationship patterns become enacted (repeated) in subsequent relationships, either consciously or unconsciously, and how they may then shape the various helping relationships.

CASE STUDY 9.1: JULIE

Julie was born to an unmarried couple. Her mother managed to keep most of her antenatal appointments and the physical birth was uneventful. The mother seemed interested in her newborn infant, as did the father. Nothing gave cause for concern to the hospital staff, the midwife or health visitor. The couple married shortly after the birth of Julie. Her parents' relationship was passionate, intense and volatile. Their marriage lasted two years. Her father found it hard to hold down a job. Though industrious and hardworking, he found relationships with superiors difficult and would frequently storm out of work or invite dismissal. During their two-year marriage Julie's parents argued and fought regularly, the father, it seemed, found it difficult to watch his daughter occupy the space he once enjoyed, close to the heart and breast of his wife.

Julie, whilst at first appearing to soothe easily when placed at the breast, became increasingly fractious at the age of about four months. The mother would attempt to soothe her baby but because of the need of her husband, would feel torn and anxious in this new love triangle. This increasingly affected her capacity to respond to her baby, as she struggled between trying to soothe her baby and satisfy her raging husband. Julie, tiny, dependent and helpless would take in and absorb this frightening atmosphere.

By the time Julie was two years old, her father had left her mother, and the initial bond with her mother had consequently deteriorated. Julie's attachment to her mother was not at all secure, she frequently felt unsafe, leading to fear of losing this most crucial attachment. The consequence for the helpless two-year-old was extreme anxiety, largely expressed in clingy attachment to her mother. Her mother, for her part, found Julie's needs unbearable and unconsciously blamed her child for the loss of her husband. Julie was subsequently subjected to pervasive neglect.

LeDoux states:

> If a significant proportion of the early emotional experience one has had are due to activation of the fear system rather than positive systems, then the characteristic personality that begins to build up from the parallel learning processes coordinated by the emotional state is one characterised by negativity and hopelessness rather than affection and optimism. (2002, p.322)

Karr-Morse and Wiley state:

> Abuse and neglect in the first years of life have a particularly pervasive impact. Prenatal development and the first two years are the time when genetic, organic, and neurochemical foundations for impulse control are being created. It is also the time when the capacities for rational thinking and sensitivity to other people are being rooted – or not – in the child's personality. (1997, p.45)

For Julie, not withstanding the neurobiological implications of surviving an unsafe environment, the emotionality of the attachments established are predominantly characterised by both *need* and *fear*, i.e. Julie had both need and fear of relationships with others.

CASE STUDY 9.2: JULIE

By the time Julie reached the age of four, her mother had met another man, again a rather intense character, and again a man prone to violent outbursts. For Julie the situation grew progressively worse, Julie was learning how not to anger her mother, how to be a 'good girl'. By now she was, in the main quiet, withdrawn, undemanding and compliant, particularly in the presence of her mother. In contact with grandparents and aunts, Julie would present as hungry and in need of attention. One particular aunt was somewhat sensitive so Julie had some sense of what acknowledgement of need was like. But Julie's development had already been skewed; her compliant or needy means of relating became the way in which she sought relationships. She was not able to put words to what she wanted or needed, thus her simultaneous compliant and clingy behaviour became her predominant means of communication and of survival. In subsequent relationships she would display the need-seeking behaviour characteristic of children vulnerable to abuse. Although aware that her needs might bring about scorn and physical abuse, much as she might try, she could not conceal it and continued to enact her need to be acknowledged and accepted.

By the time Julie was ten years old she had endured many physical punishments, had been sexually abused by her stepfather and had an overly compliant over-anxious relationship with her mother. Her main means of (psychological) survival had been achieved by dissociation and splitting; by dividing her world into good and bad, she learned to survive a hostile, unpredictable world. Her conscious feelings towards her mother were idealised, her mother merely the victim of terrifying domestic violence. Her stepfather she saw as bad. Her emotional world was divided into good guys and bad guys, monsters, demons and fairy godmothers. When she did try to elicit the protection of her mother, she was not believed. In her young mind this was yet more evidence that she must try to hide essential truths about her experiences, to be a good girl. Julie had no clear means of communication, neither a language nor secure relationship in which she could articulate or speak truthfully about her needs, as everyone else's needs superseded her own.

During normal development a child learns to tolerate both good and bad feelings towards the same person without the threat of loss of that relationship. Children are taught to speak and communicate, and when things go well enough, a child will learn to articulate their feelings. Infants and toddlers learn important processes of integration through containment of their feelings of rage and frustration. In a good parent–child relationship the attachment is not so tenuous as to communicate to the child that the attachment will end if the child expresses bad feeling or otherwise frustrates or makes demands of their parent.

SPLITTING AND PROJECTION

Splitting is a means by which a child or adult keeps separate good and bad feelings towards the same person. Splitting requires that difficult to manage feelings are dissociated (disowned) and then projected. Like the physical act of eating food, emotions can be ingested or expelled. Salzberger-Wittenberg states:

> We speak of 'taking in' knowledge and good experience, of 'distasteful' ideas, of 'digesting' facts, or 'pouring out' our troubles, of 'pushing' unwanted

thoughts out of our mind as if they were physical entities. This is more than colourful speech. We are expressing our phantasy that mental and emotional happenings can be incorporated and expelled. (1970, p.27)

Projection of feelings is a means by which infants and young children communicate. Feelings of rage and frustration are pushed out into the external world. A good enough parent will gather up (contain) fragmented and fractious feelings and thus soothe a fraught and unhappy child. Therefore a good enough environment is one in which the child is helped to tolerate a range of emotions associated with the inevitable frustrations of growing up and away from loving comfortable dependence, yet maintaining a good attachment to that carer. A parent/carer who can help the baby contain good and bad feelings through provision of constant, predictable and sensitive care giving (for example by gradually and slowly introducing the baby to separation, new people and experiences) will enable the infants to integrate, to gradually manage feelings of love and hate and of good and bad towards the same person. 'Failure to integrate good and bad feelings leads to dissociation of feeling. Splitting makes the formation of a stable identity problematic' (Misham 2005, p.141).

When an infant is helped to integrate feelings of good and bad, to tolerate conflict in relationships, they are more likely to develop a more stable identity, to be able to recognise and articulate need and to subsequently form relationships based on openness and trust. Failure to develop a stable identity means that the person is likely to have weaknesses and vulnerabilities in their relationships with others. They are less likely to be able to identify and articulate their own needs or to be able to identify and empathise with the needs of others. Therefore communication in relationships is less straightforward, needs and feelings are communicated obscurely and relationships that rely on openness, where conflict can exist without relationship breakdown, are rare. The person is unable to contain strong feelings. Unresolved feelings of need, hate and rage, can be displaced from past relationships onto subsequent and current relationships. Feelings may be communicated, consciously and/or unconsciously, i.e. projected out. In both the field of safeguarding and mental health practice, professionals will often report strong reactions, often polarised, in response to the same child or adult.

Families with very impoverished or otherwise difficult lives may have numerous professionals involved, and each professional is likely to have their own subjective sense of a family or individual or child. The professional's personal response is likely to be shaped partly by personal experiences, past and present, and partly by the context of employment in relation to specific roles and responsibilities. This will mean that different professionals will be more likely to identify with different elements of the client's characteristics or circumstance (see Salzberger-Wittenberg 1970).

Splitting can also occur between individuals, organisations and agencies and it is not unusual for one group of professionals to dislike, denigrate or misunderstand another. This does not help working together between child and adult services particularly when concerns about safeguarding children and parental mental ill-health co-exist.

When professionals are working with frightening and provocative case material and when their work depends upon building alliances with people with fragmented and chaotic lives, they are confronted with a number of dilemmas relative to management of relationships with their client as well as with other professionals.

Feelings are often communicated unconsciously and can reflect the internal world of the client group projecting a range of polarised feelings. The range of strong and polarised feelings, for example need, anger and fear, then connects or resonates, either consciously or unconsciously, with different people in the workforce. This may be shaped by professional context and primary purpose for engagement with a helping agency, or it may be shaped by personal characteristics of the professional concerned.

CASE STUDY 9.3: JULIE

By the time Julie was 23 years old she was referred into the Community Mental Health Team (CMHT) for help with anxiety, repetitive abuse in relationships and alcohol problems. Julie looked much older than her 23 years, she presented as haggard, drawn and troubled. On assessment it was found that Julie had had two children temporarily taken into care and an ex-partner in prison. She was a frequent attendee at her local surgery and had been thrown off GP lists on several occasions. Julie told the Community Psychiatric Nurse (CPN) that her problems with anxiety and alcohol were as a result of having the children taken into care. Her history revealed that she had been sexually and physically abused and had very poor family relationships. She had been on the Child Protection Register for abuse and neglect at different stages of her childhood. She was, at one and the same time, demanding, suspicious and sceptical of help. The CPN became involved as part of a rehabilitative programme as Julie was requesting her children be returned. The request from the GP was for assessment and counselling. The CPN was soon approached by the social worker (SW) for information on her progress. Julie's long term SW had recently been taken off the case because of 'over involvement' and a new SW had been assigned. In the sessions with the CPN Julie focused mainly on her anger and hostility towards abusers and the former SW and Health Visitor (HV). The CPN found it increasingly difficult not to be drawn into the web of complex relationships between professionals, finding herself empathising with Julie about the HV and SW 'ganging up' on her. The CPN also found it increasingly difficult work, she became preoccupied with feelings about fellow workers and the unfairness of it all, she found herself filled with feelings of hostility towards the SW, and hopeless and despairing in relation to the loss of the children, who the CPN believed Julie to genuinely love.

It is possible to hypothesise, at this point, that the professional network around Julie were in receipt of polarised and projected feelings. The fact that one social worker had been removed from the case may indicate that worker to be in receipt of complicated and unpleasant projected feelings. The fact that the CPN was pre-occupied with feelings about fellow workers may also be an indication of polarised, split and projected feeling.

What is *felt* in contact with families is as important as what is said. To appreciate that you can become part of the dynamic interplay of relationships between helpers and agencies can be of great benefit once a few principles of practice are accepted. Asking yourself what does a particular case or person make you feel like inside and how does that impact on the work, is an essential question, not only in the interests of the work with the family, but also as an indicator for what you may need in terms of professional support. Professional and personal support might be anything from conversation with a trusted colleague (supervisory conversation) to formal regular practice supervision.

CASE STUDY 9.4: JULIE AND THE CPN

The CPN felt the case to be troubling, but also felt embarrassed about her range of difficult feelings, in particular hostility towards the SW and HV. She was more comfortable with the empathy she felt towards Julie as a mother. The CPN, herself a single parent with two young children, felt herself to be an essential advocate for someone who had been abused, mistreated and misunderstood as a child and who was, in her mind, currently being misunderstood by other professionals. The CPN at this stage was not conscious of the fact that there was any relevance about similarities in Julie's life and her own, most notably being a single parent with two children. The CPN was conscious of the fact that the SW who had been taken off the case was middle aged and childless, but was not conscious of the fact that the SW was providing a repository for bad feelings, either her own or those projected from Julie. The CPN felt unable to forget the work when at home, the case intruded into her private life, both the empathy she felt towards Julie as a single mother and the hostilities towards the SW, who, like Julie, she experienced as persecutory. Julie had well and truly 'got under the skin' of the CPN.

In this example strong projected feelings and subsequent identifications with different aspects of the case exist, possibly in all key professionals attempting to help. It is important to reflect on what the web of feelings and actions represent. Certainly it is possible that Julie was displacing feelings from past relationships onto current relationships. In Julie's early attachments she had not been helped to reach a stage of development where she was able to integrate good and bad feelings towards the same person. In order to preserve a tenuous attachment to her unreliable and inconsistent mother she had to dissociate feelings of anger and disappointment. As mentioned earlier, when an infant is nurtured in a good enough environment he/she is helped through feelings of anger and disappointment gently and gradually. In this process he/she learns to tolerate a range of feelings towards the same person, without a threat of breakdown in that relationship. So Julie, in adulthood, having not developed the capacity to tolerate good and bad feelings towards the same person, split her world into good and bad, at this point enacted as good CPN, bad SW and HV. Similarly in her intimate relationships this basic character difficulty was evident in the way in which she formed relationships, intensely at first, idealised, then quickly deteriorating into volatile and sometimes violent affrays. This unconscious dividing up of good and bad, (splitting), is a likely consequence of unresolved conflicts, of the longed for idealised mother and the, as yet unacknowledged reality, of a neglectful abusing mother.

The social worker had necessarily focused on the needs of the children, placing Julie in a watched and judged dynamic, one in which she often and repeatedly failed. Julie's relationship with the social worker provided a catalyst for feelings of hostility, the relationship mirroring elements of her problematic relationship with her mother; being judged, her needs negated or deferred to those of others (in this case the needs of the children). The social worker also represented her abusing and cruel father and stepfather, robbing Julie of her children. The previous social worker, like the health visitor, had worked intensely with Julie. At first their relationship was idealised, but because Julie was unable to comply with the demands of the Child Protection Plan, the social worker had been judged to lack objectivity and subsequently been removed from the case. The health visitor, for her part had become increasingly anxious about the children, and unusually preoccupied with the case. Now in contact with representatives of social care and health visiting services, i.e. professionals who are more directly assessing the needs of children, Julie felt violated, vulnerable, bullied and misunderstood, she felt unsafe as a child and now as an adult unsafe with professionals concerned with the care of her children.

Strong feelings emerging from case material depend upon two main processes, first that there is a projection of unwanted or unmanageable feelings from one person to another (unconscious communication), and second that there is an identification between the helper and the person being helped (conscious or unconscious communication). It is therefore possible, in this particular case, that the social worker and the CPN had displaced some of their own needs onto Julie, which similarly may also have had their roots in childhood, but equally may echo some of their own desires or difficulties with regard to their current life circumstances (identification).

OBSERVING AND EXPLORING HIDDEN PROCESSES

When working with people with troubled childhoods, learning to speak about the actual experience of helping and the nature and characteristics of the relationship is essential. Supervision should be an opportunity to think through case work at a personal as well as a professional level. Although helpers can be forgiven for assuming that *not* attending to the difficult feelings a particular case provokes will help those feelings dissipate, in reality, and in most cases, the difficult experience is merely suppressed. It is important therefore, that all professionals working in safeguarding children and mental health services have a reliable, supportive relationship with a colleague, and that time and attention is available to reflect on confusing, frightening, intense or intrusive thoughts and feelings relative to casework.

CASE STUDY 9.5: JULIE AND THE CPN

Although aware of strong feelings in relation to this particular case, the CPN was unaware that these feelings were problematic. She took elements of the case to supervision and gained the support of her supervisor in terms of managing the boundaries of the relationship with her client. Little of her feelings about the social worker or health visitor were discussed, rather the focus related to specific work with the client and the strong empathies she felt towards her. The supervisor for her part was aware that the CPN was a single parent with two young children of similar age. However, issues relative to strong feelings of hostility towards the social worker and the health visitor and the impediments emanating from that, (difficult working together arrangements and loss of objectivity), were missed out of the session. The CPN avoided elements of the case work she felt embarrassed about, or those that she imagined might draw disapproval from her supervisor.

In the following months the children were returned to Julie for a trial period. The CPN, for her part, increased visits to twice weekly, once when the children were present and once when Julie had space of her own.

CASE STUDY 9.6: THE CPN

The perception of the CPN, on all visits, was that everything appeared to be progressing well. Julie started cooking proper meals for the children and eating meals with them. When the CPN arrived Julie would be engaged in household tasks and the children playing normally (unremarkably) close by, so she couldn't put together in her mind the information shared by the social worker about children playing abnormally and wondered what on earth the social worker could mean! At this point the CPN felt somewhat triumphant, that she had been right all along, that is until one day, whilst in the area, the CPN decided to pop in, unannounced. To her horror, on approaching the house she was to be hit with the hard evidence of a blood-stained front door. A neighbour came rushing out and said she had wanted to alert professionals but had not known who or how. The CPN, somewhat bewildered, sat with the neighbour for the next ten minutes listening to an alarming account of events that, undeniably, meant that Julie was indeed neglecting her children. They had been exposed to domestic violence following drinking binges between Julie and a new abusive partner. Julie and this man had been locking the children in a small bedroom whilst they went out. The blood on the door was from a fight the previous evening. Shaking and shocked the CPN immediately rang the SW, and waited at the house for Julie to return with the children from nursery. The SW arrived and the children were removed there and then. The CPN was party to the emotional and aggressive attacks Julie made on the SW; the CPN was then instructed to sit in the back of the car with the children, leaving Julie with another social worker. The little two-year-old child carrying a rag dolly asked the CPN if she was her new mummy.

Embarrassing hidden or obscured feelings are common in case work. They are also of huge significance. Had the CPN realised the importance of taking the more difficult feelings she had to supervision, and had the supervisor been alerted to ask certain searching questions, could those children have been protected from damaging exposure to drunken domestic violence or from further temporary placement?

It is beyond the scope of this chapter to address the hugely important subject of supervision. What I want to do is present a few practical suggestions and questions, that can be accommodated into all major supervision models or supervisory relationships to assist reflection on difficult case work. Supervision may be described as a helicopter ability, an ability to hover over a case, to have *super vision* about it, to be able to observe yourself within emotive and difficult casework. This will mean looking inside the self and outside towards others.

In the case of Julie this will mean carefully thinking through internal processes; an example of this might be the CPN's empathy and identification with her client as a single parent. Furthering understanding of the case will also require consideration of interpersonal processes. It is quite likely that Julie needed to preserve the relationship with the CPN as good, which meant that she was selective about the information she gave the CPN. This might be understood as a displacement of aspect of a past relationship, in this case Julie and her mother. This in turn shaped how the CPN judged Julie as a mother. The CPN also may have contributed by identifying with Julie as a single parent and the struggles that involved. This may then have contributed to a problematic blind spot in making a realistic appraisal of Julie's capacity to neglect her children (intentional or otherwise).

Next we might consider inter-professional processes (between the CPN, SW and HV and CPN and her supervisor). On reviewing the case of Julie and the CPN, SW and HV, powerful processes of identification were at play. Although the supervisor had some understanding of this and brought elements of this into supervision, a combination of some avoidance by the

CPN of the more bewildering or difficult elements of the material, together with no formal means for the supervisor to identify when problematic inter-professional relationships existed, may have meant that important predictors of deception, splitting and disturbed pathology were missed.

So what might usefully be taken from the case of Julie?

Supervisee/professionals tasks:

1. Strong feelings about a case are very important, they may indicate that powerful feelings are being expelled, pushed towards or into you, by a person unable to contain difficult or conflicting feelings (splitting and projection). Excesses of these processes are an indicator of disturbing pathology.

2. Feelings you may be ashamed of, confused or guilty about, are precisely the feelings you need to take to supervision.

3. It is OK to have difficult feelings about clients and other professionals, provided that you are prepared to examine them. The test is not to act upon them, rather reflect upon them, and talk about them to a trusted colleague, mentor or supervisor.

4. Having strong feelings about fellow professionals may be an indicator that the professional group are enacting the split, fragmented and tormented mind of a client.

5. Be mindful of cases that preoccupy you or follow you home from work. This is an indication that boundaries are at risk of being broken. Ask yourself: Do I behave differently towards this client in terms of information share, time spent thinking about it and degree of concern, empathy or intimacy?

6. Where possible gather information about past helping relationships.

7. Know yourself, your limitations, your strengths and your sensitivities.

8. Be healthily sceptical about your client, and continually ask yourself is it likely you are being deceived?

9. Be alert to whether your client is vulnerable to making frequent, fickle, abusive attachments.

10. Be alert to being idealised, being all important, for example a temptation to give out your personal telephone number.

11. Be alert to other professionals being denigrated.

Supervisor's tasks:

1. Ask what other professionals or volunteers are involved in the case/family?

2. Explore the history of helping relationships, e.g. is there a history of change in professionals or of difficult working relationships.

3. Ask your supervisee, do you feel able to work together with other professionals in the best interests of the family? i.e. give time to reflect on the nature of supervisee working relationships with other professionals involved in the case.

4. Is there enough 'healthy scepticism' (Duncan and Reder, 1993) relative to potential harm, intentional or unintentional? Healthy scepticism is about teasing out hidden feelings, e.g. what role might deception, self deception, deception of others play in the helping relationship? Might there also be some hidden feelings between supervisor and supervisee?

5. Examine and reflect upon the interaction of the parent/s with helpers and agencies, e.g. Is there a pattern developing? Are professional being allocated roles of good guys and bad guys? What might this mean? (splitting and projection).

6. Be alert to parents forming abusive relationships with men/women.

7. Remember abuse is perpetuated through fear, secrecy and myth.

8. Be alert to being idealised.

SUMMING UP

People who are in contact with mental health and safeguarding services often have difficult relationships with themselves, with others and with people who try to help them. In the case of Julie, in her relationships with others, and in relation to herself, her feelings were in the main polarised; that is separated into either all good or all bad. She frequently employed defences of splitting and projection, and conflict was barely tolerable. When forming attachments with others, her dependency needs were heightened. Her relationships were volatile, intense, needy and fragile. In effect her ability to form co-operative helpful relationships that contain support, empathy and some conflict was all but absent.

In her need-driven relationships Julie projected a force of different, divided feeling that would inevitably find different recipients in the workforce. Different professionals would perceive different aspects of Julie's complicated and traumatised persona. She would meet with a range of professionals all with differing life histories, some with personal struggles of their own who would unwittingly become participants in her internal and real life dramas. Her unconsciously driven and messy attempts at making relationships were perhaps an equally messy attempt to make the workforce do what her mother had been able to do, that is contain the rage and hurt of a damaged child.

Julie's mothering was messy, inconsistent and fragmented. In the absence of a dysfunctional relationship with a man she was reasonably able to provide good enough care for her children under the watchful eye of the statutory services. When forming relationships with men, typically the relationship would start intensely, idealised, like that of an infant with their mother or father, but then quickly deteriorate. Having a relationship with a man pushed Julie into a state of chaos, reawakening unconscious and conscious experiences of abuse and unmet need. This would dramatically impact on her ability to hold her children in mind and protect them. In her relationships with men Julie quickly became a victim of further abuses, thumped, dragged about and raped, re-enacting the tragedies of her childhood. In contact with professionals Julie would profess that she would care for her children; though these utterances may have been meant truthfully at the time they were spoken, she may also have been passively or actively deceiving her helpers.

That is not to say that her male partners were responsible for the neglect of her children as this was Julie's own neglect of her children. Rather, it was the dynamic interplay of factors that resulted in Julie's limited capacity to provide enough protection for her children which resulted in them suffering significant harm.

Brandon *et al.*'s (2008) child death analysis highlights Schnitzer and Ewigman's (2005) study which reports that:

> children residing in households with unrelated adults were nearly 50 times more likely to die of inflicted injuries than children living with two biological parents. Children in households with a single parent and no other adults in residence had no increased risk of inflicted-injury or death (p.87).

A SHARED FORMULATION

What might have helped professionals working with Julie and her children? First it is important that professionals have an opportunity to explore difficult experiences during the course of case work. Second it is important to come together to think about different experiences and perceptions, and third to have an opportunity to think through and talk about them, rather than react to them. In this way the differences and difficulties can be put together and thus understood as re-enactments of past experiences (shared formulation). Sharing ideas and experiences in this way can help reduce the unhelpful tendency of splits and divisions in the workforce that so often impedes child protection work. It may be helpful to invite an independent and experienced supervisor to facilitate a professionals meeting. An experienced supervisor, without direct responsibility for any one of the professionals, may be able to interpret and add meaning to the complex web of inter-professional relationships in a way that reduces the splitting and projection emanating from the uncontained and unintegrated mind of the parent.

END NOTE

It may be of help in the future to bring together vulnerable adults and vulnerable children policy and systems. In doing so, professionals may be helped to pull together their understanding about vulnerability and abuse and thus consider, in professional and theoretical context, two immensely important and related fields, safeguarding children and mental health practice.

REFERENCES

Bower, M. (2005) *Psychoanalytic Theories for Social Work Practice: Thinking Under Fire*. Oxford: Routledge.

Brandon, M., Belderson, P., Warren, C., Howe, D., Gardner, R., Dodsworth, J. and Black, J. (2008) *Analysing Child Deaths and Serious Injury through Abuse and Neglect: What Can We Learn? A Biennial Analysis of Serious Case Reviews (2003–2005)*. London: Department for Children, Schools and Families.

Hawkins, P. and Shohet, R. (1989) *Supervision in the Helping Proffesions*. Buckingham: Open University Press.

LeDoux, J. (2002) *Synaptic Self: Our Brains Become Who We Are*. London: Penguin Books.

Misham, J. (2005) 'Thinking under Fire.' In M. Bower (ed.) *Psychoanalytic Theory for Social Work Practice*. Oxford: Routledge.

Parton, N. (2004) 'From Maria Colwell to Victoria Climbié: Reflections on public inquiries into child abuse a generation apart.' *Child Abuse Review 13*, 80–94.

Reder, P., Duncan, S. and Gray, M. (1993) *Beyond Blame: Child Abuse Tragedies*. London: Routledge and Kegan Paul.

Salzberger-Wittenberg, I. (1970) *Psycho-Analytic Insight and Relationships*. London: Routledge.

Social Exclusion Task Force (2008) *Think Family: Improving the Chances of Families at Risk*. London: Cabinet Office.

STATUTE

Children Act (2004)

BIBLIOGRAPHY

Niedecken, D. (2003) *Nameless, Understanding Learning Disability*. Hove: Brunner-Routledge.

CHAPTER 10

SAFEGUARDING TRAFFICKED CHILDREN

EMMA KELLY

INTRODUCTION

Awareness amongst child protection professionals of child trafficking into, within and out of the UK, has been growing over the last ten years to the extent that it is now highlighted as a safeguarding issue in *Working Together to Safeguard Children* (Department for Children, Schools and Families 2006). Trafficking of children raises a new set of questions for child protection professionals. It is a particularly covert and clandestine activity, often arranged by sophisticated criminal gangs, in which children are subjected to extreme physical and psychological brutality (Beddoe 2007; Kapoor 2007). Children suspected to have been victims of trafficking are often extremely reluctant to talk about their experiences and a significant number disappear from public care, leaving many professionals feeling powerless (Beddoe 2007; Kapoor 2007). The tensions between safeguarding and asylum legislation only add to these difficulties, so it is no wonder that many child protection practitioners feel they are dealing with something completely new.

However, as noted in *Safeguarding Children Who May Have Been Trafficked* (Department for Children, Schools and Families 2007) 'it is essential that all professionals who come into contact with children who may have been trafficked are fully aware of the background to this activity and know how to apply the procedures for safeguarding children' (p.4). Given the differences of legislation in Scotland and Northern Ireland, this chapter only attempts to address the legislative and procedural situation in England and Wales. Throughout the term child will be used to refer to anyone under the age of 18.

WHAT IS TRAFFICKING?

The internationally accepted definition of trafficking comes from Article 3 of the United Nations *Protocol to Prevent, Suppress and Punish Trafficking in Persons, Especially Women and Children* (2000):

> (a) 'Trafficking of persons' shall mean the recruitment, transportation, transfer, harbouring or receipt of persons, by means of the threat or use of force or other forms of coercion, of abduction, of fraud, of deception, of the abuse of power or of a position of vulnerability or of the giving or receiving of payments or benefits to achieve the consent of a person having control over another person, for the purpose of exploitation.
>
> (b) Exploitation shall include, at a minimum, the exploitation of the prostitution of others or other forms of sexual exploitation, forced labour or services, slavery or practices similar to slavery, servitude or the removal of organs;
>
> (c) The recruitment, transportation, transfer, harbouring or receipt of a child for the purpose of exploitation shall be considered 'trafficking in persons'...
>
> (d) 'Child' shall mean any person under eighteen years of age.

In principle, child trafficking involves moving children across or within international or national borders for the purposes of exploitation. The definition also includes what is often referred to as 'internal trafficking', which is the trafficking of children within domestic borders. Internal trafficking in the UK can involve foreign nationals or citizen children. Trafficking is different from smuggling because of the intent to exploit; smugglers have no intent to exploit a child they are moving whereas traffickers do. Similarly, the main difference between adult and child trafficking is that 'it is irrelevant whether the child has apparently consented to being brought to the destination' (Beddoe 2007, p.12). Child trafficking is often achieved through coercion and deception; a child might believe that they are coming to the UK for legitimate reasons but are instead exploited. Human trafficking is a worldwide phenomenon with recent estimates indicating that 2.4 million people are trafficked each year, half of whom are children (UNICEF). After drugs and arms smuggling, trafficking is the largest source of revenue for organised crime (UNICEF). Human trafficking into the UK is a relatively recent phenomenon, but the UK is now a transit and destination country for child victims of trafficking.

EXTENT IN UK

In the last six years a number of research reports have been written to establish the extent of child trafficking into and within the UK (Beddoe 2007; Kapoor 2007; Somerset 2001). Collecting data about child trafficking is problematic; very few victims of this form of exploitation would describe themselves as 'trafficked'. These figures are also considered to be underestimates as we can only guess at the number of children who have been trafficked into the UK but remain undetected (Beddoe 2007).

A recent Home Office report concluded that in the space of 18 months at least 330 children have probably been trafficked into the UK (Kapoor 2007). The research by ECPAT UK into cases in three northern regions found that over 80 children were suspected to have been trafficked (Beddoe 2007). In both studies the children originate from a number of different countries with the most numerous from China, East and West Africa and to a lesser extent Eastern Europe (Beddoe 2007; Kapoor 2007). There is a considerable age range amongst such children (including pre-schoolers) but the majority are 15–17 years old at the time of discovery; less is known about their age on arrival into the UK. Until recently, it was thought that the majority of trafficked children are girls, but evidence now indicates that an increasing number of victims are boys (up to 42% in Kapoor's study). Profiling indicates that there is frequently a link between the country of origin of the child and the type of exploitation. For instance, female children from Nigeria are trafficked principally for domestic servitude whilst the majority of Russian and Eastern European girls are brought to the UK to be commercially sexually exploited (Beddoe 2007: Kapoor 2007).

REASONS WHY CHILDREN ARE TRAFFICKED INTO THE UK

The causes of child trafficking are various and complex, but can best be divided into push and pull factors. Push factors, or those which make children vulnerable to trafficking include political and economic instability, poverty, gender inequality and traditional practices in some communities and cultures (Department for Children, Schools and Families 2007). Many children who are victims of trafficking come from extremely poor or dysfunctional families or have been orphaned though parental illness or conflict. In these situations, children might be cared for by extended family or community or end up living on the streets; some of these children are then recruited by, or passed on to, traffickers who may send them to Europe. Frequently, children are deceived by their traffickers who prey on their hopes of a better life in another country. Many child victims of trafficking report being tricked into believing that they will have legitimate employment in the UK as a model or in a bar or will be setting up a home with a boyfriend (Beddoe 2007; Sillen and Beddoe 2007). The pull factors are what makes it possible for children to be exploited in the UK; put simply, children are trafficked into the UK because of the demand. This demand presents itself in a number of ways.

Trafficked for domestic servitude

It is known that a number of West African children are brought to the UK to act as domestic helps, often for Nigerian families (Ayrio 2006); a form of trafficking seen to be an abuse of long-established cultural traditions in which extended families and communities look after children other than their own. Some West African children brought into the UK find that they are not allowed to go to school, that they have to do all the household chores and care for other children, and many report being sexually abused as well. This abuse may go on for a number of years unnoticed. Such children are not identified as trafficked unless neighbours, members of the community or professionals visiting a family home become suspicious of their presence.

Trafficked for sexual exploitation

The majority of children are trafficked for the purposes of sexual exploitation, principally in brothels and saunas, or taken to clients' houses by their pimps (Beddoe 2007; Kapoor 2007). These children are frequently kept locked up, forced to service a number of clients on a daily basis (often without condoms), subject to repeated physical and sexual violence and rape, and denied basic medical attention (Kapoor 2007; Zimmerman *et al.* 2006). Such children tend to be identified through raids on premises, particularly during special police operations such as Operation Pentameter, or if they manage to escape. A number of girls have come to the attention of local authorities, often in the late stages of pregnancy, and it is thought they are evicted by their traffickers as they are no longer deemed to be attractive to clients (Beddoe 2007).

Trafficked for forced labour

Increasingly, there are reports of children being forced to work as labour, in for example restaurants, take-aways, nail bars or in suburban cannabis factories, although factual evidence remains sparse (Dowling, Moreton and Wright 2007). Clearly further work needs to be done in this area as recent estimates indicate that one child a week is being picked up during raids on suburban cannabis factories (*Independent* 2007). As well as working illegally, these children are generally deprived of their right to an education and often live in poor and cramped conditions. Professionals are likely to first identify these children after raids on premises, or if a child presents at Accident and Emergency. Sometimes, children who have been accommodated by the local authority continue to be exploited by their traffickers. The signs of this may include a child who is always out during the day and returns looking exhausted and in need of a shower, or a child who refuses educational or social opportunities stating that they are busy. There are a few documented cases of children being trafficked for illegal adoption or forced marriage but these tend to be in the minority (Beddoe 2007; Department for Children, Schools and Families 2007; Kapoor 2007).

HOW CHILDREN ARE BROUGHT INTO THE UK

Trafficked children enter the country by a variety of means; some pass through immigration control whilst others are brought in clandestinely. It is best practice to think of all children who enter the country without their parents as separated children, regardless of whether they enter alone or with an adult (Bhabha and Finch 2006). The word 'separated' is preferred to 'unaccompanied' because 'it better defines the essential problem that such children face. Namely, that they are without the care or protection of their parents or legal guardian and as a consequence suffer socially and psychologically from this separation' (Save the Children and UNCHR 2004, p.2).

Unaccompanied children

Children who arrive alone will be referred to the local authority for support including accommodation unless their age is immediately disputed (Crawley 2007). A significant number of children enter the UK unaccompanied but it remains unclear as to how many of them are victims of trafficking. A special police operation named Paladin, at Heathrow Airport, recorded during a three-month period in 2003 that 1736 unaccompanied asylum-seeking children entered, 551 of whom were deemed to be at risk for follow up, of whom 28 went missing and 14 of whom have never been recovered (Metropolitan Police Authority 2004). It is known that some children claim asylum on the orders of the traffickers and they disappear at a later stage at the demand of those that have brought them into the country (Beddoe 2007; Kapoor 2007). A key indicator is of a child presenting to immigration and social services a very similar story to other children about how they have come to claim asylum in the UK, which suggests they have been given prepared stories.

Accompanied children

Children may enter the country with an adult who claims to be responsible for them. Since 2006 tighter controls have been introduced regarding the entry of a minor to 'demonstrate that suitable arrangements have been made for his travel to, and reception and care in the United Kingdom' (Home Office 2006, p.2). If an immigration officer, after speaking to a child, is not satisfied with the purported arrangements, then they should refer the child to the local authority to undertake an assessment. However, the same difficulty presents itself, which is the means available to truly determine the relationship between a child and a carer. Many separated children will end up in a private fostering situation i.e. being care for by someone who is not a family member (as defined in the Children Act 1989). Some are likely to be exploited but remain undetected because of the current weak reporting arrangements for private foster carers in the UK. There is substantial anecdotal evidence to indicate that children are being trafficked into the UK and exploited in private fostering situations (Ayrio 2006).

Hidden children

Other separated children are brought in without being declared to immigration, so are in the UK on an illegal basis. Young people report being transported in the backs of lorries, cargo containers, or on occasions, on Eurostar. This is particularly the case for children from Afghanistan, Vietnam and some Eastern European countries (Kapoor 2007). Regardless of the means of entry many of these children will have had extremely long and often frightening journeys. They may well have been moved from place to place without knowing where they are going. They may have been kept in cramped conditions deprived of natural light and even food and water.

RECOGNISING POTENTIALLY TRAFFICKED CHILDREN

Since child trafficking was first identified in the UK in 1995, local authorities and non-governmental organisations have been developing lists of indicators to assist practitioners in recognising a trafficked child (Beddoe 2007; Somerset 2001). It is not an easy task as trafficked children rarely present in obvious ways. As with much child abuse, the indicators may be subtle and only take on any real significance when pieced together with other bits of information. Moreover, lists of indicators are often reflective of local conditions and need frequent revision as the patterns in child trafficking change. For instance, as immigration staff at the major British ports have become more aware of potential signs so there has been a shift by traffickers to bringing children in through regional ports at night time where they are less likely to be detected (Kapoor 2007). Table 10.1 details some of the general indicators which should trigger questions and concerns in a practitioners mind.

ASSESSING TRAFFICKED CHILDREN

Government guidance requires practitioners to assess vulnerable children using the Framework of the Assessment of Need of Children and their Families (Department of Health 2000). Concerns about a potentially trafficked child may well first be recorded in an Initial Assessment and this should lead to a Core Assessment being completed to gather further information. Given the very specific needs and experiences of trafficked children some local authorities are developing special assessment tools to be used in identifying

Table 10.1: Indicators of possible child trafficking	
Indicator	*Background*
Has no passport or identifying papers	Traffickers usually remove children's passports, an act that implicitly warns children to avoid exposure to officials of any kind in the country to which they have been trafficked
Does not know where they are	Trafficked children are frequently moved from country to country and city to town without being told where they are going
Tells the same or similar story to other children about their journey	Traffickers will groom their victims and convince them to give a false account of their purpose/reason for entering the UK
Goes missing	Even when trafficked children have been rescued they may have been conditioned into thinking that terrible things will happen to them or their family if they do not return to their trafficker
Refuses educational opportunities or is always out during the day	Possible that the child is being used in manual labour to pay off alleged debt bondage
Is not registered with a GP or enrolled at school	Possible that the child is being kept hidden and deprived of universal services because they are being used as a domestic help
Is being cared for by adults who are not their parents/family and the quality of the relationship is poor	Needs to be investigated as a private fostering situation but mindful that the child may have been trafficked
Has age-inappropriate clothes, e.g. skimpy items, lots of underwear and bikinis	Traffickers frequently provide their victims of sexual exploitation with 'sexy' clothes
Has a mobile phone but no money	Traffickers often provide their victims with mobile phones to ensure that they can stay in touch with the traffickers
Is seen with or driven about by a older male	This adult may well be the 'pimp'

the needs of a trafficked child, focusing on the journey, entry into the UK, the current living circumstances, household chores, health concerns, free time and the relationship between the child and those they live with.

One of the greatest obstacles facing practitioners working with child victims of trafficking is their reluctance to disclose. Many victims will have been groomed to believe that the consequences of disclosure could be fatal for either themselves or their family and friends (Department for Children, Schools and Families 2007). Practitioners need to accept that, for a variety of reasons, the child may not be forthcoming; instead practitioners should seek to find information from a number of other sources as well as drawing on key research findings in an attempt to piece the child's story together. This is time consuming and difficult. Given the above, it is essential that practitioners are supported by their agency and its systems so that they can adequately safeguard a child who may have been trafficked.

The ability to engage with the child and to maximise the chances of developing a trusting relationship with them is critical. Acknowledging that you are aware that trafficking can happen is a good place to start although the language used should be meaningful for the child. Children must also be clear about your role so time must be taken at the start of any engagement to ensure that they understand what you do. Many countries do not have equivalent welfare agencies so children may be confused and suspicious of child-care professionals. Frequently, practitioners will be relying on an interpreter. Using an interpreter in the same room is preferable to a telephone service except in exceptional circumstances. It is very important that interpreters are Criminal Record Bureau checked but more importantly that they are not part of the local community in which that young person was found. In all matters concerning a trafficked child confidentiality is of the upmost importance and the location of the child should only be divulged to those who really need to know (Department for Children, Schools and Families 2007).

SUPPORTING TRAFFICKED CHILDREN

As with all forms of child abuse the effects on the child can be complex and long lasting as well as unique to each individual. Children who have been trafficked are likely to have experienced physical, sexual and emotional abuse and possibly neglect too. Child protection professionals will be very familiar with the effects of these forms of abuse and what services exist to support children. However, trafficked children are likely to have a specific set of support needs which may be unfamiliar. These include consideration of whether the accommodation provision is safe, what strategies can be put in place to minimise the likelihood of a child going missing and a comprehensive assessment of the child's health needs including their sexual and mental health. Many victims of child trafficking may also require support with their asylum claim. A good place to start is to refer the child to the Refugee Council Children's Panel who can offer support to the child and practitioner. It will also be vital to ensure that the child is put in touch with a solicitor with experience in asylum law.

Accommodation

Currently in the UK, there is no agreement about what is the best form of accommodation for a victim of child trafficking. The idea of a 'safe house' is one option. A safe house is staffed at all times and commonly children are prevented from going out because of the risk that they will be re-trafficked. Currently there are no 'safe houses' for children although the Home Office does support safe houses for women aged over 18 (e.g. Poppy Project managed by Eaves Housing). Many local authorities are opting to place trafficked children in foster placements or in a children's home, preferably well away from the area in which they were found. Children who are accommodated on a S17 basis remain at higher risk because the type of accommodation they are placed in generally lacks the safeguards of a foster placement or residential unit. Therefore, as set out in LAC Circular 13 (Department of Health 2003), 'where a child has no parent or guardian in this country, perhaps because he has arrived alone seeking asylum, the presumption should be that he would fall within the scope of S20 and become looked after' (p.3).

Missing children

A second key support need is how to minimise the likelihood that a child will go missing, given that a recent government report highlighted that 55 per cent of trafficked children had disappeared (Kapoor 2007). Most commonly children go missing up to 48 hours after being taken into local authority care, some whilst waiting in a social services office to be assessed. Other trafficked children disappear at a later stage, probably under the instruction of their traffickers (Beddoe 2007; *Guardian* 2007; Kapoor 2007). Most such children will never be found. Therefore practitioners working with victims of trafficking need to do all they can to ensure that the child does not go missing. Many local authorities require social workers to produce a risk assessment if it is likely that a child may go missing (Department for Children, Schools and Families 2007; Department of Health 2002). It is useful to have a recent photograph of the child, along with a list of current contacts. Foster carers and residential staff need to be alert to anything suspicious, such as the same car being parked outside the property or an increase in calls to a child's mobile phone. These can be ways of exerting pressure on the child and reminding them of the possible reality of threats that have been made against them by traffickers. Clearly, it is important for whoever is working closely with such children to acknowledge that this must be a real concern and worry for them, even if they refuse to discuss it.

Mental health

Zimmerman *et al.* (2006) demonstrated that adolescents and women who have been trafficked are likely to suffer significant memory loss in relation to their abusive experiences. This memory loss can have implications for the assessment of the child as we normally rely on what children say to us about their experiences to build up our understanding of their needs. Without information about the abusive experiences such children have undergone it can be difficult to be clear as to what support or degree of safety is required. Both the police and the judiciary rely on detailed information to make their decisions in any given case and if such information is difficult to obtain from a child it may affect the authorities' capacity to act and may lead to questions about a child's credibility (Zimmerman *et al.* 2006). Post-traumatic stress disorder, depression, self-harming behaviours, attempted suicide and anxiety attacks are all common indicators of the mental health of victims of trafficking (Beddoe 2007; Zimmerman *et al.* 2006).

CHILD PROTECTION INVESTIGATIONS

If there are suspicions that a child is a victim of trafficking then standard child protection procedures must be followed. These are laid out comprehensively in *Safeguarding Children who may have been Trafficked* (Department for Children, Schools and Families 2007), supplementary guidance to *Working Together to Safeguard Children* (Department for Children, Schools and Families 2006). As the guidance makes clear, the starting point is a referral to children's social care who should follow child protection procedures if they feel a child is at risk. This may lead to a strategy discussion to share information and concerns. The Department for Children, Schools and Families (DCSF) suggests that immigration staff should be invited to the strategy discussion. A potential for conflict emerges at this point, given that the UK Border Agency are not required to consider the best interests of the child (Bhabha and Finch 2006). For this reason, some child-care services are reluctant to share information about a child because of a potential conflict of interest (Bhabha and Finch 2006). During the strategy discussion, a plan of investigation should be made as well as a plan to ensure the child's safety. As with all child protection investigations the need for a child protection medical and interview using the Home Office guidance *Achieving Best Evidence in Criminal Proceedings* (Home Office 2006a) must be considered.

In reality, there are a number of practice areas that are problematic. First, there is evidence to suggest that some practitioners do not recognise the indicators of trafficking, thereby failing to spot children who are potentially at risk. Practitioners should be supported by their employers with this through the provision of multi-agency training and local policy and procedures. Second, there exists a culture of disbelief in some geographical areas/agencies that trafficking actually happens at all. Third, the criminal element of some child trafficking can be quite daunting for practitioners. Stories of sophisticated underground networks operating throughout different groups in the UK serve to isolate responses to child victims of trafficking; despite the unusual context, trafficking is a child protection issue and should be seen within the spectrum of child abuse. Fourth, the options for child victims of trafficking are limited, which creates difficulties for frontline staff in offering appropriate needs-led services. Anecdotal evidence highlights that some practitioners have done their utmost to safeguard a child only to see them disappear from local authority care and return to their traffickers.

ENABLING TRAFFICKED CHILDREN TO REMAIN IN THE UK

Child victims of trafficking are governed both by child-care legislation and asylum legislation. Whilst the former should predominate many child-care practitioners feel that such children are at the mercy of Home Office decisions. The DCSF (2007) supplementary guidance makes it very clear:

> The nationality or immigration status of the child does not affect agencies' statutory responsibilities under the 1989 or 2004 Children Acts. These issues should be addressed in discussion with the BIA **only when** the child's need for protection from harm has been addressed and should not hold up action to protect the child from harm (p.23).

Unfortunately, the tendency is for age disputes to take precedence over the needs of a child as a victim of trafficking which can significantly affect the level of support and safeguarding a trafficked child receives.

Recent research indicates that some trafficked children have been treated as adults for the purposes of asylum and some have been held in detention centres (Bhabha and Finch 2006; Crawley 2007). It is only through successful legal challenges that the true age of some of these children has been accepted and their right to local authority support has been recognised. The potential for child victims of trafficking to be mistaken for adults renders them extremely vulnerable in a number of ways. First, they will not receive the support and care that they are likely to need. Second, they may well go missing if they are dispersed as an adult asylum seeker and placed in inappropriate accommodation. Third, the stress of waiting for an asylum appeal can exacerbate any mental and physical health problems. Fourth, they may actually be returned to their country of origin as an adult where it is possible that they will be re-trafficked (Department for Children, Schools and Families 2007).

Age assessments

Currently, separated children are age assessed initially by immigration officers and then in some cases by social workers (Crawley 2007). It is a complex area of practice, made more difficult in the case of trafficked children by the fact that they are very unlikely to have any documents that prove their age. Under current legislation, children who are victims of trafficking are not automatically granted discretionary leave to remain until they are 18. Children who have been trafficked are treated like any other unaccompanied child and required to make an asylum claim.

The UK government has always maintained a distinct position on separated children which puts it at odds with most of Europe and causes daily practice tensions for those working with child victims of trafficking. First, the UK maintains its reservation on the UN Convention for the Rights of the Child on Immigration and Nationality (22), meaning that the right to protection for child victims of trafficking is not guaranteed (Bhabha and Finch 2006; Crawley 2007; Sillen and Beddoe 2007). Fortunately, the government has recently announced its intention to review the reservation. Second, the government has yet to ratify the Council of Europe Convention on Action against Trafficking of Human Beings, which sets out the basic standards of victim protection (Sillen and Beddoe 2007). It is expected that the UK government will ratify this Convention at the end of 2008. Third, the UK Border Agency does not have a statutory duty to safeguard children and promote their welfare as they are exempt from S11 of the Children Act 2004. In some areas immigration staff have been invited to sit on the local safeguarding children boards; however they are not mandatory partners (Bhabha and Finch 2006). Attempts are currently being made to strengthen the UK Borders' Agency responses to children through the *Code of Practice – Keeping Children Safe from Harm* (2008) which is out for consultation.

The net effect is confusion and frustration for practitioners as they try to manage and make plans for a child amidst these contradictory responses to victims of child trafficking. Fortunately there are a number of specialist agencies and resources that can be utilised by practitioners. Lists of agencies that can provide support and advice and electronic resources can be found at the end of the chapter:

TWO CASE STUDIES WITH POINTS FOR DISCUSSION

CASE STUDY 10.1: IDENTIFICATION

Aim: To consider whether or not Hung is a victim of child trafficking.

Instructions: Divide participants into groups of four and give them one role each, preferably on pre-prepared cards. Ask each participant to consider the information they have and to share it with the group. The group then needs to consider the questions below, making notes on a flip-chart with one person in the group being ready to feed back the group's thoughts.

Roles:
Police: You find Hung in a raid on a suburban property in a city in England. The property has been converted into a cannabis factory where there are 500 cannabis plants with an estimated street value of £250,000. Two adult Vietnamese men were arrested along with Hung on suspicion of possessing a controlled drug.

UK Border Agency: You have no record of Hung entering the country. Hung has no passport or documents to prove his identity.

Social Services: You have completed an Initial Assessment with an interpreter present. Hung has said very little except that a guardian brought him into the UK. You have placed Hung in temporary accommodation on a S17 basis and age assessed him as 17.

Refugee Council Children's Panel worker: You have supported Hung in claiming asylum and finding a solicitor. Engaging with him has been hard as he is very quiet and reluctant to speak. However, you are concerned as you have read a number of reports in the local press about Vietnamese children going missing.

Questions:
1. Is Hung a victim of child trafficking? Please identify what factors influenced your decision-making in this situation.
2. What support does Hung need?
3. Do any safeguarding measures need to be put into place?

CASE STUDY 10.2: SUPPORT

Aim: To consider what protection and support Grace might need.

Instructions: Break the group into smaller groups, preferably in fours, ask them to consider the information and answer the questions below. Prepare each group to feed back on at least one question.

Case study: Grace is found wandering the streets of a city centre late one night. Grace is extremely distressed, speaks very little English and appears disorientated as she does not know what country she is in. Grace is also heavily pregnant. Grace claims to be 15 but there is no supporting documentation and the midwife thinks she must be older than that. Grace is originally from Togo and speaks French. Grace is unable to account in full about what has happened to her in the last couple of years, although it becomes clear that she has been kept locked up in this country by a distant family member and forced to have sex with men on a daily basis.

Questions:

1. What steps should be taken to safeguard Grace?

2. What are Grace's immediate support needs?

3. How can you ascertain if Grace is at further risk?

4. Will Grace be allowed to remain in the UK?

5. What are Grace's longer term support needs?

CONCLUSION

Practitioners across the country must be alert to the possibility of child trafficking as evidence increasingly shows that trafficked children are found throughout the UK including in areas that do not have a large asylum seeking population (Beddoe 2007; Department for Children, Schools and Families 2007; Kapoor 2007). As with much child abuse, the indicators of child trafficking are rarely clear cut, therefore those that work with separated children must complete a full and holistic assessment of a child. Even without a disclosure from a child, aspects of their story may well cause suspicion and concern and these must always be acted on. Children who have been trafficked are extremely vulnerable; the majority go missing on a permanent basis after being identified by statutory services, therefore every safeguard should be put into place if there are concerns that a child may have been trafficked (Beddoe 2007; Department for Children, Schools and Families 2007; Kapoor 2007). There is no doubt that this is a complicated and challenging area of practice but maintaining a focus on the child's needs throughout is the key to developing a plan that both safeguards and promotes the welfare of a child victim of trafficking.

REFERENCES

Ayrio, D. (2006) 'Select Committee on Home Affairs, Examination of Witnesses (Questions 718–719).' Available at www.publications.parliament.uk/pa/cm200506/cmselect/cmhaff/775/6050908.htm, accessed 12 August 2008.

Beddoe, C. (2007) *Missing Out: A Study of Child Trafficking in the North-west, North-east and West Midlands.* London: ECPAT UK.

Bhabha, J. and Finch, N. (2006) *Seeking Asylum Alone in the UK.* Cambridge, MA: Harvard University. Available at www.humanrights.harvard.edu/conference/SAA_UK.pdf, accessed 12 August 2008.

Crawley, H. (2007) *When is a Child Not a Child? Asylum, Age Disputes and the Process of Age Assessment.* London: Immigration Law Practitioners Association.

Department for Children, Schools and Families (2006) *Working Together to Safeguard Children.* London: Stationery Office.

Department for Children, Schools and Families (2007) *Working Together to Safeguard Children – Safeguarding Children who May Have Been Trafficked.* London: Stationery Office. Available at http://publications.everychildmatters.gov.uk/default.aspx?PageFunction=productdetails&ProductId=HMG-00994-2007 &, accessed 12 December 2008.

Department of Health (2000) *Framework of the Assessment of Children in Need and Their Families.* Available at www.dh.gov.uk/en/Publicationsandstatistics/Publications/Publications PolicyAndGuidance/DH_4003256, accessed 12 December 2008.

Department of Health (2002) *Local Authority Circular (2002) 17: Children Missing from Care and from Home; Good Practice Guidance.* Available at www.dh.gov.uk/en/Publicationsandstatistics/Lettersandcirculars/LocalAuthorityCirculars/AllLocalAuthority/DH_4004872, accessed 12 August 2008.

Department of Health (2003) *Local Authority Circular (2003) 13: Guidance on Accommodating Children in Need and their Families.* Available at www.dh.gov.uk/en/Publicationsandstatistics/Lettersandcirculars/Localauthoritysocialservicesletters/DH_4003946, accessed 12 August 2008.

Dowling, S., Moreton, K. and Wright, L. (2007) 'Trafficking for the purposes of labour exploitation: A literature review.' Home Office online report, available at www.homeoffice.gov.uk/rds/pdfs07/rdsolr1007.pdf, accessed 12 August 2008.

Guardian (2007) 'Vanished: The child victims of trafficking.' 20 September. Available at www.guardian.co.uk/2007/sep/20/children.immigration, accessed 12 December 2008.

Home Office (2006a) 'Achieving Best Evidence in Criminal Proceedings: Guidance for Vulnerable or Intimidated Witnesses, including Children.' Available at www.homeoffice.gov.uk/documents/ach-bect-evidence, accessed 12 December 2008.

Home Office (2006b) 'Explanatory memorandum to the statement of changes in immigration rules laid on 23rd January 2006 (HC 819).' Available at www.ukba.homeoffice.gov.uk/sitecontent/documents/policyandlaw/statementsofchanges/2006/hc819.pdf?view=Binary, accessed 12 August 2008.

Independent (2007) 'Children trafficked from Asia to UK to work in cannabis factories.' 23 September. Available at news.independent.co.uk/uk/crime/article2990151.ece, accessed 12 August 2008.

Kapoor, A. (2007) *A Scoping Project on Child Trafficking in the UK.* London: CEOP.

Metropolitan Police Authority (2004) *A Partnership Study of Migration into the UK via London Heathrow.* Available at www.mpa.gov.uk/downloads/committees/ppr/ppr-040712-14-appendix01.pdf, accessed 18 August 2008.

Save the Children and UNHCR (2004) *Separated Children in Europe Programme Statement of Good Practice,* 3rd edn. Available at www.separated-children-europe-programme.org/separated_children/good_practice/index.html, accessed 12 August 2008.

Sillen, J. and Beddoe, C. (2007) *Rights Here, Rights Now.* London: UNICEF and ECPAT UK.

Somerset, C. (2001) *What the Professionals Know: The Trafficking of Children into and through the UK for Sexual Purposes.* London: ECPAT UK.

United Nations (2000) 'Protocol to Prevent, Suppress, and Punish Trafficking in Persons, Especially Women and Children, Supplementing the United Nations Convention on

Transnational Organised Crime.' Available at http://untreaty.un.org/English/TreatyEvent 2003/Texts/treaty2E.pdf, accessed 12 August 2008.

UNICEF 'End Child Trafficking'. Available at www.unicef.org.uk/campaigns/campaign_sub_ pages.asp?page=54, accessed 12 August 2008.

UK Border Agency 'Code of Practice for Keeping Children Safe from Harm – a Consultation'. Available at www.ukba.homeoffice.gov.uk/sitecontent/documents/aboutus/consultations/ keepingchildrensafe/, accessed 12 August 2008.

Zimmerman, C., Hossain, M., Yun, K., Roche, B., Morrison, L. and Watts, C. (2006) *Stolen Smiles: The Physical and Psychological Health Consequences of Women and Adolescents Trafficked into Europe*. London: London School of Hygiene and Tropical Medicine.

AGENCIES THAT CAN PROVIDE SUPPORT AND ADVICE[AQ]

AFRUCA – Africans Unite Against Child Abuse
Unit 3/DF Leroy House, 436 Essex Road, London, N1 3QP
020 7704 2261
www.afruca.org.uk
Online resources, training and drop in

ECPAT UK – End Child Prostitution, Child Pornography and Child Trafficking
35–37 Grosvenor House Gardens, Grosvenor Gardens, London, SW1W 0BS
020 7233 9887
www.ecpat.org.uk
UK's only specialist NGO on child trafficking; resources, information, campaigning and extensive training programme

NSPCC Child Trafficking Advice and Information Line
0800 107 7057
www.nspcc.org.uk
Advice line for any practitioner with any concerns about a child who may have been trafficked

Refugee Council Children's Panel
240–250 Ferndale Road, Brixton, London, SW9 8BB
Advice line: 0207 346 1134
www.refugeecouncil.org.uk
Works directly with separated and trafficked children, as well as giving advice to those involved in their support

UKHTC – UK Human Trafficking Centre
PO Box 4107, Sheffield, South Yorkshire, S1 9DQ
www.ukhtc.org.uk
Resources, training and victim care programme

ELECTRONIC RESOURCES

ATLeP – Anti-Trafficking Legal Project
www.ein.org.uk/resources/printfriendly2.shtml?x=227892
Information about legal practice on child trafficking in England and Wales

Crime Reduction Toolkits: Trafficking of People
www.crimereduction.homeoffice.gov.uk/toolkits/tp00.htm
A multi-agency resource with information and practical tools

CHAPTER 11

CRIMINAL INVESTIGATION AND SAFEGUARDING: DILEMMAS FOR POLICING

JEFF BOXER

PART 1: THE CHANGING CONTEXT OF CHILD ABUSE INVESTIGATION

Introduction

Protecting children and investigating child abuse can be difficult and challenging, not just because the subject is upsetting, but because good judgements are characteristically complex despite the existence of detailed guidance. Decisions about children's safety are tough and any uncertainty in one's judgement can provoke anxiety.

A child abuse investigation can entail many tough decisions, often presented as one dilemma after another, often in quick succession. The object of this chapter, therefore, is to provide an insight into how some of these dilemmas might be resolved with a degree of confidence, by examining a case study. However, to put these dilemmas into current context, the first part of this chapter will consider the importance of the police's law enforcement role before moving on to the case study in Part 2.

Frameworks and guidance

Child abuse as a social concept has evolved over time through changing experiences, attitudes and a series of key milestones. In their seminal study of fatal abuse, *Beyond Blame*, Reder, Duncan and Gray take a huge slice of time to illustrate the cyclical phenomenon they term the 'social construction of child abuse' (1993, pp.6–8) but we will focus on the last two decades from 1987. Since that time child protection processes have been moulded by guidance that has emerged from successive child abuse tragedies and reports from the public inquiries that examined them. The *Cleveland Inquiry Report* (Butler-Sloss 1988), the *Victoria Climbié Inquiry Report* (Laming 2003) and the *Bichard Inquiry Report* (Bichard 2004) gave rise to two Children Acts

(1989 and 2004); three editions of *Working Together* guidance (1991, 1999 and 2006) complete this evolving picture. Additionally, the changing criminal justice landscape has provided better access to the courts for victimised children and greater rigour and clarity around the capture of their testimony (Criminal Justice Acts 1988, 1992 and 2003; Youth Justice and Criminal Evidence Act 1999; *Memorandum of Good Practice* Home Office and Department of Health 1992 and *Achieving Best Evidence Guidance* 2002 and 2007 (Home Office 2002 and Criminal Justice Service 2007).

Thus a robust statutory and procedural framework developed that provided the platform for good inter-agency practice to become firmly established throughout the 1990s. It is not reassuring to find then, that despite this guidance and well established joint working framework, none of the key services were able to prevent the death of Victoria Climbié by the time she encountered the child protection establishment during the summer of 1999. As the chair of the Victoria Climbié inquiry, Lord Laming, stated; 'Having considered the response to Victoria from each of the agencies, I am forced to conclude that the principal failure to protect her was the result of widespread organisational malaise' (Laming 2003, p.4). To understand this malaise we will now examine some significant features of the inquiry, particularly those concerning agency roles.

Joint practice or blurred vision?

In the 1990s the widespread creation of specialist local 'child protection teams' (CPTs) provided the police focal point for the inter-agency arrangements and with responsibility for investigating and prosecuting identified abusers. *Working Together* (Department of Health 1991) describes this function as being 'to determine whether a criminal offence has been committed, to identify the person or persons responsible and to secure the best possible evidence in order that appropriate consideration can be given as to whether criminal proceedings should be instituted' (p.16).

Working practices, though, are often less to do with protocol and more to do with what becomes established over time by the workforce itself through familiarity. Arguably, this happened during the 1990s with police officers and social workers carrying out the same investigative tasks with the same intended outcome and with neither agency assuming responsibility for its own functions. Laming refers to this as a 'blurring' of roles (2003, p.306) with the uncertainty about what the police actually do being reinforced by some officers' perceptions that child protection policing and ordinary policing were different (p.318).

So, although joint *processes* may have improved, the developing collaborative *practices*, it is argued, masked a problem. The terminology used and the emphasis on 'joint' investigations encouraged a lack of demarcation between agency functions, a lack of responsibility for bespoke investigative activity and, significantly, a lack of *accountability* for particular decisions.

The term 'joint' investigation illustrates this. Broadly speaking, a local authority's section 47 (Children Act 1989) duty is to determine the likelihood of 'significant harm' and to try to effect change in a child's life for the better: the purpose of a police investigation is to establish whether criminal offences have been committed, to identify offenders and to gather evidence for prosecution if required. So there are potentially conflicting methodological features of a 'joint' investigation based on remedial *versus* disciplinary outcomes. For the former, information is gathered without constraint by rules of evidence so informed decisions about positive outcomes can be made. The burden of proof if the case gets to family court is the 'balance of probabilities'.

For the latter, material is gathered within the rules of evidence so it is tested in the criminal courts 'beyond reasonable doubt'; a burden of proof far harder to satisfy demanding a much tighter investigative approach. Police investigators might not appreciate the importance of this if they believe they are carrying out a 'joint section 47 investigation' alongside social work counterparts. The potential cost is a failure to gather evidence in a way that ensures its probative value is not lost, which does the investigation, and ultimately the child, a disservice.

So a 'joint' investigation is really two different inquiries carried out simultaneously. The 'joint' context simply relates to activity that takes place at the interface of each agency's functions: sharing information, decision-making and some tasks occurring at the same time, albeit for different purposes (e.g. joint visits or child forensic interviews).

Lastly, the Children Act's (1989) welfare principle ('the welfare of the child is paramount') is *the* critical influence on this 'joint' environment. A criminal investigation may initially be uncomfortable for a child but this does not mean it is not in the child's long-term interests. Identifying and prosecuting offenders can sometimes be the best way of ensuring remedial or beneficial outcomes; making decisions that criminal investigations are 'not in the child's interests' too early can, it is argued, have the opposite effect.

Specialist skills and status

The status, skills and experience of police CPT investigators was also an issue for the Victoria Climbié inquiry. The inquiry heard that serious crimes against children were often investigated by officers with no previous detective training (Laming 2003, p.311) and that child victims received less of a law enforcement service than adult victims in similar circumstances (p.298 and pp.305–6). One suggested cause was the way that CPTs were perceived by police officers generally. Some forces traditionally only recruited trained detectives to CPTs whilst others found it difficult to attract such officers. There was a, sadly, often expressed view that CPTs did not *really* investigate crime and that this was not real police work.

This derogatory view was not just held by non-CPT officers. Many CPT officers themselves, particularly some of those experienced staff who had helped shape inter-agency practice during the 1990s, were uncertain about their criminal investigation role (cf. 'blurring' of roles above). Whilst this assertion is largely anecdotal, it is supported by Lord Laming who comments on one officer's view 'that social services were the lead agency in the investigation of Victoria's case would appear to be reflective of a common view held by child protection officers in the [Metropolitan Police Service]' (2003, p.306).

As a result, the police reconsidered the remit, resourcing and skills of CPTs and undertook initiatives to raise both the investigative skill-base of CPTs and the perception of their investigative function.

- The 'CPT' label was dropped in favour of a designation reflecting the investigative role – 'child abuse investigation unit' (CAIU).

- The Association of Chief Police Officers (ACPO) published guidance emphasising the investigative function (ACPO/Centrex 2005a).

- The training programme issued by Centrex (the former Central Police Training and Development Authority) supporting the guidance focused on the investigation of abuse as a serious crime and stipulated a professional development route incorporating detective training. (Centrex 2006).

It is too early to assess any benefits from these initiatives as they are largely dependent upon the changing perceptions of both existing specialist officers and those who aspire to the role. Time will tell whether this cultural change has taken place.

Part 1 summary

Our first dilemma is about the police's safeguarding role. In part one, we have seen how collaborative child protection work evolved in the 1990s; largely, it must be said, to the benefit of thousands of children. We have seen how the 'joint' nature of the work tended to 'blur' agency roles affecting, detrimentally, the police's law enforcement response and the perception of the police function by others. Finally, we have touched on the police efforts to re-establish their investigative focus.

The changing context of police investigation is best summed up by reference to the way successive editions of *Working Together* describe it. *Working Together* (Department of Health 1991, p.16) refers to police investigation in terms of its potential lack of success, stating 'Failure to conduct child abuse investigations in the most effective manner may mean that the best possible protection cannot be provided for a child victim.' Ironically, just before Victoria Climbié died, *Working Together* (Department of Health, Home Office and Department for Education and Skills 1999) provided greater clarity on the investigative role by stating: 'The police have a *duty* and *responsibility* to investigate crimes committed against children and such investigations should be carried out sensitively, thoroughly and professionally' (p.23, emphasis added). Lastly, *Working Together to Safeguard Children* (Department for Education and Skills 2006) further reinforces investigation by stating 'The police are responsible for the gathering of evidence in criminal investigations. This task can be carried out in conjunction with other agencies, but the police are ultimately *accountable* for the product of criminal enquiries' (p.62, emphasis added).

So the police contribution is to provide a law enforcement response; the fact that each agency is responsible for its own aspect of the problem is arguably what *Working Together* is all about. If they are expected to perform their role in any other way (i.e. to simply support social services led inquiries under the Children Act), there is little point in them being at the inter-agency table.

PART 2: DECISIONS AND DILEMMAS – A CASE STUDY

Introduction

Part 2 loosely follows the initial stages of an individual case described by *Working Together to Safeguard Children* (Department for Education and Skills 2006, pp.142–146) and requires some work from you, the reader. You will be asked about your 'safeguarding' expectations of the police before going on to consider three successive case-study dilemmas.

Safeguarding and the police

Part 1 examined the current context and established the criminal investigation responsibility of specialist police units as a 'given'. In Part 2 we broaden our scope to the whole-force 'safeguarding' responsibility. The Every Child Matters (ECM) programme, the Government's response to the Victoria Climbié inquiry, describes five key outcomes, two of which relate specifically to the criminal justice services. These outcomes and the term 'safeguarding' suggest a wider policing response than just crime investigation and a greater range of activity than the established phrase 'child protection' did through the 1990s.

At one end of this range 'safeguarding' might mean the initial encounter with a child in adverse circumstances by a patrolling police officer or community support officer (PCSO) and the follow-on actions for ensuring the child's safety or meeting the child's needs. At the other end 'safeguarding' might be the deployment of resources on a massive scale over some years as part of a widespread investigation into child abuse images online (see numerous internet references and commentaries on Operations Ore and Landslide since 1999).

Finally, safeguarding also relates to the police's strategic position towards children in the round. This might include, for instance, setting specific 'safeguarding' priorities in a strategic policing plan; funding and resourcing for specialist units; reporting and investigating infrastructures; information sharing protocols; representation within multi-agency governance structures, etc.

Now consider the activity below in light of your knowledge of the police and the discussion within Part 1.

A reader activity

Think about the five ECM outcomes below. Jot down some key words about *your* expectations of the police safeguarding responsibility for the underlined Criminal Justice System outcomes.

The focus of agencies providing a service to children, including the police, should be to ensure that children have the support and opportunities they need to:

- be healthy
- stay safe
- enjoy and achieve
- make a positive contribution
- achieve economic wellbeing.

(Adapted from HM Government 2004, p.9
and Home Office 2004, p.1 *et seq.*)

As you read further you will examine three aspects of a case study: initial contact; referral and initial investigation; sharing information. Use your list of key words to guide your thinking on the case study.

This section has introduced the police safeguarding role. However, just because the police's ECM responsibilities stipulate *more* than just investigating crime, this does not mean that the 'law enforcement' functions discussed in Part 1 have any less significance to *Working Together*. In fact, it is the police's unique position as the principal law enforcement agency that enables their safeguarding role to be meaningful.

We will now begin the case study. The circumstances, police officers and other people referred to are fictitious; contrived so as to illustrate relevant points. The police actions described within the narrative are also contrived and do not necessarily represent typical policing responses.

Initial Contact
BACKGROUND

All public-facing police officers and staff sometimes encounter children in adverse situations but only a small proportion of these become subject of a child abuse investigation. From truants to runaways and from anti-social youths to children who witness domestic violence, all are children who require the police to consider the processes that might ultimately lead to a positive outcome. The initial police response is vital to the effectiveness of those processes. Now consider the activity below.

The bus station

Think about the following scenario and the ensuing dilemma.

Constable Green sees David, 14, 'hanging around' the bus station during the afternoon. She speaks to him and, somewhat anxiously, he says he was sent to the head teacher's office for misbehaving but has sneaked out of school because he will be in trouble with his father. PC Green suggests that she take him home to explain his worries to his parents but David becomes angry and frightened, pleading with her not to tell. He runs off, crying, before she can ask his full name and address but she knows which school he attends.

PC Green has a number of calls to attend before her shift ends. Although David is still a schoolboy, she thinks he is a typical difficult youth making too much of the situation. If she identifies him she will have to tell his parents and complete lots of forms; hardly worth the effort as he is only 'bunking off' school – she sometimes did that herself when younger. This is not really serious compared to the other things she has to do that day. Anyway, he is a big lad and resourceful enough to look after himself.

Review your list of key words about your expectations from the beginning of this section and consider the following:

- What do you expect PC Green to do?
- Who else needs to know about this?

DISCUSSION

PC Green's dilemma is whether the police should actually be involved at all. Her perspective is skewed due to poor understanding of her safeguarding responsibilities and a lack of investigative approach, albeit her suggestion to take him home seems sensible in the circumstances. She has a number of barriers preventing her taking further action and has some preconceptions of the incident based on her childhood experiences. Her view of David as a typically troublesome but resourceful teenager might be tainted by previous dealings with other youngsters in similar situations and her frame of reference affects her objectivity. In this way she minimises the true nature of the incident. This phenomenon, derived from personal experience, is known as 'the unconscious development of working rules' (ACPO/Centrex 2005b, pp.58–59) which leads, inevitably, to individual bias and faulty decision-making.

PC Green has gaps in her knowledge of the incident; for example, she does not know why David is fearful of his father. If she is to make an informed and objective decision she should adopt an investigative approach to fill those gaps. She will only be able to assess David's needs properly if she adopts an inquiring mind set and asks the right questions.

Reder and Duncan (1999, pp.142 and 145) suggest a 'dialectic mindset': a process that guides practitioners to consider information known, identify gaps in knowledge, ask relevant questions to seek further information, synthesise that information towards greater understanding and, finally, choose an appropriate professional response. This sounds like a complex method for dealing with something apparently straightforward but these are the very thought processes underpinning good police investigative practice.

Consider the 5WH questions that police officers learn to use during their initial training (what, when, where, who, why and how) and which are the basis of a 'state of mind' that defines all investigations. One must ask questions to establish what happened, when, where and how it happened, who was involved and, often the hardest, why it happened. Meaning is attributed to information obtained by assimilation – putting new information into context and alongside information already known. Completing this is the investigator's decision about the most appropriate course of action. This questioning approach reflects the dialectic mindset because it establishes the most rational way of responding to new, increased knowledge.

So PC Green needs an investigative mindset; not just for this incident but because it is a 'state of mind or attitude...developed over time through continued use' (ACPO/Centrex 2005b, p.60). This approach would have helped her place greater significance on David's anxiety about being in trouble with his father and would have opened up further lines of enquiry. Had she tactfully explored his feelings she would have understood his fear (see the next section) and possibly suggested an alternative short-term solution to taking him straight home.

Finally, PC Green is obliged to consider David's needs. Safeguarding children is not just the duty of specialist units; Part 2 of the Children Act 2004 applies to the duty of all police officers and staff to discharge their functions 'having regard to the need to safeguard and promote the welfare of children' (section 11 and *Working Together* (Department for Education and Skills 2006) p.61). PC Green has to consider, first, whether David is safe, and second, whether he has any needs that can be met by particular services. She should then pass that information on to someone best placed to deal with it.

A SOLUTION?

A possible solution to this dilemma relies on two things:

- The adoption of an investigative mindset by front-line police officers and staff so that informed, rationalised decisions are made at initial contact.

- The application of recognised safeguarding processes designed to promulgate the flow of information about children.

The former would have prompted PC Green to explore David's anxiety and gather further information from his school. This would help to establish his short-term safety and to determine if he had any other needs. The latter would have ensured she made a proper record of her encounter that could be passed to a specialist unit for further investigation and onwards referral to the appropriate agency if necessary.

Referral and the initial police investigation

BACKGROUND

The word 'referral' means different things to different police units but we will use the police guidance definition, that is, 'a communication between agencies which alerts the agency to concern for a child [in respect of that agency's functions]' (ACPO/Centrex 2005a, p.75).

Other agencies are expected to refer any suspected criminal offences to the police so they can consider their investigative function (Department for Education and Skills 2006, p.62). Note, though, that although the police must *record* all allegations they receive (ACPO/Home Office 2007) there is no absolute requirement to pursue each investigation to its ultimate conclusion. The extent of the investigation depends on the individual circumstances and on reasoned decisions about continuance, whether it was referred 'in' to the police or was referred 'out' to another agency having come directly to police notice – more on this later. Consider the activity below.

Referral 'out'

Our case study continues...another dilemma!

PC Green investigates a little deeper into David's circumstances so she can, first, ensure that urgent action is not required and, second, inform the child abuse investigation unit (CAIU) about her concerns. David's school provide his identity; they confirm he was sent to the head teacher for an unprovoked 'slapping' incident but never arrived and that his attendance is being monitored due to a recent truanting history. She also establishes that David has a six-year-old brother named Zack in the primary school next door. PC Green decides that urgent action is not required and so submits a 'notification' report to the CAIU.

The following morning the CAIU referral manager, Detective Sergeant Douglas, has a number of notifications to consider including PC Green's report. DS Douglas has arranged for a series of checks on these reports so he can assess whether they warrant police action or referral onwards.

Those checks reveal two calls for police to David's home about suspected domestic violence in the past six months. Both calls were made by a neighbour who believed the boys' father was assaulting their mother. Each time police officers attended the disturbance had abated and there was no evidence or complaint of assault, despite both parties being questioned separately. On the second occasion, three months ago, David's father was arrested but has not been charged with any offences. The children were not seen by the attending officers on either occasion.

Over 20 years ago, David's father was convicted for residential burglary and spent two months in a young offenders' institution. Last month he was charged with seriously assaulting another man outside a night club and three days ago he was arrested for driving his car whilst drunk. Neither of these matters has yet been to court.

DS Douglas telephones both schools. He is told that David is in his classroom but the school also reports that David came into school five weeks ago with two bruised eyes saying he was accidentally head-butted playing football at the weekend. The school is increasingly concerned about David's attendance and he seems more withdrawn and isolated lately.

Zack's school states that he has a good attendance record but his PE teacher noticed some bruising on his back and arms some weeks ago; Zack said he had fallen off his bicycle.

Finally, DS Douglas telephones the social work duty team to make a telephone referral but is unable to speak to a manager. He passes an outline referral to the duty clerk without sharing any significant information. He is uncertain about his next actions.

Once again, think about your list of key words and consider the following:

- Describe what you expect DS Douglas to do now?
- What is the extent of the police's ongoing role in this case?

DISCUSSION

This dilemma is about the extent of police involvement in a 'joint' investigation.

The school's information raises the level of concern but not to the extent that warrants immediate action as the children are at school and DS Douglas has time to think carefully about his response. As this discussion relates to the police *investigative* role we will accept DS Douglas' initial assessment that an urgent response (e.g. police protection) is not required at this point.

Safeguarding processes stipulate key decision points for individual cases (Department for Education and Skills 2006, p.123), however, in order to provide a rationale for those decisions it is often useful to take a problem-solving approach. The dangerous practice of making decisions 'by checklist' is *never* advocated but three simple generic questions help police supervisors make sense of existing information and which apply at each point where the police make a decision about their continued role in an investigation. Let us consider DS Douglas' methodology.

The first question establishes the nature of the referral: *Do these circumstances indicate a likelihood of significant harm?* To keep it simple we will not discuss the concept of 'significant harm' in detail here as we are more concerned with the importance of the threshold in determining the police role than the assessment of harm itself.

The information about the father's recent offending suggests current family stressors; together with David's increasing withdrawal at school, this indicates that the local authority would probably consider their section 17 duty (Children Act 1989) to undertake an assessment of need at the least. Such a matter would not require police involvement beyond referral. However, the father's recent violence and alcohol related offending, uncharacteristic recent bruising to both children – albeit explained to a degree – and the suspicion of domestic violence all combine to raise the concern towards the significant harm threshold.

We should make it clear that DS Douglas cannot answer this question unilaterally. Lord Laming was unequivocal in his recommendation for supervisory involvement in joint investigations where harm is suspected (2003, pp.303–304). DS Douglas must speak to his social services counterpart to help him confirm his concerns and identify factors he might have overlooked or attributed less significance to. Thus, a 'referral' is not simply one agency passing information to the other and expecting the other to get on with it, it is also the first strategy discussion where the first joint decisions are made. So, having decided to make a 'significant harm' as opposed to an 'in-need' referral, DS Douglas is bound to involve the social work manager in discussion to inform his decisions.

The second question goes to the heart of the police investigative function: *Is a criminal offence against a child alleged or (still) suspected?* This forces the third question onto the agenda: *What is the continuing extent of the police's criminal investigation?* If one could say, categorically (unusual at referral), that a criminal offence is *not* alleged or suspected then it is difficult to justify police collaboration beyond the initial assessment. For example: significant harm relating to chronically poor or inadequate parenting as opposed to *wilful* neglect would not be a criminal offence and would not require continued police involvement.

However, if a criminal offence is immediately clear or apparent after further enquiries the decision to continue with the police investigation will depend on a range of other factors such as the nature or gravity of the offence and its effect on the child, the probative value of facts available (or likely to become available), the welfare of the child, etc. Lastly, other agencies' views should be considered provided that *accountability* for decisions about criminal investigation rests with the police (Laming 2003, recommendation 99; Department for Education and Skills 2006, p.104).

It must be emphasised that these three questions apply equally throughout the investigation as at referral. If at any stage it becomes apparent that a better outcome for the child can be achieved from an intervention that does not involve criminal proceedings then it is the police's decision whether to discontinue (this does not mean 'terminate') the criminal investigation (Department for Education and Skills 2006, p.104). Note, though, that the too early use of the phrase 'not in the child's best interests' to justify discontinuing the criminal investigation may result in the loss of opportunities to secure vital evidence.

A SOLUTION?

A possible solution relies on key questions about identifying significant harm and criminal offences. In a linear fashion those questions and their responses are summarised below.

1.   *Do these circumstances indicate a potential for significant harm?*

     Yes – Refer to social services as a significant harm case and consider question 2 (as in our case study).

No – refer to social services as an in-need case and, generally, take no further action other than to share information.

2. *Is a criminal offence against a child alleged or (still) suspected?*

Yes – consider question 3 (as in our case study – potential assault).

No – generally take no further police action beyond initial assessment (unless urgent action is required regarding a child's safety).

3. *What is the continuing extent of the police's criminal investigation?*

Consider a range of other factors including but not limited to the nature and gravity of the offence; the effects upon the child; the probative value of available evidence, the welfare of the child; the views of other agencies; etc. All things considered, in our case study DS Douglas should allocate an investigating officer to make further enquiries and determine what evidence is available.

Finally, as the police are accountable for the criminal investigation, nothing in this method should prevent the police from acting quickly and unilaterally to preserve evidence where necessary.

Information sharing
BACKGROUND

Relevant information should always accompany referrals so the receiving agency can consider its responsibilities. Where the police decide that for the time being they have no investigative role, they are still required to contemplate sharing information on an ongoing basis. Consider the activity below.

Request for information

Yet another dilemma!

Ms Joyce, the social services manager, calls DS Douglas. He makes a verbal 'significant harm' referral and states his intention to allocate an investigator. Ms Joyce asks for a full, written, breakdown of all police information on all family members to help her make an initial assessment.

Once more, think about your list of key words and consider the following questions.

- Describe what you expect DS Douglas to do now?

- Explain how much information DS Douglas should supply to Ms Joyce and why?

DISCUSSION

This dilemma is about the amount of information shared with social services. Nowadays society and individuals are more aware of their rights to privacy than ever before. Two Data Protection Acts (1984 and 1998) and the Human Rights Act 1998 have engendered a culture of extreme caution, even fear, about disclosing personal information. As Sir Michael Bichard states 'It is evident that police officers were nervous about breaching the legislation' (Bichard 2004, p.4). In 2006, in response to the Bichard Inquiry, the government issued inter-departmental guidance – the *Information Sharing: Practitioner's Guide* (HM Government 2006) – as part of the ECM programme.

The open sharing of information across agency boundaries and the help in its interpretation given by the agency having provenance over it gives strength and effect to 'working together'. Information management lies at the heart of safeguarding processes and is supported by some key concepts: lawful authority, proportionality, relevance and accountability. We will now examine these.

'Lawful authority' has its roots in ethics and human rights. The police have certain obligations to fulfil in preserving rights conferred by the 'European Convention on Human Rights' (ECHR, through the 'Human Rights Act' 1998). The well cited European Court's 'Osman' ruling (*Osman* v. *UK* [2000] 29 EHRR 245) provides a positive obligation to take all reasonable steps to safeguard life (Article 2). The case of Z (*Z and others* v. *UK* [2001] 34 EHRR 97), a child neglect case, provides the mandate to prevent torture and inhuman and degrading treatment (Article 3) in a private setting. The right to respect for private and family life (Article 8) includes recognition of the right to a childhood and the development of that childhood (Drew 2000, p.31). Lastly, the 'United Nations Convention on the Rights of the Child' (United Nations General Assembly 1989) emphasises a child's inherent right to life and the state's duty to ensure a child survives and develops to the maximum possible extent, a duty fulfilled by the provision of services that support ECM.

The authority in law has two principal aspects. Sections 10 and 11 of the Children Act 2004 require local authorities and their partners to develop and co-operate with safeguarding arrangements including information exchange. Section 115 of the 'Crime and Disorder Act' 1998 allows the disclosure of information to relevant authorities for the purpose of preventing and reducing crime or apprehending offenders.

We should also consider 'proportionality'. The proportionality principle is inherent in the police's common law duty of confidence, the Data Protection Acts and the Article 8 right to privacy and underpins the lawful management of police information. This is not just about the amount of information shared; it is primarily about balancing the protection of individual rights with the interests of the wider community. In other words, would the benefit of disclosing a piece of information outweigh the possible harm caused by its disclosure? (HM Government 2006, p.9). Any interference with individual rights must be proportionate to the legitimate aim and policing purpose being pursued and should not go beyond what is strictly necessary to achieve that purpose, particularly if the police consider sharing personal information without the subject's consent, ostensibly breaching their common law duty of confidence.

Next, we consider 'relevance'; important because it requires the police to look at information on an individual, ongoing, case-by-case basis guiding 'proportionality' decisions at a given point in time. So, what is not relevant today might be relevant tomorrow. For instance, it might not be relevant that a child's parent was suspected of receiving stolen goods if *today's* allegation is neglect. If the social worker discovers *tomorrow* that frequent callers to the home suggest a chaotic lifestyle, then the relevance of the police information is worthy of further exploration.

Finally, we consider 'accountability'. We stated earlier that, historically, police officers worked in a culture of caution, uncertain about the legality of information sharing practices. Nowadays, though, the police are used to recording decisions and the reasons for making them. Rather than being an additional administrative burden, this auditable decision making process enables officers to have confidence in those decisions demonstrating accountability and integrity. Thus, investigators can be comforted to know they have considered lawful authority, proportionality and relevance and have documented their thought processes in a way that stands up to scrutiny.

We can now look at a practical template based on these concepts and apply it to our case study.

A SOLUTION?

Our template is in two stages: assessing the information (relevance) and assessing the need to share it (proportionality). Auditable record keeping (as above) is a 'given' for this exercise.

DS Douglas' first task is to consider the information and its 'relevance'; does it currently have a bearing on the investigation? He should also consider whether it is factual (or sustainable by other facts) and whether it is accurate and up to date. DS Douglas has a number of pieces of information, not all of which are relevant or up to date. Our subject's time in a Young Offenders' Institution over 20 years ago for burglary does not seem relevant at the moment and would not be disclosed. However, apart from the initial information that constitutes the referral itself, there is some additional relevant information about the boys' father and home life. Clearly, the domestic violence reports and the facts surrounding the father's arrest are relevant – this is one of the reasons for the 'significant harm' referral. The arrest for a serious assault is also relevant because it is suggestive of a propensity to violence. The arrest for drink-driving is also relevant because it suggests potential recent stressors within the family as well as the use of alcohol, an aggravating feature. We know these facts are accurate because they emanate from police arrest records where the identity of the arrested person would have been confirmed. Lastly, the information is timely as it relates to recent incidents.

DS Douglas' second consideration is the need to share the information and 'proportionality': does the need to share this information (the public interest) outweigh the rights of the subject and if so, how much can he share and with whom? It is safe to say that *all* this information will be valuable in helping to assess the likelihood of significant harm because it has more meaning when viewed as a 'gestalt'. However, in relation to the domestic violence incidents, it is not clear whether the father knows the identity of the neighbour who originally called the police and until the police are sure there are no extraneous safety issues, care must be taken not to unintentionally reveal the caller's identity.

The *Information Sharing: Practitioner's Guide* (HM Government 2006) has a well crafted flow chart that takes a linear approach to sharing information which ought to be followed as the current, definitive guide.

Part 2 summary

Part 2 asked you, the reader, to do some thinking. Taking into account the ECM outcomes you considered your expectations of the police for three case study dilemmas in succession.

The first, uncertainty about what to do following initial contact, was resolved by suggesting the patrol officer adopt an investigative mindset and apply correct 'notification' procedures for alerting relevant people about the children.

The second, ambiguity about the nature and extent of police involvement in a 'joint' investigation, was resolved by suggesting that the police referral manager ask a series of key questions about significant harm, the suspicion or allegation of crime and the necessity for pursuing the investigation.

The third dilemma, the ever-present worry about the extent of information exchange, was resolved by suggesting that the referral manager consider a two-stage test based on the relevance of the information and the extent to which it should be shared.

This is only a snapshot of the initial stages of a typical case seen daily by specialist child abuse investigation units and the dilemmas reflect those occurring throughout an investigation's life-cycle. Despite some solutions being proposed there is no 'one-size-fits-all' template to cover every eventuality. As the start of this chapter alluded to, all the guidance in the world cannot bring about good judgements; that comes through experience and knowledge of what investigating child abuse is all about. More importantly there is no substitute for an enquiring mind and sound detective work, at least to the same standard that one would expect if the victim were an adult. As Laming recommends, 'Chief constables must ensure that the investigation of crime against children is as important as the investigation of any other form of serious crime. Any suggestion that child protection policing is of a lower status than other forms of policing must be eradicated' (2003, p.311).

REFERENCES

ACPO/Centrex (2005a) *Guidance on Investigating Child Abuse and Safeguarding Children*. Bramshill: Centrex.

ACPO/Centrex (2005b) *Practice Advice on Core Investigative Doctrine*. Bramshill: Centrex.

ACPO/Home Office (2007) *National Crime Recording Standards*. London: Home Office. Available at www.homeoffice.gov.uk/rds/countrules.html, accessed 13 August 2008.

Bichard, M. (2004) *The Bichard Inquiry Report*. London: Stationery Office. Available at www.homeoffice.gov.uk/pdf/bichard_report.pdf, accessed 13 August 2008.

Butler-Sloss, E. (1988) *Report of the Inquiry into Child Abuse in Cleveland 1987*. London: HMSO.

Centrex (2006) *The Specialist Child Abuse Investigator's Development Programme*. Bramshill: Centrex.

Criminal Justice System (2007) *Achieving Best Evidence in Criminal Proceedings: Guidance on Interviewing Victims and Witnesses, and Using Special Measures*. London: Criminal Jusrtice System.

Department for Education and Skills (2006) *Working Together to Safeguard Children: A Guide to Inter-agency Working to Safeguard and Promote the Welfare of Children*. London: Stationery Office.

Department of Health (1991) *Working Together under the Children Act 1989: A Guide to Arrangements for Inter-agency Co-operation for the Protection of Children from Abuse*. London: HMSO.

Department of Health (2000) *Framework for the Assessment of Children in Need and their Families*. London: Stationery Office.

Department of Health, Home Office, Department for Education and Skills (1999) *Working Together to Safeguard Children: A Guide to Inter-agency Working to Safeguard and Promote the Welfare of Children*. London: Stationery Office.

Drew, S. (2000) *Children and the Human Rights Act*. London: Save the Children.

HM Government (2004) *Every Child Matters: Change for Children*. Nottingham: DfES Publications.

HM Government (2006) *Information Sharing: Practitioner's Guide*. Nottingham: DfES Publications.

Home Office (2002) *Achieving Best Evidence in Criminal Proceedings: Guidance for Vulnerable or Intimidated Witnesses, Including Children*. London: Home Office.

Home Office (2004) *Every Child Matters: Change for Children in the Criminal Justice System*. Nottingham: DfES Publications.

Home Office and Department of Health (1992) *Memorandum of Good Practice on Video Recorded Interviews with Child Witnesses for Criminal Proceedings*. London: HMSO.

Laming, H. (2003) *The Victoria Climbié Inquiry: A Report of an Inquiry by Lord Laming*. London: HMSO.

Reder, P., Duncan, S. and Gray, M. (1993) *Beyond Blame: Child Abuse Tragedies Revisited*. London: Routledge.

Reder, P. and Duncan, S. (1999) *Lost Innocents: A Follow Up Study of Fatal Child Abuse*. London: Routledge.

United Nations General Assembly (1989) *Convention on the Rights of the Child*. Available at www.everychildmatters.gov.uk/strategy/uncrc/articles/, accessed 13 August 2008.

USEFUL WEBSITES

www.everychildmatters.gov.uk

http://police.homeoffice.gov.uk/publications/operational-policing/bichard-inquiry-report, accessed 5 December 2008.

http://www.homeoffice.gov.uk/rds/countrules.html

www.victoria-climbie-inquiry.org.uk

CHAPTER 12

GOOD PRACTICE IN UNDERTAKING SOCIAL WORK ASSESSMENTS

ROSIE JAKOB

INTRODUCTION

Assessments are an integral part of practice for any professional working with children. For those working in the safeguarding arena they are essential. An assessment can be a one-off visit or can involve a series of structured meetings. A professional will begin making assessments from the moment they become aware of a situation, be it through an initial meeting or reading through a referral. Good practice in undertaking social work assessments involves building on the information they have and taking into account all the contributory factors. It involves gathering information from a variety of sources and combining that information with their professional knowledge and the use of a number of tools, as well as taking into account up to date research.

Assessment is important in ensuring that professionals are making informed decisions about the needs and safety of children. Professionals working in safeguarding can make life changing judgements about children and their families. It is important, therefore, that such decisions are supported by evidence. An assessment is the most effective way of gathering evidence and assisting in making such decisions. If done well it can offer clarity of thought and reassurance for the worker that their recommendations are validated.

Following *Child Protection Messages From Research* (Department of Health 1995) there was a refocusing of children's services towards meeting the resources required for children in need and of social workers becoming more holistic in their assessments. Alongside this was a recognition that other professionals, such as health visitors and teachers, often hold significant information about children and should be more involved in any process of assessment. The result was the current guidance for professionals, *Framework for the Assessment of Children in Need and their Families* (Department of Health 2000). This is known as the 'Lilac Book' because of its cover. This guidance seeks to have a more 'ecological' approach to assessment, and includes an exploration of three specific domains: parenting capacity, child developmental needs and environmental factors (p.17). The domains are set out in the shape of a triangle and this is known as the Assessment Framework.

REQUIRED ASSESSMENTS BY THE LOCAL AUTHORITY SOCIAL WORKER

Within this guidance, a structure is laid out for the process of assessments, including timescales. The guidance reinforces the critical factor of time in a child's life.

A timely response to responding to a child's needs means that the process of assessment cannot continue unchecked over a prolonged period without an analysis being made of what is happening and what action is needed, however difficult or complex the child's circumstances (Department of Health 2000, para. 3.7).

The guidance begins by making clear that a decision about the need for further action is to be made within one working day of information being received. Any decision to gather more information is described as an *initial assessment* (Department of Health 2000, para 3.9).

An initial assessment must be completed within seven working days. It is a brief assessment by social services of each child included in the referral. This is often a highly sensitive piece of work where the family may be feeling particularly agitated and distressed. It is essential, therefore, that such an assessment is conducted sensitively and that every attempt is made to form a positive working relationship with the family. Being open and honest about the procedure can aid this relationship and begin to develop a trusting partnership between worker and family member.

The assessment is based on the Assessment Framework dimensions. It must involve seeing the child(ren) and talking to the child, if of an appropriate age and understanding. It can involve interviews with family members and talking to other agencies. An initial assessment can be very brief where there is deemed to be no need for any further action, or it is obvious the child is suffering significant harm, or it can require the full seven days of information gathering. At the end of an initial assessment a decision must be made about whether there is a need for further action. This could be a referral on to an appropriate agency or it could be a decision to continue social services involvement and complete a *core assessment* (Department of Health 2000, para 3.11).

A core assessment is expected to be completed in 35 working days, or seven weeks. It is an in-depth assessment which 'addresses the central or most important aspects of the needs of a child and the capacity of his or her parents or caregivers to respond appropriately to these needs' (Department of Health 2000, para 3.11). The core assessment usually begins when the initial assessment ends, when a S47 enquiry is begun, or when new information has emerged. A S47 enquiry is made under S47 of the Children Act 1989, where there is a concern that a child may be at risk of or is likely to suffer significant harm. If care proceedings have been initiated, specialist assessments may well have been commissioned by social services or other parties. In this circumstance it is accepted that a core assessment cannot be completed until these specialist assessments have been received and analysed, therefore going over the 35-day guidance.

CHILD IN NEED AND/OR IN NEED OF SAFEGUARDING

The Assessment Framework very clearly brought back into focus the aspects of S27, Part 111 of the Children Act 1989 relating to children in need. A child in need is defined by the Act:

a. He is unlikely to achieve or maintain or to have the opportunity of achieving or maintaining, a reasonable standard of health or development without the provision for him of services by a local authority.

b. His health or development is likely to be significantly impaired, or further impaired, without the provision for him of such services; or

c. He is disabled. (Children Act 1989, S17 (10))

This refocusing of services led to many local authorities developing policies for *children in need forums* in addition to *child protection case conferences*. The decision about which route is the most appropriate can be made at different stages of an assessment process, and can change if circumstances within the family change. There may, for example, be a decision that a child should become the subject of a child protection plan initially but later to deregister the child and move the support to a child in need forum. Assessment, therefore, is organic and professional approaches need to be flexible and open-minded if clear judgements are to be made.

Children who are in need of safeguarding because they are suffering or likely to suffer significant harm fall under S47 of the Children Act 1989. S47 makes it clear that where there is such a concern, a local authority has an obligation to consider initiating enquiries to find out what is happening to that child:

Where a local authority –

a. are informed that a child who lives, or is found in their area –

    i   is the subject of an emergency protection order; or

    ii is in police protection; or

b. have reasonable cause to suspect that a child who lives, or is found in their area is suffering, or is likely to suffer, significant harm,

the authority shall make, or cause to be made, such enquiries as they consider necessary to enable them to decide whether they should take any action to safeguard or promote the child's welfare. (Children Act 1989 S 47(1))

Assessment can play a crucial role in deciding whether safeguarding is a factor in considering the needs of a child. Although the Assessment Framework is a useful guide to considering the many aspects of the dynamics of a family, it is very important to note that it does not consider risk specifically. The Assessment Framework does provide a selection of tools that can be used when gathering information, including a Family Pack of Questionnaires and Scales (Cox and Bentovim 2000). It is important though, that practitioners have other assessment tools to draw upon when assessing risk and making an analysis of a family's strengths and difficulties.

CASE STUDY 12.1: ASSESSING RISK

This exercise is designed to stimulate discussion about how we assess risk and what resources we can draw upon to help us analyse a situation.

Marcus is a five-year-old boy with cerebral palsy. He is wheelchair dependent and struggles with his fine motor skills. He has just started part time at mainstream school. Marcus has medication to help him control his involuntary movements but health professionals have expressed concern that his parents are over-medicating him. His teacher has noticed that Marcus often nods off in class and finds it difficult to concentrate. She has spoken to the parents about Marcus's sleepiness but they appear unconcerned. His parents often talk about him negatively in front of him and are desperate for his educational statement of special needs to come through so that he can attend school full time. Recently Marcus has started to shout out in class and ignore the teacher. She has a policy of placing naughty children on a carpet square for five minutes. The teacher has had to do this with Marcus. Whilst lifting him today, however, she has noticed that he has bruising all along his back. The teacher has expressed her concern to the named child protection teacher who has taken the decision to contact social services.

Factors to consider

- What information would be useful in assessing the risk to Marcus?

- Where can the information be obtained?

- What knowledge will you draw on?

- Is there research that will be of value?

- Can you use specific tools to assist your analysis?

Further questions:

- What do you consider to be the most significant features of concern in this situation?

- What would be the most appropriate course of action?

- What are the disadvantages/advantages of each course of action?

USING THE FRAMEWORK FOR ASSESSMENT

Figure 12.1 Framework for Assessment (Department of Health 2000, p.17)

As Figure 12.1 illustrates, the Framework considers three significant aspects of a child's life which need to be balanced in order that the best outcome is identified to safeguard and promote the child's welfare. These are described as domains within the guidance and cover:

- child's developmental needs

- parenting capacity

- family and environmental factors.

The areas to be considered in an assessment are quite comprehensive and, if completed thoroughly, can give a good basis for forming judgements and making decisions. The essential principles underpinning the Framework are that it:

- is child-centred

- is rooted in child development

- is ecological in approach

- ensures equality of opportunity

- involves working with children and families

- builds on strengths as well as identifies difficulties

- is inter-agency in approach to assessment and provision of services

- is a continuing process, not a single event

- is carried out in parallel with other action and providing services

- is grounded in evidence-based knowledge. (Department of Health 2000, para 1.33).

One of the key messages from the guidance is that assessment is not an isolated process. The inclusion of other agencies and of the family is essential for good practice. Alongside this is the recognition that services need to be put in place as an assessment progresses. It is not helpful to make an assessment of a family without offering any intermediate support. In fact it may well be detrimental to the child to be left in a situation where no services are being provided.

CASE STUDY 12.2: USING THE FRAMEWORK

Tim and Andrea are both white, aged 17. They have been together for three years and have one child, Marty. When Marty was six weeks old he sustained a broken arm. At the time of the injury the couple were living with Tim's dad and his wife. Also in the house were Tim's three younger siblings, aged 14, seven and five. The house has three bedrooms and so Tim and Andrea have been sleeping in the front room with Marty. They live in a predominately white inner city estate. They are claiming benefits. During the initial assessment the couple were not able to give an acceptable explanation for the injury to Marty and Marty has been placed in foster care under an Interim Care Order. A core assessment has begun.

During the course of the core assessment certain services have been put in place:

- The parents are being offered contact six days a week, both at a contact centre and in the foster carer's home.

- A parenting course has been identified for both parents.

- A referral has been made to the teenage parent service.

After the core assessment
It is discovered from the assessment that:

Child's developmental needs:

- The health visitor was not concerned about Marty's health prior to his injury. He was developing well and putting on weight. He was being bottle fed. The health visitor did comment that Marty was the focus of all of the family members and often the younger children's friends would want to hold him. He was very much loved and fussed over in the home. At times she had felt that Marty was not getting enough rest.

- Marty was recovering from his broken arm quickly. He did not appear to be in too much discomfort. On week four of the assessment, his cast was removed. He did require some simple physio exercises which had been shown to the foster carers and the parents.

- The paediatrician was clear that Marty would have cried out in pain when the injury occurred.

Parenting capacity:

- Both parents were very warm and affectionate with Marty. They gave him lots of cuddles and often praised him. It was noted however, that when Andrea held Marty, she was a little awkward and tended to be quite rough with him. This had been pointed out to her in contact but little had changed in her handling of him.

- The parents were competent at preparing bottles and at sterilising the bottles, although Tim tended to do this most of the time. Tim often did the feeding. He would offer Andrea the opportunity but she would refuse. Tim also liked to bathe Marty whilst Andrea's lack of confidence held her back.

- The parents tended to argue with each other over minor issues. They tended to forget Marty was there with them at times when they were engrossed in point scoring. Tim was often preoccupied with how Andrea behaved in front of other men and what she was wearing.

- Both parents are deeply concerned about Marty's injury. They have made a number of suggestions about how he broke his arm, none of which have been accepted by the medics. In week seven of the assessment, Tim says that he may have picked up Marty by the arm when he was crying at night. The medics say that this could possibly account for Marty's broken arm. Further exploration reveals that Tim was doing all the night time feeds and was exhausted. Andrea has said that she has difficulty waking up at night time.

Family and environmental factors:

- Andrea was estranged from her family, who lived in another town. She had had a difficult early life and disclosed during the assessment that she had been sexually abused by a cousin who was ten years older than her. She had told her mother who did not believe her.

- Tim's dad and his wife were viewed as a significant support by the couple. They had a good relationship with them but wanted to prove that they could parent Marty without grandparents' interference. Tim's dad and his wife both work shifts. When they are both out Tim was expected to look after his younger siblings. He felt quite resentful of this when Marty was born but felt obliged because he was living in their house rent free.

- Tim's mum lived on the other side of town. She appeared to be genuinely concerned for her son and his family. She offered to care for Marty if he did not return to the couple's care but would have preferred to offer them support.

Questions:

- The core assessment revealed a number of strengths with this young couple, as well as a number of difficulties – what were they?

- Using the assessment to inform the planning, what would need to be done to ensure Marty's safe return to his parents?

- Is this a viable option?

- What are the alternatives?

GATHERING EVIDENCE

The Assessment Framework makes clear how important evidence is in making any assessment: 'The combination of evidence based practice grounded in knowledge with finely balanced professional judgement is the foundation for effective practice with children and families' (Department of Health 2000, para 1.59).

Evidence can be gathered in a variety of ways:

- agency records

- other professionals

- observation

- interviews

- research

- the use of theory and theoretical models/tools.

1. Agency records

Agency records can include huge amounts of useful information about a family. If the family has been known to children's social care then there will be documentation. It is worth going through all of this if possible. It may involve travelling from one area of the country to another if the family has moved about. Not only can it give a historical context to the family dynamics, it can also provide the worker with a better understanding of the family's experience of services. Using systems theory (see Howe 1987, p.21), this can give ideas as to why, for example, there may be some resistance from family members. The worker can then empathise with the family members and be able to approach their relationship with the family sensitively, offering an alternative, more positive experience of the service.

Agency records can often be forgotten when a family has been previously assessed. Workers may tend to rely on the most recent assessment completed to base their actions on and the questions asked. Although time consuming, it is always important to read all the information available to the worker. Without this thorough approach mistakes can be made and children can be placed in dangerous situations.

It is also important to access the records of other agencies who have been involved if at all possible. These can include health records, education, probation, youth justice and police. If at all possible best practice is to gain the consent of the individual concerned to access confidential information. If the assessment relates specifically to a child who may be suffering or at risk of suffering significant harm, then it is likely to be in the public interest to share this information even if consent from the parent or carer has not been obtained. There are times when seeking consent is likely to further endanger a child and consideration must be given to this beforehand. S10 and S11 of the Children Act 2004 place a duty on a number of agencies to co-operate with each other regarding the improvement of children's wellbeing and to make arrangements to ensure that there are clear agency guidelines regarding the sharing of information. *Working Together to Safeguard Children* (Department for Education and Skills 2006a) explains how agencies should work together. The Government has produced *Information Sharing: Practitioner's Guide* (Department for Education and Skills 2006b) which can help professionals who are unsure about when to share information. There is also a useful website which explains the law regarding information sharing at www.ecm.gov.uk/informationsharing (Department for Education and Skills 2006c).

2. Other professionals

As well as gathering information through written records, it is important to speak to the people who are working with the family if at all possible. Often, further information that is not written down can be obtained through these discussions. The observations of a teacher, for example, on how a child behaves before and after contact may well be essential to an assessment but not recorded anywhere.

3. Observation

Observation can be critical to understanding how a child is functioning. It can give clues about the child's developmental stage but also regarding their integration with others. Observing contact between the child and other family members can assist in the assessment process. It can also be useful to observe a child at school or nursery. Such an approach is child centred and reminds us of the reason for the assessment. Observation skills are often under-used and it is important to keep accurate records of what has been observed to refer to later.

4. Interviews

Interviewing family members is one of the main aspects of assessment. It is through the interview process that a relationship is built between the professional and the family member. If we are able to use our skills in communication and rapport building, the interview process can in itself be an enlightening experience for families. The exploration of often difficult and painful backgrounds requires a heightened sensitivity and a willingness to go at the interviewee's pace. If the assessment involves issues of safeguarding, such interviews may include revisiting possible harm that the child may have suffered or is likely to suffer. There is likely to be a need to challenge some of the individual's perceptions. If there is a willingness to examine the issues then the assessment process can be experienced as therapeutic for the family (although this is obviously not its primary function) and may lead to positive changes being made. As in all interactions, it is always necessary to record what is being said.

Direct work with children is another style of interviewing. If a child is able to engage in direct work, this can be a very productive element of the assessment. Again it ensures that our practice is child centred and offers an opportunity to get to know the child far better. Direct work can involve a number of different techniques such as playing, life story work, drawing, etc. (see Shah and Argent 2006). With some children the use of interactive computer programmes can help and may be a familiar activity to them (see Calam *et al.* 2007).

5. Research

Research can play a key role in supporting assessment decisions and subsequent planning. New research is always being produced and can be particularly helpful when decisions are finely balanced. Although practitioners often struggle to find time to keep up to date with recent developments it can be useful to explain why certain judgements are being made. This is particularly beneficial when the assessment is being completed as part of care proceedings. The use of established research such as *Children's Needs – Parenting Capacity – The Impact of Parental Mental Illness, Problem Alcohol and Drug Use, and Domestic Violence on Children's Development* (Cleaver, Unell and Aldgate 1999) can be very helpful with regard to ideas about interventions and the analysis of the information gathered. The research produced by Sturge and Glaser (2000) regarding domestic violence is very useful when considering the impact of domestic violence on children.

6. Theory and theoretical models/tools

Theory underpins professional practice in safeguarding on a daily basis. It is often said to be an area in which professionals lack confidence or understanding as to how those theories are used in practice. If the professional steps back however, it can support them in analysing information and making sound judgements. When observing family interactions for example, professional knowledge of attachment theory (Bowlby 1982) is essential. In interviews with family members professionals may be using a client-centred approach – workers may draw on theories of psychodynamics to interpret the effects of a person's upbringing on their current behaviour (Freud 1923). Professionals may make use of theories of loss and bereavement (Kübler-Ross 1969) or task-centred models (Reid 1972). Whatever approach taken, there is a theory that is being worked from. The use of theories helps professionals to understand and interpret different behaviour and information. It can provide evidence for the way in which assessment material is analysed.

There are numerous tools that have been developed to help workers make practical use of theory and to order information systematically. The use of attachment checklists provided by Fahlberg (1994) can be useful in analysing the behaviour of children of all ages. Howe *et al.* has also produced a clear and comprehensive guide to different styles of attachment and the behaviours that may be found (1999). Prochaska and DiClemente's 'Comprehensive model of change' (1982) has proved a very useful model for assessing motivation, particularly with regard to drug and alcohol users. Calder *et al.* (2000) provide a number of theoretically based tools for assessing different types of sexual abusers. The 'Signs of safety' model developed by Turnell and Edwards (1999) is a particularly helpful way to approach the information gathered, looking specifically for solutions rather than problems.

CASE STUDY 12.3

A mother of two children has schizophrenia. The children are ten and seven. The children have a positive view of both parents. Their father has recently left the family home. The children have been exposed to domestic violence between their parents over a number of years. When their mother is well, they enjoy a positive relationship with her. When she becomes ill she becomes neglectful of their basic needs and can become harsh and negative towards them. The children have usually turned to their grandparents when this has occurred as their father's excessive use of cannabis has led to him being unresponsive and preoccupied. The oldest child often refuses to go to school and can become aggressive. She is described as emotionally immature. The younger child cries often and is clingy to adults.

In considering this scenario, one could use *Children's Needs – Parenting Capacity* (Cleaver *et al*. 1999) pages 40–41 and 45–46 to evaluate the strengths of this family and the difficulties.

Strengths: Positive relationship with both parents; separation of parents has led to an end to domestic violence; supportive grandparents.

Difficulties: Long-term exposure to domestic violence; unpredictable nature of mental illness; children do not appear particularly resilient; possible insecure attachment.

Decision-making in assessment is rarely easy or straightforward, particularly where children require protection. Although the suggested tools can be used to assist in making a decision, professional judgement also involves the use of their own and others' experience in practice. It will contribute to the decisions about what weight should be given to different pieces of information. It is crucial that regular supervision is provided to all practitioners. When undertaking an assessment the supervisor is more detached from the family dynamics and is therefore in a position to see things that the practitioner may have lost sight of. Again this provides a further check in the assessment process and the efforts made to make the correct decision for a child.

WORKING WITH RESISTANCE

We are all likely to have some level of professional involvement in our lives, be it our children's teachers on parents' evening or the need to visit our GP. An assessment, however, will be far more intrusive, with professionals often questioning a family's whole way of functioning. Alongside this, it will often be happening at a particularly stressful point in that family's life. As such, workers may not be welcomed with open arms by family members and there may well be a degree of resistance.

Cleaver and Freeman (1995) examined the reasons why people may be unwilling to co-operate with professionals when there is a suspicion of child abuse. Some of the factors were as follows:

- Lack of trust – this may well be related to past experiences of services, possibly a parent having been in care themselves.

- Lack of choice – it may be that the family members are undergoing an assessment through the court process and therefore feel that they are left with no option.

- Rights not being respected – family members may feel that their privacy is being invaded (which it is) and/or that their right to bring up a child the way they want to is being disrespected. Balancing the welfare of the child (who is the worker's client) with the rights of parents and caregivers is often challenging.

- High level of intensity – assessments can be very intense and workers attempt to explore every angle of a situation. It may involve revisiting extremely painful histories and can be quite frightening for family members.

- Fear of betrayal – the relationship between the assessor/s and the assessed is usually brief but intense. The skilled worker is likely to draw out significant information from the family. If this is information is obtained and the consequence is not what the family hoped for, there can be a strong sense of being betrayed by someone who they may have felt close to previously. Alternatively, the family member may have a personal history of being betrayed and is not willing to take such a risk with a professional.

- Worker disliked – as unpalatable as this is to most of us, some people may just not like the worker they have been allocated and may be deliberately obstructive because of this.

- Race, culture, gender – the question of who assesses different families and the possible barriers that may be inherent in that can be particularly relevant.

CASE STUDY 12.4: WORKING WITH RESISTANCE

Delia is the 40-year-old mother of eight children, aged between 17 and 6. Their father is a violent man and a heroin addict. He has returned to the family intermittently because Delia holds the view that all her children should have the same father. Delia has moved from place to place, fleeing violence and the involvement of social services in her life. There are aspects of Delia's parenting which are very positive – she always makes sure the children are clean and well-fed; she is warm and affectionate towards them; and she would spend her last breath protecting them from their father – in fact this is why she has finally separated from him permanently. When he was last with the family, he hit his oldest son, Jamie, then aged 16. Although these are admirable qualities, Delia has allowed her children to be exposed to frequent periods of domestic violence. Delia and her children have led a chaotic lifestyle, often living in fear of their lives; they have had many different addresses and attended school only on occasion. The longest any of them has ever remained in the same place and attended the same school is five months. As a consequence the children have limited social skills and seven of the eight children have behavioural problems.

As the concerns for the children have increased, a decision was made to begin care proceedings. The oldest daughter, Dena, was quite happy to come into care as she and her mother clash frequently. Jamie and his younger brother Brian, aged 14, have refused to come into care. Attempts to place them in care were thwarted as they have just returned home each time. The five younger children are in three separate placements. Delia is deeply angered by the actions of social services and sees no reason why they had to take this action. She views herself as a good mother and has only limited insight into the effect her lifestyle has had on her children. She wants all her children together again but sees no reason why she should work with the social worker. She was in care herself and feels it damaged her. The only person Delia is willing to talk to at all is the children's guardian ad litem.

Points to consider:

- Why is Delia so resistant?

- What can be done to move the situation on?

- Are there tools and/or theories that can be drawn on and used to help facilitate the assessment?

Even though some families may be resistant, professionals do need to keep working with them in order that the welfare of the children is secured. Maintaining a balance between working in partnership with parents and ensuring that the child's welfare is paramount can present something of a dilemma for workers at times. A recent study by Forrester *et al.* (2006) found that social workers who participated in their study tended to be 'highly confrontational and rarely showed what might be considered good listening skills. The picture was so consistent that it cannot be about individual practice, it is a systemic issue' (p.48). The pressure of workloads and the recognition that workers need to be honest and open with families can cause their practice to be compromised. If professionals are to successfully assess families it is important that their communication skills are maintained at a high level. The use of approaches such as solution-focused therapy and motivational interviewing (Miller and Rollnick 2002) can help the worker to engage with the family member and begin to explore incentives for moving beyond resistance.

It may be of value to make use of a respected family member to move people on. Their opinion is likely to hold far more weight than the professional's and their motivation will be more likely to be in the interests of the family member than not. If there are no such family members it may be worth exploring if there are other professionals who already have a reasonable relationship with the family. They may act as an agent to introduce the assessor or they may be willing to co-work the assessment. Co-working is often a positive way forward for all concerned, allowing the family to feel that they are not having to begin from the beginning again, offering the new worker an opportunity to begin building a relationship and ensuring that what is discussed is verified by the presence of a second worker.

Of basic importance is that the professional ensures they are consistent, predictable and available, that they keep appointments, are not late and inform people if there is likely to be a delay. Offering practical support is often a way to begin to develop trust. Families are often not aware of resources available to them which might alleviate some of their stress, for example, holiday play schemes. Offering to obtain information for them can not only indicate a supportive approach but can also help families feel listened to.

THE IMPACT OF VICTORIA CLIMBIÉ

Since the Assessment Framework guidance was published in 2000, there have been further child death tragedies, the most well-known being that of Victoria Climbié who died at the hands of her aunt and her aunt's partner. The inquiry into her death (Laming 2003) revealed similar themes to those that had emerged in previous inquiries, namely poor communication between professionals, poor co-ordination, lack of training and resource pressures on frontline workers. In response to this the Government produced the green paper *Every Child Matters* in 2003 and the Children Act 2004. The aim of both of these was to secure more integrated services around the needs of children. As a consequence, a data base known as ContactPoint, containing information on all children, is being established as a means of monitoring children.

A joint Chief Inspectors' Report on Safeguarding Children was published in July 2005. The report's findings are summarised in *Working Together to Safeguard Children* (Department for Education and Skills 2006a, p.1.9). It found that safeguarding children has become more of a priority across agencies and that agencies are working better together to identify concerns. It also found that children are better listened to and consulted but expressed some concern about the safeguarding of particular groups of children such as disabled children and those living away from home.

What happened to Victoria Climbié highlighted that the intention that the Assessment Framework would be used as a common language across agencies had not really happened. Although it is acknowledged that social care is the lead agency when there are issues of protection, the responsibility to safeguard children should be shared. As a result, the Integrated Children System and the Common Assessment Framework have been developed.

The Integrated Children System (ICS) is described as a 'conceptual framework for assessment, planning, intervention and review which builds on the Assessment Framework and the Looked After Children system' (Department for Education and Skills 2006d). The intention is to ensure that information gathered from individual children's records can be used as the basis for the sharing of common information between relevant agencies and to make it easier to review and assess progress made by individual children. It involves every local authority putting in place an ICT system that is compliant with the ICS.

The Common Assessment Framework (CAF) is a simplified version of the Assessment Framework. It should be fully in force by March 2008 (Department for Education and Skills 2006e). It is designed to be used by practitioners from all settings and agencies working with children at an early stage of assessing needs. It is completed with the voluntary agreement of a child, depending on their age and understanding, and its family. The intention is to ensure that any practitioner can become the lead professional in an assessment using a standardised national approach and a common language. This offers an opportunity for early intervention and involves sharing responsibility. It is also designed to ensure an improved recording of information gathered which can then be accessed by any professional working with the family. This is intended to reduce the number of times a family has to repeat information to different professionals. The Common Assessment Framework is designed to ensure that decisions about whether to refer a child on to a more specialist agency such as social services are evidence-based. If it is not appropriate to refer on it is hoped that appropriate services can be co-ordinated via the lead professional.

The changes being made to ensure improved communication between agencies are at a relatively early stage. It is to be hoped that they will ensure a better co-ordination of services and of assessment material. They may even prevent possible future tragedies for some children. The fact remains, however, that it is the person who killed the child who is ultimately responsible, rather than a social worker or agency. There will always be people who harm or murder children. Regardless of the changes being made to the systems, the factors involved in undertaking assessments of children and their families remain constant. Assessments involve more than just the gathering of information, but also an ability to systematically analyse that information using a combination of professional experience, knowledge and judgement to make safe decisions for a child's future welfare.

REFERENCES

Bowlby, J. (1982) *Attachment and Loss*. New York: Basic Books.

Calam, R., Cox, A., Glasgow, D., Jimmieson, P. and Groth Larsen, S. (2007) *In My Shoes: A Computer Assisted Interview for Communicating with Children and Vulnerable Adults*. York: Child and Family Training.

Calder M. with Goulding, S., Hanks, H., Regan, L., Rose, K., Skinner, J. and Wynne, J. (2000) *The Complete Guide to Sexual Abuse Assessments*. Lyme Regis: Russell House Publishing.

Cleaver, H. and Freeman, P. (1995) *Parental Perspectives in Cases of Suspected Child Abuse*. London: HMSO.

Cleaver, H., Unell, I. and Aldgate, J. (1999) *Children's Needs – Parenting Capacity – The Impact of Parental Mental Illness, Problem Alcohol and Drug Use, and Domestic Violence on Children's Development*. London: Department of Health.

Commission for Social Care Inspection (CSCI), HM Inspectorate of Court Administration, The Healthcare Commission, HM Inspectorate of Constabulary, HM Inspectorate of Probation, HM Inspectorate of Prisons, HM Crown Prosecution Service Inspectorate, The Office for Standards in Education (2005) *Safeguarding Children: The Second Joint Chief Inspector's Report on Arrangements to Safeguard Children*. Available at www.safeguardingchildren.org.uk/Safeguarding-Children/2005-report, accessed 13 August 2008.

Cox, A. and Bentovim, A. (2000) *Family Pack of Questionnaires and Scales*. Norwich: Department of Health.

Department for Education and Skills (2003) *Every Child Matters – Green Paper*. Norwich: DfES.

Department for Education and Skills (2006a) *Working Together to Safeguard Children*. Norwich: DfES.

Department of Education and Skills (2006b) *Information Sharing: Practitioners Guide*. London: DfES.

Department of Education and Skills (2006c) *Information Sharing*. London: DfES. Available at www.ecm.gov.uk/informationsharing, accessed 13 August 2008.

Department for Education and Skills (2006d) *Integrated Children's System – Fact Sheet*. DfES. Available at www.everychildmatters.gov.uk/ics, accessed 13 August 2008.

Department for Education and Skills (2006e) *The Common Assessment Framework – Delivering Services*. DfES. Available at www.everychildmatters.gov.uk/deliveringservices/caf/, accessed 13 August 2008.

Department of Health (1991) *Children Act 1989*. London: DoH.

Department of Health (1995) *Child Protection Messages from Research*. London: DoH.

Department of Health (2000) *Framework for the Assessment of Children in Need and their Families*. Norwich: Department of Health, Department for Education and Employment, Home Office.

Fahlberg, V. (1994) *A Child's Journey Through Placement*. London: BAAF.

Forrester, D., McCambridge, J., Rollnick, S., Strang, J. and Waissbein, C. (2006) *Child Risk and Parental Resistance: Can Motivational Interviewing Improve the Practice of Child and Family Social Workers in Working with Parental Alcohol Misuse?* Available at www.aerc.org.uk/documents/pdf/finalReports/AERC_FinalReport_0016.pdf, accessed 13 August 2008.

Freud, S. (1923) *The Ego and the Id*, trans. J. Riviere (1962) New York: Norton.

Howe, D. (1987) *An Introduction to Social Work Theory*. Burlington, VT: Ashgate.

Howe, D., Schofield, G., Brandon, M. and Hinings, D. (1999) *Attachment Theory, Child Maltreatment and Family Support*. London: Macmillan.

Kübler-Ross, E. (1969) *On Death and Dying*. New York: Macmillan.

Laming, H. (2003) *The Victoria Climbié Inquiry: Report of an Inquiry by Lord Laming*. London: Stationery Office.

Miller, W.R. and Rollnick, S. (2002) *Motivational Interviewing: Preparing People for Change*, 2nd edn. New York: Guilford Press.

Prochaska, J.O. and DiClemente, C.C. (1982) 'Comprehensive model of change. Transtheoretical therapy: towards a more integrative model of change.' *Psychotherapy: Theory, Research and Practice 19*, 3.

Shah, S. and Argent, H. (2006) *Life Story Work: What It Is and What It Means*. London: BAAF.

Sturge, C. and Glaser, D. (2000) 'Contact and domestic violence: the expert court report.' *Family Law 30*, 615–623.

Turnell, A. and Edwards, S. (1999) *Signs of Safety: A Solution and Safety Oriented Approach to Child Protection Casework*. New York: W.W. Norton.

CHAPTER 13

THE MOST IMPORTANT PROFESSIONAL RELATIONSHIP

LIZ HUGHES

This chapter is based on a Delphi study (Gordon 2004) in which members of an English Health Authority regional group of child protection specialist nurses/child protection supervisors were asked to identify the factors which they believed may affect health visitors' capacity to make good assessments and decisions in their work with vulnerable children (Hughes 2005). Although the study focused on health visitors, the resulting model and assessment process could be used with frontline workers in any agency.

Every time there is a serious case review in the United Kingdom following the death of a child from abuse or neglect, the same issues of poor quality assessments, poor inter-agency communication, poor information collection, poor analysis, poor management and lack of resources are identified (Sinclair and Bullock 2002; DCSF 2008).

This is despite the steady flow of government guidance and advice since 1974 escalating to a bewildering level with the 'Every Child Matters, Change for Children' programme (HM Government 2004), following the publication of Lord Laming's report into the death of Victoria Climbié (Laming 2003). Much of the early guidance relates to the proceduralisation of the child protection system. Some elements concern the proper care and treatment of children who have suffered significant harm through abuse or neglect whilst others deal with the concept of partnership, or the care of parents (Children Act 1989).

More recently, central government's focus has been on the move from 'protection' when a child has already suffered harm, to 'safeguarding the welfare' of children by early identification and intervention in order to prevent harm. Notably, none of the guidance is concerned with the proper care or wellbeing of those staff members who undertake work with children who are vulnerable to abuse and neglect.

Despite the development, for well over a decade, of specialist child protection nurse posts providing expert advice, support and supervision, the questionable quality of assessments and decision making by frontline workers remains a recurring theme in serious case reviews.

Practice note

Could it be that the focus in supervision sessions is on the management/accountability function rather than the supportive function, meaning that supervisors do not have the opportunity to recognise the emotional impact of the work and its influence on practitioners' competence to make good quality assessments and interventions?

THE ROLE AND RESPONSIBILITIES OF HEALTH VISITORS IN CHILD PROTECTION WORK

Primarily focusing on family health education and health promotion, health visitors have a crucial role to play in the promotion of children's health and development and the protection of children from harm (Department of Health 2001).

The role of health visitors

- Primary prevention of child abuse and neglect
- Recognition of vulnerability
- Early intervention
- Risk assessment
- Information sharing.

Their unique role in providing a universal non-stigmatising service gives them access to and regular contact with children and families. Health visitors are well placed to recognise family stresses and circumstances that may lead to abuse or neglect and to identify children who have suffered or who are likely to suffer significant harm.

Health visitors currently provide a service to all families where there are children under the age of five years, though home visiting has in many areas been reduced to a 'birth visit' followed by clinic attendance and client initiated contact (Dickens 2001).

THE ROLE OF THE CHILD PROTECTION ADVISOR/SPECIALIST NURSE

The role of the child protection named nurse is described in full in *Working Together to Safeguard Children* (Department for Education and Skills 2006). The development of specialist nurse and child protection named nurse posts has evolved over the last 15 years or so. Usually not line managers, the main functions of specialist/named nurses are to provide expert advice, support, training and supervision to frontline health practitioners and to assist primary care trusts with internal management reviews.

The early child abuse inquiry reports make little reference to, or specific recommendations relating to, nursing professionals even though health visitors were involved with most cases. It was not until the mid 1970s that the work of the nursing professions in the protection of children was formally recognised in government guidelines (Department of Health and Social Security 1975).

Partly as a result of the increasing number of child sexual abuse registrations, the then Department of Health and Social Security asked its Standing Nursing and Midwifery Advisory Committee to consider the implications of child abuse for the profession. This led to the consideration of the work of 'senior nurses, who in the course of their duties, supervise and assist in the training of practitioners in matters relating to child abuse' (Department of Health and Social Security 1988a). The committee's chair noted that the circumstances in which children's deaths occurred demonstrated certain recurring characteristics in the management arrangements, particularly of health visitors and school nurses. These characteristics included uncertainty about incident reporting, confusion about case conference decisions and outcomes and inadequate monitoring of incidents and concerns.

THE ROLE AND RESPONSIBILITY OF HEALTH ORGANISATIONS TO SAFEGUARD CHILDREN

Child protection as a discrete area of responsibility for the National Health Service has a relatively short history. A significant change in the last few years has been the devolvement of accountability for child protection from health authorities to primary care trusts (Department of Health 2002), PCT chief executives becoming legally responsible for safeguarding children in the same way as they are for other services. Section eleven of the Children Act 2004 describes in detail the responsibilities of health trusts to safeguard and promote the welfare of children. These responsibilities include ensuring safe recruitment of staff in line with the recommendations of the Bichard enquiry (2004) and the provision of child protection training to staff.

It has long been recognised that organisations rely heavily on the quality of the workforce to achieve their corporate aims (Bates, Pugh and Thompson 1997, p.189). An organisation that fails to pay serious attention to staffing or human resource issues is one that seriously risks a breakdown in its ability to achieve its ends. Where this applies to a child protection system, there is a very real danger that children will be unnecessarily harmed as a result of staff-related issues not being addressed. It is relatively easy in health services to attach considerable importance to the needs of service users and yet to devote little or no time, thought or energy to the needs and concerns of staff. This is especially so in the case of child protection work (Morrison 1990).

It is therefore necessary to challenge organisational cultures that neglect the staff dimension and allow discontent and other problems to fester. Morrison raises a number of issues about the harm that can be caused by employing organisations that are unaware of and insensitive to the complex emotional dynamics that characterise child protection interventions. Workers get paid for 'Doing tasks, outcomes and so on. Thinking and feeling were off organisational limits' (p.193). The consequences for health and social care organisations are deeply damaging in terms of critical reasoning, planning, work relationships, reflective analysis, staff stress and motivation.

Within a risk management environment such as child protection, says Morrison (in Bates *et al.* 1997, p.193), the consequences are blunted emotional responsiveness, reduced sensitivity, inadequate reflection and dangerous decision-making. Emotional competence is therefore not simply a challenge for individual managers or practitioners; it is also a corporate issue for organisations. Child protection work is being undertaken in an organisational environment which for many staff is characterised by rapid and continuous change, occupational insecurity and a preoccupation with survival at both institutional and personal levels (*ibid.* p.196).

Practice note

We know that children suffer more harm in 'high criticism, low warmth' families (Department of Health 1995); we can expect that organisations reflecting that culture will cause similar harm to workers.

SUPERVISION, THE CORNERSTONE OF GOOD PRACTICE

Supervision is a process in which one worker is given responsibility to work with another worker in order to achieve certain professional, personal and organizational objectives. These objectives include competent, accountable practice, continuing professional development and personal support.

(Harries 1987, cited in Morrison 2001)

There is a large amount of literature and practice guidance relating to the subject of supervision which is useful in facilitating understanding of the process which is supposed to ensure best practice. Supervision has four functions.

The functions of supervision

- *Managerial function*: to monitor performance and accountability.

- *Educative function*: to explore knowledge and identify training needs.

- *Supportive function*: to explore emotional responses and to manage stress.

- *Mediation function*: to facilitate information sharing and communication up and down the organisation, ensuring that the individual worker is linked to the wider organisation.

In the National Health Service, because health professionals are accountable both to managers who may not be from the same discipline and to professional bodies for their clinical practice, supervision may be separated into its different components and delivered by different people as appropriate to the discrete needs of the individual stakeholders. Thus, a health visitor with access to 'performance review' by a manager, 'clinical supervision' from a professional colleague, 'child protection supervision' from a specialist nurse, 'peer group support' and 'ad hoc' support from members of the primary health care team may receive as many different pieces of advice as the number of people involved. This may leave the individual more confused and stressed than before, and the potential for effective decision-making compromised. Conversely, the practitioner may find, from a variety of perspectives, an option that is more acceptable to her particular way of operating and the particular circumstances of the situation. Health visitors in most areas in the UK have regular, proactive, one-to-one child protection supervision with a specialist nurse. They are asked to identify children in need and children at risk of significant harm, using the *Framework for the Assessment of Children in Need and their Families* (Department of Health 2000), in conjunction with the known risk factors for child abuse and neglect (Department of Health 1995), their professional experience and intuition.

The supervisor records the main points of the discussion about the child and family, the agreed action plan and the date for review, but little about the factors which may influence and affect the practitioner's capacity to comprehend and analyse complex information in order to make valid assessments of risk.

Practice note

If supervision is meant to be the cornerstone of good practice, and it evidently doesn't always result in good practice, could it be something to do with the process? Do organisations recognise the importance of supervision in quality assuring the competence of frontline staff in child protection work and ensure that it is a priority?

This would be evidenced by the existence of robust, unambiguous policies and procedures to support and guide frontline practitioners in this very complex and emotive area of work and by the development of a supervision policy supported by a child protection training programme which allows for the needs of individuals.

Practice note

It is not usually helpful to have a blanket policy that applies to all. For example a newly qualified worker or a worker with a high caseload of vulnerable families is likely to need more frequent supervision than an experienced practitioner working in a less demanding area.

Do practitioners understand the purpose of supervision, and how to make the most of the opportunity? Is training for supervisees provided? Are practitioners correctly identifying the families who should be discussed in supervision? What guidance is given regarding the factors which may be indicators of abuse and neglect? Do supervisors check that practitioners learn from training and that learning influences practice? How do supervisors know that what is a time-consuming and therefore expensive process is effective in improving practice?

Do supervisors focus on the management/accountability function at the expense of the supportive function?

Reder and Duncan (2004) remark that the consequences of focusing on tasks and outcomes in child protection work at the expense of thinking and feeling are damaging in terms of critical reasoning, working relationships, planning and reflective analysis.

> Child protection can cut across our feelings and experience in some of the most personal parts of our lives, those experiences and feelings can have a powerful effect on our professional behaviour. (Murphy 1995)

Practice note

Frontline practitioners who visit families at home will experience first hand, the abusive and neglectful circumstances which some children endure, in today's parlance, 24/7, for much of their early years. The impact on staff will be different depending on personality, emotional maturity, professional experience, colleague and management support and other internal and external resources. How many health visitors have been heard to say that they would like to take such and such a child home with them? No doubt social workers and teachers have felt this way too.

> Anxiety runs like a vein throughout the child protection process.' (Morrison 1994, p.196)

Anxiety may result in a practitioner's avoidance of supervision because the supervisor's involvement may be perceived as interfering and unhelpful. Anxiety may result in loss of self-confidence and dependency on the supervisor. It may result in disguised compliance, the practitioner appearing to engage in the process, but not being completely open and honest with the supervisor. Are supervisors too ready to accept practitioners' assessments and not asking enough probing questions?

Anxiety exists not only at the level of the individual, but also as an organisational phenomenon. Failure at an organisational level to contain anxiety appropriately can permeate all aspects of the agency's work as well as affecting its relations with the outside world and other agencies. In this environment,

---

Probing questions

Domestic abuse has been identified as a vulnerability factor.

- What does the practitioner know about the level of violence?

- Is she aware of the SPECCS or similar model of assessment? (Metropolitan Police risk assessment model)

- Is she aware of the literature relating to the effects of domestic abuse on children?

- Has she attended training on the subject?

- Has she assessed the impact on the children in this particular family?

- Has she shared information with other workers involved with the family?

- Are there any other risk factors, for example, alcohol abuse?

- What intervention has been identified as appropriate and how will that be monitored?

---

anxiety is seen as unprofessional, a sign of weakness or not coping. This may result in uncertainty being suppressed through fight and flight mechanisms.

The culture of nursing in which many older health visitors 'grew up' was very much as Morrison (1996) describes. It was expected that a nurse would get on with the work, however difficult, without complaining and without becoming emotionally involved with patients. It is therefore not surprising that some practitioners find supervision alien to that culture, threatening rather than helpful. Supervisors must be sensitive to these issues if supervision is to be effective.

Managing individual supervision sessions

Practice note

Consider the following factors when assessing the supervision needs of an individual practitioner:

- Recently qualified or new to the area
- Working in isolation
- Supervision history
- Caseload numbers
- Sickness record
- Characteristics of the local area.

Many health visitors have caseloads in excess of 400 children; some have as many as 20 families where there are health or lifestyle issues that may adversely affect parenting capacity. There is a risk that in order to get through the pile of records within the allotted supervision session, not enough time is given to the emotional impact on the practitioner of the workload, how a particular child or family makes the worker feel, why that might be and the thought processes and principles used which have resulted in the assessment (Appleton and Cowley 2003).

It can be very daunting to be confronted with a big pile of records. It is very important that supervisors read records to be aware of the quality of record keeping. Don't try to go through every file in one session, it might mean that because time is limited the last few files in the pile do not get the level of attention needed.

Practice note

Choose one or two files, and go through them in detail. Encourage the practitioner to apply the same principles to the remaining cases. If it is obvious that the fattest file is on the bottom of the pile, choose that one first; it is likely to be the most difficult case!

Boundary setting

A clear supervision contract describing the responsibilities and expectations of both parties is helpful in setting boundaries to avoid misunderstandings and feelings of rejection.

Practice note

Whilst being clear that supervision is not about personal therapy or counselling (Morrison 2007), it emphatically is about the person in the context of their work.

When exploring thought processes and reasoning leading to the assessment and analysis of risk to vulnerable children, it is essential that supervisors consider the effects of practitioners' personal as well as professional circumstances: for example, having young children of their own, the availability and quality of peer support, or organisational issues such as management style, provision of resources and staffing levels.

Practice note

Supervisors must be mindful of the emotional needs of staff, but clear that supervision is not a therapeutic forum in which to address personal issues. Staff should be sensitively signposted to a more appropriate service, e.g. workplace wellbeing or occupational health.

Keeping supervision records

Practice note

Separate supervision records into those that relate directly to the child and family and 'process notes' which relate to the practitioner and are not to be shared with the family.

Careful and thoughtful documentation of supervision sessions recording precisely how and why decisions have been made and actions agreed are vital if practitioners are to be supported if things go wrong. Parents have the right of access to health records relating to their children including supervision records.

It is best practice to be open and honest with parents about concerns before referral to supervision unless to do so would put the child at increased risk. Concerns should be recorded in the parent held record along with proposed interventions. Practitioners should explain that they have a professional responsibility to discuss concerns with a supervisor; the parents' consent for referral to supervision is not needed.

There are two types of supervision record to be kept. First, the record relating to the child and family, including the assessment, plan of intervention and review date. This should be kept with the main health record for the child and is subject to the law relating to the keeping of health records. Second, the supervisor's record of professional issues relating to the worker's professional practice (process notes) which are confidential to the supervisor and the practitioner and not to be shared with families. Both parties have a copy. These records should be securely kept.

TOWARDS IMPROVED PRACTICE

The Delphi group identified a number of factors, the presence of *and especially a combination of which*, may impact on the capacity of practitioners to think about and reflect on their practice. The factors identified were classified under three key headings.

Issues relating to the practitioner

- Mental health/stress
- Family commitments/responsibilities
- Other personal issues not specified
- Ability to think/reflect
- Observation skills
- Ability to learn from experience
- Ability to seek advice
- Time management skills
- Ability to work across professional boundaries

- Experience of child protection work
- Perception of clients
- Uptake of child protection training
- Attitude to work
- Self-awareness
- Ability to challenge
- Supervision history
- Over-optimism
- Overwhelmed
- Burn-out.

Issues relating to caseload/workload

- Staff shortages
- Caseload demands
- Fear of violent families
- Quality of colleague support
- Anxiety about complaints from families.

Issues relating to the organisation

- Organisational change
- Availability of child protection training
- Accessibility of supervision
- Management style/arrangements.

The *Framework for the Assessment of Children in Need and their Families* (Department of Health 2000) considers the child's developmental needs in relation to the parents' capacity to meet those needs and the influence of family and environmental factors, providing practitioners with a model within which to systematically assess risk whilst maintaining the focus on the child.

A similar three-domain model can be constructed, focusing on:

1. The practitioner in the context of personal and professional development needs.

2. The capacity and culture of the organisation to meet those needs.

3. The impact of caseload/workload and other workplace issues.

This model may be of use in assessing the competence of frontline practitioners to think about their cases, identify vulnerable children, assess risk and to intervene effectively and appropriately to prevent abuse and neglect.

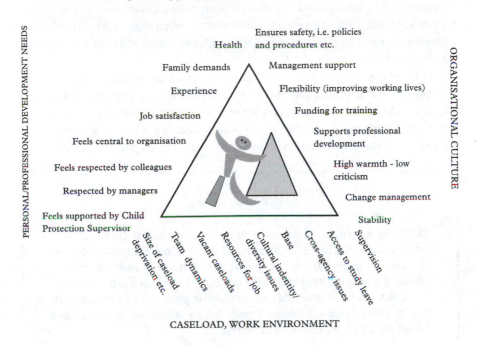

Figure 13.1 Framework for the Assessment of Practitioners

A BRIEF RUN THROUGH THE LITERATURE
Thresholds for concern/intervention

It is important that supervisors are aware of the characteristics of individual caseloads. It is likely that within the same city or geographical area, thresholds for concern about vulnerability are different depending on what is perceived as being the norm for that area. One of the factors identified in the Delphi study was practitioners working in areas of social deprivation for years and years being likely to accept lower standards of child care than those working in more affluent areas. It is possible that in the context of communities from diverse backgrounds, child-rearing practices that would not be generally acceptable may be difficult to challenge. Reder, Duncan and Gray(1993) refer to this as 'cultural relativism'.

Throughout history, children and young people have been exploited and physically injured, but this has not always been construed as child abuse or necessarily wrong. Public concern about child cruelty and neglect began at the end of the nineteenth century, when social conditions were in a state of great change. It was against this background that some degree of state intervention in family life was seen as justified in order to protect children. Nowadays there is public concern about protecting children at risk, but also about professionals over reacting and removing children from their families too readily. There is intense media interest when a tragedy occurs, often followed by a campaign to seek out those to be held responsible (Department of Health and Social Security 1988b; Laming 2003).

Differences of perception exist across social class and culture, between generations and genders, and between professionals and agencies. A concern to protect children from serious injury or death, coupled with a concern not to intervene unless necessary, has resulted in a primary focus of resources and energy on those families where the risks appear serious and immediate.

Practice note

Decision-making in child protection is about balancing harm; it is not about protection from all risk. When children are removed from the care of their parents, they may be protected from the risk of physical harm, but they may also be separated from a range of positive influences, for example the continuing presence of a parent with whom there is an emotional bond. Many decisions are therefore based on a judgement of relative risk.

PROFESSIONAL COMPETENCE
'Learning occurs in the context of its use'
Knowledge, values and skills acquired during formal training represent only the beginning of professional learning. Several studies of professional development in social care, health, education and other settings suggest that professional competence is only partly a conscious process. Significant elements of professional competence are held at a tacit or intuitive level, and are shaped as

much by workplace experiences as formal training (Eraut 1994; Morrison 2001, pp.134–136; Yelloly and Henkel 1995).

Appleton and Cowley (2008) focuses specifically on health visitors' use of professional judgement in the assessment of family health need. An important feature of her analysis was the fact that, even when guidelines exist, in practice most health visitors reported using their own professional judgment in making family assessments. The worker cannot by definition know what unconscious habits and beliefs s/he is picking up or the extent to which such unconscious learning is more rather than less healthy.

The quality and culture of the workplace and the degree of positive modelling therefore have a powerful impact on the shaping of professional competence. Thus in a positive work environment in which there are models of sound knowledge, evidence-based practice, appropriate values and co-operative working relationships, the worker is likely to pick up good habits, styles and beliefs. The negative modelling of behaviour that occurs in less healthy, highly stressed or dysfunctional work environments might include less desirable, less transparent, less evidence-based approaches, providing tacit permission for staff to treat others with disrespect and to engage in a range of practices that fail to put the needs of service users first.

Given that the nature of professional competence is powerfully shaped by the worker's experience doing the job, and that a significant proportion of this occurs below the level of conscious awareness, it is vital that supervision enables workers to step back and reflect, to translate the work they do into accurate observations, feelings, knowledge, understanding, analysis, skilled behaviour, planning and evaluation (Kolb's 1988 'learning cycle').

Practice note

It is worth bearing in mind that most health practitioners do not choose to become involved in child protection work. For many, child protection work gets in the way of the work that they were trained for, and really want to do. For some it is too difficult and, because of the anxiety it causes, they may actively avoid becoming involved. Fear of complaints from families was identified as being a factor likely to influence decision-making. It is vital that supervisors ask questions about workload and how it makes practitioners feel if they are to identify such problems.

Professional dangerousness (Bates *et al.* 1997)

Our understanding of the ways in which the dynamics of abusing families interact with professional systems to increase the dangerousness of such situations, resulting in the mismanagement of high risk families, has been enriched by Reder *et al.*'s analysis of child death inquiries (1993, p.200).

Many parents of abused children have themselves been subject to emotionally depriving care and/or physically abusive punishment which are subsequently manifested in their own adult and parenting relationships in the form of unresolved dependency needs and major conflicts about control. Reder *et al.* suggest that these care/control problems are further played out through the interactions between such families and the child protection network. Four specific processes in family–professional relationships are identified: dependency; closure; flight and disguised compliance.

Processes in family–professional relationships

Dependency: Professionals are drawn into meeting more and more demands from parents, thereby obscuring the child's needs and issues of risk. When for whatever reason this support is withdrawn, this triggers in the parents early feelings of abandonment, anger and withdrawal.

Closure: Parents who have a precarious feeling of control over their own lives may, when forced to engage in mostly involuntary relationships with the child protection system, respond by distancing and closing in on themselves in an attempt to regain control over the outside world by keeping it out.

Flight: Parents move home in an effort to maintain control over the child protection system by running away from and thus fragmenting the professional network.

Disguised compliance: Parents offer an overt verbal compliance whilst maintaining a covert agenda of delinquent and rebellious behaviour towards the child protection agencies.

Morrison (2001) points out that there is a parallel narrative in Reder *et al.*'s (1993) story of the way in which professionals can be drawn into dysfunctional family processes which has its starting point in dysfunctional organisational processes (p.201). In agencies where anxiety is not attended to, where thinking and feeling are off-limits and where management processes may be experienced as non-contingent, neglectful or punitive, care and control conflicts can be an endemic feature of agency life. Thus when such agencies encounter child abuse, their staff's own organisational and personal care and control conflicts may be unwittingly triggered by the same dynamics in the families whose children they seek to safeguard. Morrison summarises by stating that the frontline of today's child protection work is potentially a partnership between families and professionals, neither of whom feels understood, valued, respected, prepared or supported. This he says, has potentially highly damaging consequences not only for practice, but also for the wellbeing of staff.

Attachment theory

Described by Bowlby (1969), attachment theory offers an account of how early childhood experience with caregivers influences the development of interpersonal relating and relationships with others in adulthood. Bacon and Richardson (2001) describe a parallel theme being the effect of working in the field of child protection on professionals' own attachment systems, and the necessity to be aware of the interplay between the individual professional's response, the role of the organisation and the ability to make useful clinical interventions.

The practitioner's need for a secure base and the impact on practice of defensive reactions in the public and professional domains are key issues.

Practice note

It is imperative that the supervisor considers the effects of the practitioner's relationship with and attachment to families where there are concerns about child welfare. It may be difficult for a worker who has a warm relationship with such a family to believe that a child may be at risk.

Professional accommodation syndrome

In 1983 Roland Summit published a seminal paper, 'The child sexual abuse accommodation syndrome,' which offered a model to explain both why children take so long to disclose sexual abuse, and the reasons for some children subsequently retracting their statement (Bates et al. 1997, p.204). Summit showed how the sexually abused child, living in a family system regulated by the perpetrator's dominance and by secrecy, feeling helpless and entrapped by the abuse, sought to resolve this psychological crisis by shifting responsibility for the abuse from the adults to the child. The function of this accommodation is that, by choosing to take responsibility for their own abuse, the child can attempt to regain some control over the situation.

Summit's model can be adapted to help us to understand more general processes of victimisation and staff stress. It is particularly useful for child protection staff because it draws on the dynamics of abuse. The model, which can be applied to managers, teams and organisations, is based on five stages.

The five stages of staff stress

- **Secrecy**: Many staff hesitate to speak about the impact of the work on them because they feel or know that the agency or colleagues covertly or overtly deny them permission to do so.

- **Helplessness**: Staff who feel helpless in relation to their work, or in the face of stress arising from it, feel a sense of shame. They experience the agency's rejection and dislike of their helplessness and receive the message that those in the helping professions are paid to be 'copers'. The agency's belief system is that uncomplaining workers are OK.

- **Entrapment and accommodation**: Staff are trapped in a dilemma in which telling the truth about their stress is seen as unprofessional, whilst denying that they feel stress is seen as coping and professional. In the face of this, staff are forced to accommodate by then deciding that the fault lies not with the agency's insensitivity, or with the nature of their work, but with themselves for feeling as they do, failing to cope and generally not being sufficiently robust. The answer appears then to lie in suppressing their feelings, invalidating their experiences and working harder.

- **Delayed or unconvincing disclosure**: Disclosure of the distress may eventually be triggered by conflict, training, illness or talking to colleagues. Where conflict is the trigger, this may be in the form of unpredictable behaviour such as atypical aggression, lateness, sickness or sudden resignation. If this behaviour is only understood at a superficial level, it may result in actual or perceived responses such as 'if you can't stand the heat get out of the kitchen'.

- **Retraction**: The delayed or confusing nature of the disclosure, if followed by insensitive, ignoring or disbelieving responses in the agency, leaves the worker psychologically and professionally abandoned, fearing that he or she will be written off as incompetent. In the face of this threat to their whole career the only solution appears to be retraction.

CHANGING THE FOCUS OF SUPERVISION

The Delphi group reflected one of the findings of *Child Protection, Messages from Research* (Department of Health 1995), that in the same way that children experience abuse, it is the coming together of several 'triggers' rather than one issue in isolation which may result in health visitors being vulnerable to suboptimal decision-making. This was illustrated by the following definitions of 'overwhelmed' and 'burn-out' offered by two members of the Delphi group, which include several of the other factors where consensus was achieved.

> Overwhelmed: overpowered by work demands. Burn-out: high work demands, poor resources, little support from colleagues and managers.

> Burn-out: emotionally exhausted; no interest any longer in caseload or work; feeling of being unable to rise to the occasion (yet again), no longer stimulated by the job. Overwhelmed: still interested, still keen; case numbers too high; too many problem families; too many vulnerable children; short staffed, poor management support.

It is recognised that vulnerability is a dynamic concept in families, affected positively and negatively by many factors; so it is too, with practitioners.

Practice note

It is important, when preparing for and during supervision sessions, that supervisors bear in mind the emotional impact on their supervisees of changes in circumstances both at work and in their private lives (Murphy 1995, pp.163–40) and that they encourage reflective practice with the aim of getting workers to think critically about their perceptions and actions (Gibbs 2001).

In practice, the perceived need to discuss all of the cases which a practitioner brings to a supervision session can result in a focus on the tasks identified in Gibbs' study (2001) checking what they had done on cases and giving out the next set of instructions. There may not be time to find out what life in all of its aspects is like for the practitioner, and how that may be impacting on his or her capacity to function.

CONFIDENTIAL

FRAMEWORK FOR ASSESSMENT OF HEALTH VISITORS AND SCHOOL NURSES IN CHILD PROTECTION SUPERVISION

Date this assessment started	Date completed

DETAILS OF PRACTITIONER

Name	Home address
	Postcode
Job title	Base address
	Postcode
Date of birth ☐ Male ☐ Female	Previous base address (use sperate sheet for more previous addresses if necessary) Postcode
Contact telephone no(s)	NMC number

Date of qualification for current role:
Length of time in current post:

LINE MANAGER

Name	Current address
	Postcode
Contact telephone no(s)	

DETAILS OF PERSON(S) UNDERTAKING ASSESSMENT

Name	
Role	
Contact telephone no(s)	Address
	Postcode
Dates of supervision	

If you need more space the boxes will expland as you type.

DEVELOPMENT OF HEALTH VISITOR OR SCHOOL NURSE

	Domain	Comments
H **E** **A**	General Health Sickness recorded etc	
L **T** **H**	Communication skills Expression, questioning, listening, hearing, responding, understanding	
	Emotional and social development Feeling respected within the organisation, supervision history, coping with stress, motivation, positive attitudes, confidence	
	Behavioural development Lifestyle, self-control, behaviour with peers	

Domain	Comments
Identity, self-esteem, self-image and social presentation Perception of self, sense of belonging, experiences of discrimination due to race, religion, age, gender, sexuality and disability	
Team relationships Building stable relationships with colleagues and wider health community, collaboration with other agencies	
Skills and experience Developing confidence, adherence to policies, procedures, asking for help, decision making, engaging in supervision, benefiting from CP training	

	Domain	Comments
L **E** **A** **R** **N** **I** **N** **G**	**Understanding, reasoning and problem solving** Organising, making connections, being creative, exploring, experimenting	
	Participation in learning, eduction Access and engagement, attendance, participation, organisational support, access to appropriate resources	
	Progress and achievement in learning Progress in basic and key skills, available opportunities, support to access eduction	
	Aspirations Ambition, practitioner's confidence and view of progress, motivation, perseverance	

ORGANISATIONAL CAPACITY

Basic care, ensuring safety and protection Provision of basic tools of trade, base/work environment, awareness of personal safety issues	
Emotional warmth and stability Stable, respectful, stimulating organisational environment, praise and encouragement of best practice. Change management	
Guidance, boundries and stimulation Encouraging autonomy, effective and appropriate disciplinary procedures, support for professional development	

CASELOAD/WORKLOAD

Team history, functioning and well-being Size and composition of team, sickness absence management support, relationships within team	
Wider issues Formal and informal support networks from colleagues, manager, supervisor and others, wider caring and employment roles and responsibilities	
Base Adequately equipped, appropriate size, quiet space, comfortable, warm, geographically convenient	
Professional resources, including education Size of caseload, numbers of vulnerable children, numbers of children on CPR, staff vacancies, access to training, conferences etc.	

SUMMARY OF ASSESSMENT

Summarise the strengths and needs of the practitioner

Action needed
Practitioner's comments on the assessment and actions identified:
First meeting with manager (if appropriate) Date   Venue

CONSENT FOR INFORMATION STORAGE AND INFORMATION SHARING

Tick boxes as appropriate

☐ I understand the information that is recorded on this form, and that it will be stored and used to provide services for me

I agree that this assessment may be shared as appropriate:

☐ All ☐ As specified below

Agency Service

☐ I agree that the existence (not details) of this assessment can be included in my personal file

Practitioner signature	Print name	Date
Assessment author's signature	Print name	Date
Manager's (as applicable) signature	Print name	Date

Any additional information about renewed or altered consent
Date

CONCLUSION

Health service organisations depend on the process of supervision to quality assure the competence of frontline staff to assess need and intervene effectively with vulnerable families to prevent abuse and neglect. Most frontline health practitioners now have regular proactive child protection supervision with a specialist child protection supervisor in which those families where vulnerability to abuse and neglect has been identified are discussed.

Child protection supervisors depend on practitioners making accurate assessments and being in possession of up-to-date information in order to be able to offer useful guidance and support. This in turn depends on the competence of the practitioner to gather and process complex information in order to understand what might be going on in the family. There are many factors, personal, emotional, psychological, professional and organisational relating to the practitioner that may impact on his or her ability to do this. The practitioner may be newly qualified or new to the area. S/he may be over-whelmed by the demands of a heavy workload; s/he may be covering for a sick colleague. S/he may be working in an area where all families are vulnerable and have a higher threshold for concern. S/he may be worried about her own sick child at home. S/he may be bewildered by the current rapid rate of change at both local and national levels.

We all come to work leaving our private lives behind. Sometimes it feels as though we have done a day's work before we leave home in the morning. In such circumstances it is likely that our capacity to make complex assessments and decisions may be affected. This applies to supervisors as well as supervisees. It is important that we are all aware of those things in our private lives that may impact on our work. Part of the supervision session should be devoted to finding out how the practitioner is feeling and who/what may be making him or her feel that way.

It is vital that the practitioner feels respected by his or her colleagues, the supervisor and the organisation. This is demonstrated by ensuring that super-vision sessions are not cancelled unless it is absolutely unavoidable, that sessions take place in an environment which facilitates thinking and reflection, where both parties feel comfortable and where they will not be disturbed. It is important to set ground rules for the session including how long it will last; the circumstances in which confidentiality may be broken; recording of the dis-cussion and so on. It is useful to have a contract setting out exactly what is expected of both parties and signed by both. Practitioners should be encour-aged to prepare for supervision sessions in advance by reading the records, visiting the family and revisiting the action plan agreed at the last session. Any changes in circumstances should be documented by the practitioner so that the supervisor's time can be spent in listening, reflecting and asking probing questions rather than writing copious notes. Supervisors should prepare for sessions in the same way.

Practice note

Remember to begin the session by asking about the supervisee. Consider using the adapted CAF form for this purpose, it is proba-bly not necessary to do it on every occasion, but useful if there are significant changes in the practitioner's circumstances.

This approach would constitute a change in the current culture and practice of supervision which some may find difficult to embrace. Some practitioners may find the asking of personal questions intrusive and inappropriate and some supervisors may agree.

Both practitioners and managers should see supervision as a priority. In some trusts, supervision is mandatory but, in practice, when workloads are high and there are shortages of staff, direct client contact activities and other service commitments are seen as more important and supervision sessions are cancelled. The likely outcome of this is that anxiety levels escalate, workers become overwhelmed, sickness absence increases and services are reduced to 'core business'. Children and families are not seen, assessments are not made and vulnerability goes unrecognised. The rest, as they say, is history.

REFERENCES

Appleton, J.V. and Cowley, S. (2003) 'Valuing professional judgement in health visiting practice.' *Community Practitioner 76*, 215–220.

Appleton, J.V. and Cowley, S.(2008) 'Health visiting assessment. Unpacking critical attributes in health visitor needs assessment.' *International Journal of Nursing Studies 45*, 232–245.

Bacon, H. and Richardson, S. (2001) 'Attachment theory and child abuse: An overview of the literature for practitioners.' *Child Abuse Review 10*, 377–397.

Bates, J., Pugh, R. and Thompson, N. (1997) *Protecting Children: Challenges and Change.* Aldershot: Arena.

Bichard, M. (2004) *The Bichard Inquiry.* London: Stationery Office.

Bowlby, J. (1969) *Attachment and Loss Volume 1*, reprinted 1978. London: Penguin.

Department for Children, Schools and Families (2008) *Analysing Child Deaths and Serious Injury through Abuse and Neglect.* London: The Stationery Office.

Department for Education and Skills (2006) *Working Together to Safeguard Children.* London: Stationery Office.

Department of Health (1995) *Child Protection Messages from Research.* London: HMSO.

Department of Health (2000) *Framework for the Assessment of Children in Need and their Families.* London: Stationery Office.

Department of Health (2001) *The Health Visitor and School Nurse Development Programme: Health Visitor Practice Development Resource Pack.* London: Stationery Office.

Department of Health (2002) *NHS Reform and Health Care Professionals Act 2002, Guidance to Primary Care Trusts and Strategic Health Authorities.* London: Stationery Office.

Department of Health and Social Security (1975) *Working Together in Child Protection. An Exploration of the Multi-Disciplinary Task and System Arena.* London: HMSO.

Department of Health and Social Security (1988a) *Report of the Joint Standing Nursing Advisory Committee.* London: HMSO.

Department of Health and Social Security (1988b) *Report of the Inquiry into Child Sexual Abuse in Cleveland 1987.* London: HMSO.

Dickens, J. (2001) 'The Role of the Health Visitor.' In Polnay, J. (ed.) *Child Protection in Primary Care.* New York: Radcliffe Medical Press.

Eraut, M. (1994) *Developing Professional Knowledge and Competence.* London and New York: Routledge.

Gibbs, J. (2001) 'Maintaining front-line workers in child protection: a case for refocusing supervision.' *Child Abuse Review 10*, 323–335.

Gordon, T.J. (2004) 'The Delphi Method.' In J.C. Glenn and T.J. Gordon *AC/UNU Millennium Project Futures Research Technology Version 2.* Available at www.acunu.org, accessed 17 November 2008.

Harries, M. (1987) *Discussion Paper on Social Work Supervision.* West Perth: Australian Association of Social Workers.

HM Government (2004) *Every Child Matters.* London: The Stationery Office.

HM Government (2006) *Working Together to Safeguard Children: A Guide to Inter-agency Working to Safeguard and Promote the Welfare of Children*. London: The Stationery Office.

Hughes, E. (2005) 'Determining the factors which influence health visitors' assessments of vulnerable children.' Unpublished dissertation submitted in partial fulfilment of the regulations for the MA Child Protection and Child Welfare, University of Huddersfield.

Kolb, D. (1988) 'The Process of Experiential Learning.' In D. Kolb (ed.) *Experience as the Source of Learning and Development*. London: Prentice Hall.

Laming, H. (2003) *The Victoria Climbié Inquiry, report of an inquiry by Lord Laming*. London: Stationery Office.

Morrison, T. (1990) 'The emotional effects of child protection work on the worker.' *Practice 4, 4*, 253–271.

Morrison, T. (1996) 'Partnership and collaboration: rhetoric and reality.' *Child Abuse and Neglect 20, 2*, 127–140.

Morrison, T. (1997) 'Emotionally Competent Child Protection Organisations: Fallacy, Fiction or Necessity?' In J. Bates, R. Pugh and N. Thompson *Protecting Children: Challenges and Changes*. Aldershot: Arena.

Morrison, T. (2001) *Staff Supervision in Social Care*. Brighton: Pavilion.

Morrison, T. (2007) 'Emotional intelligence and social workk, context, characteristics, complications and contribution.' *British Journal of Social Work 37*, 245–263.

Murphy, M. (1995) 'Delivering Staff Care in a Multi-disciplinary Context.' In J. Bates, R. Pugh and N. Thompson (1997) *Protecting Children: Challenges and Change*. Aldershot: Arena.

Reder, P. and Duncan, S. (2004) 'Making the most of the Victoria Climbié Inquiry Report.' *Child Abuse Review 13*, 95–114.

Reder, P., Duncan, S. and Gray, M. (1993) *Beyond Blame, Child Abuse Tragedies Revisited*. London: Routledge.

Sinclair, R. and Bullock, M. (2002) *Learning From Past Experience; A Review of Serious Case Reviews*. London: Department of Health.

Summit, R.C. (1983) 'The Child sexual abuse accomodation syndrome.' *Child Abuse and Neglect 1*, 177–193.

Yelloly, M. and Henkel, M. (1995) *Learning and Teaching in Social Work towards Reflective Practice*. London: Jessica Kingsley Publishers.

CHAPTER 14

DOING SERIOUS CASE REVIEWS WELL: POLITICS, ACADEMIA, RISK MANAGEMENT AND STAFF CARE

HILARY OWEN

INTRODUCTION

This is a difficult area of work which I think is made more difficult by defensive local and national politics and by the government's limited approach. Whilst it is necessary to begin this chapter with a description of the statutory guidance which governs serious case reviews, so that we know precisely what it is we are dealing with, the discussion which follows is, I hope, rather more stimulating and optimistic. Many of the brightest academics in health and social care are arguing for a radical change in approach, which is both reassuring and exciting. As Munro says, 'Don't keep banging your head against a brick wall' (2005).

THE STATUTORY GUIDANCE

What is a serious case review? Statutory guidance in *Working Together to Safeguard Children* says:

> When a child dies, and abuse or neglect is known or suspected to be a factor in the death, local organisations should consider immediately whether there are other children at risk of harm who need safeguarding. Thereafter, organisations should consider whether there are any lessons to be learnt about the ways in which they can work together to safeguard children. Consequently when a child dies in such a circumstance, the LSCB [local safeguarding children board] will always conduct a review into the involvement with the child and family of organisations and professionals. Additionally LSCBs should always consider whether a serious case review should be conducted where:

- a child sustains a potentially life-threatening injury or serious and permanent impairment of health and development through abuse or neglect; or

- a child has been subjected to particularly serious sexual abuse; or

- a parent has been murdered and a homicide review is being initiated; or

- a child has been killed by a parent with a mental illness; or

- the case gives rise to concerns about inter-agency working to protect children from harm. (HM Government 2006, p.169)

The guidance is clear about the purpose of serious case reviews. They are to:
- establish whether there are lessons to be learnt from the case about the way in which local professionals and organisations work together to safeguard and promote the welfare of children

- identify clearly what those lessons are, how they will be acted on, and what is expected to change as a result; and

- as a consequence, improve inter-agency working and better safeguard and promote the welfare of children. (p.170)

The guidance also clearly states that

> Serious case reviews are not part of any disciplinary enquiry or process, but information that emerges in the course of reviews may indicate that disciplinary action should be undertaken under established procedures. Alternately, reviews may be conducted concurrently with disciplinary action. (p.175)

Once a decision is made that a serious case review is to be undertaken, then each agency that has had involvement with the family must nominate an independent professional internally to carry out an individual management review (IMR). *Working Together* (HM Government 2006) gives broad, rather formulaic guidance about how this should be done (p.176), saying that the aim should be to 'look openly and critically at individual and organisational practice to see whether the case indicates that changes could and should be made and, if so, to identify how those changes will be brought about' (p.174).

FOUR STARS, BUT WILL ANYTHING CHANGE?

As Ofsted gets more involved in the evaluation of serious case review reports written by independent authors, and reports are graded 'outstanding', 'good', 'adequate' or 'inadequate', the emphasis is on the quality of the end product. Political reputations will be made or destroyed by the grades, which contribute to the overall annual performance assessments of local authority children's services. One may imagine a fair amount of 'blame prevention engineering' (Hood and Rothstein 2001) being levered into place by senior officers. In addition, it is worth remembering that, as Reason indicates, 'Seeking as far as possible to uncouple a person's unsafe acts from any institutional responsibility is clearly in the interests of managers. It is also legally more convenient, at least in Britain' (2000, p.768). No attention, however, is being paid to what makes a good quality serious case review *process*. There is nothing in the grade descriptors used by Ofsted that would indicate any thinking has been done about either the methods by which a serious case review should be carried out, or the areas of academic research and discussion which might be relevant. Surprisingly, there has been no attempt so far to learn lessons from other high risk areas of work which have extremely well-established processes for learning from all adverse incidents and errors, like the aviation industry, the armed forces and the NHS. This is disconcerting. The circumstances in which children are killed or seriously injured by their parents or carers are by definition complex. The skills and knowledge required from practitioners to prevent a child's death by working with parents and carers who may attack their children are extraordinary. It is a mistake to think that these situations can be analysed properly by simply looking at 'individual and organisational practice to see whether the case indicates that changes should be made' (HM Government 2006, p.174). We need to ensure that our serious case reviews are carried out using the very best analytical tools and remedial processes available, and it is clear that, at the moment, this is not happening. The same general problems and failures keep being identified, without an improvement in outcomes. Reder and Duncan (2003) indicate that 'Since the 1970s, virtually all reviews of fatal child abuse cases in the United Kingdom report that there was evidence of communication failures between professionals'. Munro (2005, p.533) states:

> The cumulative results of thirty years of child abuse inquiries have created the traditional solutions: psychological pressure to avoid mistakes, increasingly detailed procedures and guidelines, strengthened managerial control to ensure compliance, and steady erosion of the scope for individual professional judgement...the solutions are not working as expected but appear to be creating new problems.

Whilst the government commissions a very helpful biennial analysis of all serious case review reports in England, which picks out messages for future practice (see the latest one, by Brandon *et al.* 2008, covering 2003–2005) there is very little ongoing routine analysis and reporting of adverse incidents or 'near misses' to add to our knowledge.

There has been no research carried out on the effects of the serious case review process on the practitioners involved. Neither has there been any attempt to apply relevant disciplines like clinical psychology and psychiatry to the process, despite the obvious secondary trauma and post-traumatic stress some professionals suffer because of the child's death. Good, experienced practitioners who have been praised for the quality of their work with families in the course of a serious case review have been lost from organisations simply because the process of the review was so stressful. Also, however, as Reason (I would say an aptly named man) indicates 'it is often the best people who make the worst mistakes – error is not the monopoly of an unfortunate few' (2000, p.769). When these practitioners leave the field, we cannot learn from their experience. There is a high level of children's social work vacancies nationally (11.8% in 2005, up from 11.4% in 2004, according to Community Care online, 30.6.08) and difficulties in recruiting appropriately qualified and experienced paediatricians to child protection posts (see 'Paediatricians Reluctant to Court Backlash', *Guardian* 2008).

All of this means we cannot afford to let the current situation continue: we can learn how to do serious case reviews well, and we deserve assistance from the government to do it.

PILOTS, SURGEONS, GPS, TEACHERS, HEALTH VISITORS, POLICE OFFICERS AND SOCIAL WORKERS: GETTING OUR ACT TOGETHER

In recent years the NHS and other healthcare organisations around the world have funded research to learn from the aviation industry's risk management techniques. There are indeed marked parallels between the two areas of activity, as Helmreich and Davies indicate:

> There are similarities in the on-going struggle for safety in both healthcare and aviation. First, although safety is the primary goal, cost drives decisions. Second, both domains have, in part, become safer because of technological innovation. Third, there are multiple sources of threats to safety in both systems – technological, human, and environmental. Fourth, disasters are always followed by furious bouts of second-guessing. Fifth, teamwork is essential in reducing, trapping and mitigating or treating errors... When human error is cited as a major contribution in an air crash, this occurs most often in the form of failures in teamwork, in such areas as communication and shared mental models (2004, pp.1–2).

There are obvious similarities here with child protection work, particularly where communication and teamwork are concerned, and in fact many of the research findings in the aviation field would assist the analysis of services provided to children who die, and provide solutions to problems identified. For example, there are consistent findings about the effects of stress on judgement: 'an individual's thought processes and breadth of attention narrows' (Sexton, Thomas and Helmreich 2000, p.745). There are findings about systems and organisations 'the same set of circumstances can provoke similar errors, regardless of the people involved' (Reason 2000, p.769). Many studies have indicated the importance of flat hierarchies in safe team working

(Helmreich and Davies 2004; Sexton *et al.* 2000): think consultant paediatrician's view versus senior house officer's, as in the Victoria Climbié inquiry. However, there is one consistent finding in the aviation industry which, I think, could improve work with vulnerable children significantly: 'Highly effective cockpit crews use one third of their communications to discuss threats and errors in their environment, regardless of their workload, whereas poor performing teams spend about 5% of their time doing the same' (Sexton *et al.* 2000, p.748). This in itself is helpful. However, the aviation industry and, increasingly, the health care economy, have developed their risk management techniques in a way which maximises the benefits of this finding. As Gawande states:

> The Federal Aviation Administration has a formalised system for analysing and reporting dangerous aviation incidents, and its enormous success in improving airline safety rests on two cornerstones. Pilots who report an incident within ten days have automatic immunity from punishment, and the reports go to a neutral, outside agency, NASA, which has no interest in using the information against individual pilots. (2003, p.66)

The health care community has its own ways of analysing serious untoward incidents. One is based on a systems approach, called 'root cause analysis', training in which is available online (via the National Patient Safety Agency).

IMR authors in health care organisations might benefit from completing the root cause analysis training before they undertake their reviews.

Another approach is the regular confidential 'M&M' (morbidity and mortality) meeting, at which doctors can discuss their errors with colleagues and ask the question 'What would I have done differently?' Gawande describes how these meetings work in the United States:

> it takes place, usually once a week, at nearly every academic hospital in the country... Surgeons, in particular, take the M&M seriously. Here they can gather behind closed doors to review the mistakes, untoward events, and deaths that occurred on their watch, determine responsibility, and figure out what to do differently next time... In its way, the M&M is an impressively sophisticated and human institution. Unlike the courts or the media, it recognises that human error is generally not something that can be deterred by punishment. The M&M sees avoiding error as largely a matter of will – of staying sufficiently informed and alert to anticipate the myriad ways that things can go wrong and then trying to head off each potential problem before it happens. (2003, pp.57–62)

What is clear is that to develop a comprehensive programme of learning from all adverse incidents in safeguarding children, not just the fatal ones, as the aviation industry has done so successfully, would be a step in the right direction.

Reviewing adverse incidents

Some general practices, adopting this approach of reviewing all adverse incidents on a regular basis for the whole range of their work, have naturally applied it to their work in safeguarding children. They have identified situations where children have been placed at risk by poor practice and have convened local meetings of all involved professionals to examine what went wrong and put improvements in place. Where these meetings are instigated by NHS or primary care organisations, chairing them is clearly a task for named or designated health professionals, who have the specialist knowledge and strong inter-trust and inter-agency links needed to ensure all the learning from the incidents is put to good use. Other organisations like children's social care, police, and schools have professionals in similar specialist roles who could chair.

For local professionals involved in reviewing their own adverse incidents, the learning can be uncomfortable and challenging, and therefore it stays with them for longer and has a greater beneficial effect on their practice. The government could assist by developing a national reporting network from which all practitioners working with children or parents could learn. 'Highly effective cockpit crews…'

DID YOU MEAN WHAT I THINK YOU SAID, EVEN THOUGH YOU SHOULD REALLY SPEAK TO MY SECRETARY AND I REALLY DON'T WANT TO HEAR IT BECAUSE I'VE GOT TOOTHACHE AND I'M JUST ABOUT TO LEAVE FOR THE DENTISTS? SHALL I CHECK BACK WITH YOU OR JUST LEAVE IT BECAUSE AMBIGUITY IS MORE COMFORTABLE?

A second area of academic study which could improve our analysis of agency involvement when children die from abuse, and subsequent outcomes for other children, is that relating to communication. Reder and Duncan (2003) indicate that:

> a major concern is that precisely the same failures are occurring now as in the past, despite numerous inquiry recommendations to improve communication and, presumably, deliberate local and national strategies to implement

them. How can this be explained? Does the problem lie in the nature of the recommendations, the way they are implemented, a lack of sophistication of professionals to follow the implementation strategy adequately, a lack of resources to allow this to happen, or something else? (pp.83–84)

Reder and Duncan attempt to find the answer to their question by applying some of the learning from the psychology of communication to the Victoria Climbié Inquiry Report (Laming 2003). Their findings indicate clearly that communication is a far more complex issue than the statutory guidance would suggest, involving many different processes that need to be managed by practitioners if there is to be an unambiguous outcome to their interaction. They conclude that it would be possible and of great benefit to train practitioners in how to communicate unambiguously. Whilst the spirit of this has been included in the government's recommended training programme for the children's workforce, the *Common Core of Skills and Knowledge* (HM Government 2005), there is no acknowledgement of the complexity good communication involves, nor of relevant research findings. In addition, there is no attempt to address the fact that practitioners do not generally have the time to communicate well: they are lucky to be able to snatch a few words on the telephone.

Communication

If we are to prevent child abuse deaths, then it is essential that these two key issues, communication training and having the time to communicate well, are addressed nationally as well as locally.

SUPPORTING STAFF

It is an unfortunate truth that individuals, including practitioners, involved with families where child abuse deaths occur sometimes suffer secondary trauma. If practitioners do suffer it, the symptoms can be made worse by the way their senior managers treat them in the course of a serious case review.

Supporting staff

Local safeguarding children boards (LSCB) could ensure that their members receive training in how to manage serious case reviews in such a way that secondary trauma symptoms suffered by practitioners are not exacerbated. Members with professional backgrounds in mental health services may well be able to assist with this.

It is helpful in considering how best to support staff involved in a serious case review first to think through the emotions of individuals whose work is about to be reviewed. The exercises below will help managers to do this.

Exercise 14.1

Imagine you are a practitioner working in children's services. You visited a vulnerable young family two days ago and in the course of your visit entertained the two-year-old whilst his mother prepared a bottle for her new baby. He is very cute, learning to talk, and is interested in everything. Today you come to work and receive the news that he has been killed by his stepfather. What are your feelings? Shock; grief; great sadness for family members; guilt for not preventing the death; failure of confidence in your ability to do your job; fear that you have missed something significant in your risk assessment and will be disciplined by your employer; fear of the press coverage. Do you trust your manager to behave with integrity when her reputation may be questioned?

You must become a member of the Rapid Response Team (see Chapter 7 of *Working Together to Safeguard Children* (HM Government 2006)) convened to support the family, and attend a planning meeting this afternoon with other professionals involved.

- What will help you deal with all these issues today, in the next week, in the next year?

Exercise 14.2

Imagine you are a first line manager in an organisation providing children's services. Today you come to work to discover that a member of your team has had a child on her caseload die at the hands of his stepfather. What are your feelings? Shock; great sadness for family members; fear that you have missed something in supervision and will be disciplined by your employer; fear of the press coverage; anxiety about your team member's state of mind, particularly since she needs to attend a planning meeting this afternoon; anxiety about any action you will have to take to ensure her practice is safe in the foreseeable future. Do you trust your staff member's professionalism?

- What will help you deal with these issues today, in the next week, in the next year?

Exercise 14.3

Imagine you are the Chief Executive Officer. Today you come to work to discover that a child to whom your organisation provided a service has died at the hands of his stepfather. What are your feelings? Again, shock; great sadness for family members; anxiety. You are legally responsible for ensuring your agency discharges its safeguarding responsibilities in accordance with Section 11 of the Children Act 2004. Do you know how well your organisation is currently doing? Will anything come out of the ensuing serious case review to threaten your position as CEO? Will your anxiety affect the way you manage the situation?

- What do you need to do today?
- How will you ensure you don't cause staff unnecessary additional stress?
- How will you ensure your staff are supported?

The larger local safeguarding children board areas instigate two or more serious case reviews per year, and their processes for administering them have started to become refined and businesslike as they learn from experience. This is helpful: it is important for staff involved with the families to know that there are individuals around in the system who know how things happen, who can be accessed for advice, and who can provide some certainty in the midst of a scary situation. People who have had little contact with the field of child protection, and still less with children's traumatic deaths, experience a very human shock reaction when they become involved for the first time. This is as true for senior officers of LSCB organisations as it is for members of the general public. Many senior officers behave in an uncharacteristically anxious way when faced with a serious case review, and it is important that they remain open to the advice of LSCB managers and Chairs. An anxious chief executive officer can inadvertently exacerbate the anxiety of practitioners.

Some LSCBs have protocols for managers carrying out IMRs which draw attention to the support needs of involved staff.

An example from Sheffield LSCB

Agencies are responsible for ensuring staff are provided with/ given access to emotional support. This support should be clearly identified and communicated to staff involved. The death or serious injury of a child will have an impact on staff and needs to be acknowledged by agencies. The impact may be felt beyond the individual staff involved and throughout the team, organisation or workplace.

The serious case review process itself provokes anxiety in many professionals.

The nature, scope and timescales of the case review should be made clear at the earliest possible stage to staff that have been involved with the case, and their line managers. It should be made clear that the serious case review process can be a long process.

Information should be provided about sources of independent support staff may wish to use in connection with their involvement in the review, e.g. organisations' staff support schemes, human resources departments, occupational health services, workplace wellbeing schemes, trade union or professional body, etc.

It is important that all relevant members of agencies are interviewed and given an opportunity to share their views on the case.

It would in most cases be appropriate to interview the staff member and manager for the case separately.

Staff can choose not to partake in the interview process.

Staff members providing information and attending interviews about their role and actions in relation to the case should wherever possible be given at least two weeks notice of the interview, and invited to be accompanied by a manager (though not one who is also directly involved in the review), their trade union or professional association representative.

Agencies need to ensure staff feel the process is transparent and staff involved feel their views have been represented. Therefore it may be appropriate or useful to share the record of the interview with the staff member.

Whilst this example is written from a supportive perspective, it is very much about a process which is 'done to' staff. The root cause analysis approach compares very favourably with this in that it involves the practitioner more in helping to find the problems or errors which could have contributed to the incident. This has a dual benefit. First, it ensures practitioners' experience and often specialist expertise is applied to the incident. Second, it leaves practitioners with more influence and power in the process, ameliorating some of the effects of secondary trauma.

A PLEA FOR THE FUTURE

It is important to remember that, just as a pilot does not intend to crash his/her aeroplane, no children's services practitioner ever intends that their work should contribute to a tragedy. When an aeroplane crashes, the pilot is just as likely to die as the passengers. When medical error occurs in the field of child protection these days, the doctor concerned is likely to have his/her career and/or mental health ruined. When a child is killed and children's services practitioners have their practice examined by a serious case review, it is likely their careers and mental health will be compromised. The knowledge and skills are available to enable us to up our game when we carry out serious case reviews, both in terms of healthy process and prevention of future deaths. Let's make sure we use all the tools we have: we owe it to children, their families and the practitioners helping them.

REFERENCES

Brandon, M., Balderson, P., Warren, C., Howe, D., Gardner, R., Dodsworth, J. and Black, J. (2008) *Analysing Child Deaths and Serious Injury through Abuse and Neglect: What Can We Learn?* Research Report DCSF-RR023. Nottingham: Department for Children, Schools and Families.

Community Care (2008) 'Expert Guides: Social care workforce.' Available at www.communitycare.co.uk/Articles/2008/06/30/104621/social-care-workforce.html, aaccessed 18 December 2008.

Gawande, A. (2003) *Complications: A Surgeon's Notes on an Imperfect Science.* London: Profile Books.

Guardian (2008) 'Paediatricians reluctant to court backlash.' (19 March).

Helmreich, R.L. and Davies J.M. (2004) 'Culture, threat and error: Lessons from aviation.' *Canadian Journal of Anesthesia 51,* R1.

HM Government (2005) *Common Core of Skills and Knowledge for the Children's Workforce.* London: DfES.

HM Government (2006) *Working Together to Safeguard Children.* London: Stationery Office.

Hood, C. and Rothstein, H. (2001) 'Risk regulation under pressure: Problem solving or blame shifting?' London: LSE Research Articles Online. Available at http://eprints.lse.ac.uk/archive/00000335/, accessed on 23 November 2008.

Laming, H. (2003) *The Victoria Climbié Inquiry: A Report of an Inquiry by Lord Laming.* London: HMSO.

Munro, E. (2005) 'A systems approach to investigating child abuse deaths.' *British Journal of Social Work 35,* 4, 531–546.

Reason, J. (2000) 'Human error: models and management.' *British Medical Journal 320,* 768–770.

Reder, P. and Duncan, S. (2003) 'Understanding communication in child protection networks.' *Child Abuse Review 12,* 82–100.

Sexton, J.B., Thomas, E.J. and Helmreich, R.L. (2000) 'Error, stress, and teamwork in medicine and aviation: cross sectional surveys.' *British Medical Journal 320,* 745–749.

STATUTE

The Children Act (2004) London: Stationery Office.

LIST OF CONTRIBUTORS

Dipti Aistrop Specialist Health Visitor, Sheffield Primary NHS Care Trust. Dipti Aistrop has been a health visitor since 1983. She completed a Post Graduate Diploma in Promoting Mental Health of Young Children in 1999 at St Georges Medical school and has held a specialist health visitor post in Sheffield since 2002. She has a specific interest in maternal and infant mental health and has worked in partnership with the local Child and Adolescent Mental Health Service to develop support for first time parents and their infants towards early secure attachments.

Flora Bandele Education Safeguarding Children Co-ordinator, Sheffield City Council. Flora Bandele is a Safeguarding Children Service advisor and trainer for education and school staff in Sheffield. She is an ex-teacher who has also worked as an Education Welfare Officer. She has had several years experience of working with children and young people, many of whom have been either victims of abuse or abusers themselves, as well as working with their parents. She is involved in various safeguarding children board and council committees including those dealing with safeguarding policies and procedures, child sexual exploitation and domestic abuse. She also has experience in advising investigations into allegations against staff and is an active member of the Sheffield Safeguarding Children Board Multi–agency training pool.

Jeff Boxer National Investigative Training Co-ordinator, National Policing Improvement Agency (NPIA). Jeff Boxer, BSc (Hons) Policing and Police Studies, PGCE Post Compulsory Education, is a serving police officer with over 12 years experience of safeguarding children which includes; conducting and supervising child abuse investigations as a detective sergeant within a child abuse investigation team; managing specialist child abuse investigation training for the Metropolitan Police and writing policy and guidance for the Metropolitan Police on child protection. He contributes to the Association of Chief Police Officers (ACPO) Investigating Child Abuse National Steering Group and is also the author of the national learning programmes for police specialist child abuse investigators and for investigative interviewers.

Mandy Craig Substance Misuse Development Project Co-ordinator, Sheffield Safeguarding Children Board. Mandy Craig has been working in the field of substance misuse for the last 13 years. Mandy is currently the substance misuse development project manager for Sheffield Safeguarding Children Board, organising and delivering training, developing policies and protocols, initiating campaigns to highlight issues that affect the children of substance misusers and offering advice and support to all agencies working with families where substance misuse is an issue. A major achievement for Mandy has been the development of a safe storage box for Methadone and other prescribed medications which has been produced by Remploy for use in the homes of service users.

Gail Gumbrell Adult Social Worker, Community Learning Disability Team, Bradford. Gail Gumbrell has worked as a social worker with adults with learning disabilities for many years, based in Bradford. Over the past four years her interest in parents with learning disabilities has increased and she is currently involved in offering training for her local safeguarding board on this subject.

Liz Hughes Consultant Nurse, Integrated Safeguarding Children Service, Sheffield. Liz Hughes was a health visitor for 11 years, a child protection specialist nurse for ten years and has been a Consultant Nurse, Safeguarding Children, for five years. Liz Hughes is a consultant nurse in the Integrated Safeguarding Children Service in Sheffield.

Rosie Jakob Family Court Advisor, Children and Family Court Advisory and Support Service. Karen Johnson (CAFCASS). Rosie has worked in social care for 18 years, and as a social worker with children and families since 1994. She currently works as a Family Court Adviser for CAFCASS and as a lecturer practitioner.

Karen Johnson Lead Nurse, Safe-guarding Children at Derbyshire Mental Health Services. Karen Johnson has worked for 34 for years in Mental Health Services. She is a qualified psychotherapist and nurse. For the past five years Karen has specialised in the field of safeguarding children and parental mental health. She contributes to advancements in the field to encourage workforce development by providing consultation on the relationship between mental illness and childhood trauma and neglect.

Emma Kelly Programme Co-ordinator, ECPAT UK (End Child Prostitution, Child Pornography and the Trafficking of Children). Emma Kelly is a qualified social worker with a master's degree in social work from the University of Glasgow. She has a background in child protection social work and multi-agency learning in Manchester working for the ACPC and Manchester Safeguarding Children Board. Emma joined ECPAT UK in August 2007 where she co-ordinates and delivers training on child trafficking across the UK and is currently undertaking research on the incidence of child trafficking in Wales.

Hilary Owen Assistant Executive Director of Safeguarding and Welfare, Barnsley Metropolitan Borough Council. Hilary Owen was a court social worker for five years, a child protection co-ordinator for seven years, child protection specialist adviser in the NHS for nine years and is now a service manager in an integrated safeguarding children service which employs social work, health, education, and early years qualified professionals. She is vice chair of Sheffield's Safeguarding Children Board Operational Executive Committee. Hilary Owen is Assistant Executive Director of Safeguarding and Welfare, Barnsley Metropolitan Borough Council. She was also vice chair of Sheffield's Safeguarding Children Board's Operational Executive Committee for two years. Hilary has written several articles and edited or contributed to several books including *Good Practice in Child Protection* and *One of the Hardest Jobs in the World: Attempting to Manage Risk in Children's Homes*, both published by Jessica Kingsley Publishers.

Ruth Pearson is a Senior Lecturer in Social Work Studies at Sheffield Hallam University. She has a background in Child Protection Social Work and multi-agency safeguarding children training and development. She has worked for Rotherham ACPC and Sheffield ACPC/LSCB in training and in policy development. She has an MA in Child Protection and Welfare from Huddersfield University.

Sue Peckover is a Senior Research Fellow at the Centre for Applied Childhood Studies at the University of Huddersfield. She has a background in health visiting and a research interest in domestic violence, child welfare and public health. Sue is currently working on ESRC funded research examining aspects of information sharing, assessment and decision-making in child welfare.

SUBJECT INDEX